W9-AAT-267

2205150068

Bitter Fruit

Bitter Fruit

Black Politics and the Chicago Machine, 1931–1991

William J. Grimshaw

The University of Chicago Press

Chicago and London

The University of Chicago Press, Chicago 60637
The University of Chicago Press, Ltd., London
© 1992 by The University of Chicago
All rights reserved. Published 1992
Printed in the United States of America
01 00 99 98 97 96 95 94 93   5 4 3 2
ISBN (cloth): 0-226-30893-6

Library of Congress Cataloging-in-Publication Data

Grimshaw, William J.
    Bitter fruit : Black politics and the Chicago machine, 1931–1991/
William J. Grimshaw.
        p.   cm.
    Includes bibliographical references and index.
    1. Afro-Americans—Illinois—Chicago—Politics and government.
2. Chicago (Ill.)—Politics and government—To 1950.   3. Chicago
(Ill.)—Politics and government—1951–   I. Title
F548.9.N4G73   1992
323.1'196073077311—dc20   92–4489
                                                                                             CIP

⊗ The paper used in this publication meets the minimum requirements
    of the American National Standard for Information Sciences—Per-
    manence of Paper for Printed Library Materials, ANSI Z39.48-1984.

This is for you, Chris:
Stay the course,
the way our friend taught us to do it.

Contents

Preface

This is one of those books that started out as one thing and wound up as something else. Initially it was to have been an update of the black-machine relationship in Chicago politics. Harold F. Gosnell's classic pair of studies about machine politics and black politics—*Negro Politicians: The Rise of Negro Politics in Chicago* (1935) and *Machine Politics: Chicago Model* (1937)—described the machine in its early formative stages and explored a black politics deeply rooted in the Republican "party of Lincoln, the emancipator" (1935, 36).

Some twenty-five years later, James Q. Wilson updated Gosnell's pathbreaking work with his widely influential *Negro Politics: The Quest for Leadership* (1960). Wilson chose not to explore the bases for the extraordinary differences he found; but the changes were indeed profound. In place of Gosnell's ambitious and highly contentious black elite, which generated a kaleidoscopic leadership structure, Wilson found a stable and firmly unified black elite under the command of a single man, the legendary Congressman William "Boss" Dawson, "the Man," as many of his followers referred to him. Black voters were hardly any less unified, standing as solidly behind the Daley-Dawson machine as they once had stood behind the "party of Lincoln." In the space of but a single generation, black politics appeared to have shifted a full 180 degrees.

I was not introduced to the problem of the black-machine relationship through the literature, however, but in a practical way, as a starry-eyed volunteer in independent campaigns against the machine in the early 1970s. For a University of Chicago graduate who had spent much of his time reading political philosophy at the feet of Joseph Cropsey and Leo Strauss, it was an eye-opening experience. Indeed, in my first campaign I was thrown out the door of a polling place by a couple of tough machine goons for objecting to some voting irregularities. Chicago politics lacked the subtlety and profundity of political theory, but its raw and direct ways were entic-

ing nevertheless. I even convinced my wife, Jacky—bent on a career
in medicine, who eventually would wind up as Mayor Harold Washington's chief political adviser and campaign manager—to jump into
the ring.

What struck me as I came to think about the black-machine relationship was how profoundly it had changed since the time of Wilson's research in the late 1950s. Massive school boycotts by black
students in the early 1960s produced the first cracks in the relationship. Martin Luther King's celebrated foray into the city for open
housing created more cracks. A destructive series of ensuing upheavals created still more cracks: the devastating West Side riots following Dr. King's assassination, accompanied by Mayor Daley's infamous "shoot-to-kill" order; the appalling "police riot" at the 1968
Democratic convention; the brutal murder of Black Panther leaders
by the police; and Mayor Daley's long and bitter feud with Congressman Ralph Metcalfe, a machine hack who was transformed into a
folk hero by that confrontation. Clearly, an updating of the once firm
black-machine relationship was in order, and that was what I set out
to do as the tumultuous 1970s drew to a close.

Heeding the sage counsel of the veteran machine watcher and
"insider" Milton Rakove, I began the inquiry by interviewing a
couple of politicians who "owed me" a candid orientation interview.
(Rakove's rule for interviewing amounted to an application of the
machine's exchange principle. In order to get help from a politician,
you had to first help him. In short, work a precinct, win an interview.) Fortunately, I had knocked on a few doors for Leon Despres
in the Fifth Ward, when he served as the "dean" of the anti-machine
alderman. Despres was an "outsider," but he was a seasoned and
shrewd observer of both machine politics and black politics. I had
even more "credit" with a former machine insider, Harold Washington. Harold and I first met while I worked for Democratic Governor
Dan Walker in the early 1970s, and after he broke with the machine
in the late 1970s, my wife and I worked in all of his campaigns.

To my utter dismay, both men, one by one, knocked my feet out
from under me. Much of what I knew to be the case did not square
with their views at all. In characteristic fashion, the intellectually inclined Despres dismissed Wilson's "abstract theorizing" as misleading and unhelpful, and he urged me to go back to Gosnell's far richer
empirically grounded work for a firmer grounding. The practical
Washington sent me to the precinct captains. I would learn from
them, he said, just how limited "Boss" Dawson's hold had been over
the other black ward bosses. "Do you really believe," he asked me,

"that old man Daley would have given a black man all the power that Bill Dawson was supposed to have had?"

Properly censured, and more than a little perplexed, I did some digging and wound up going back to the beginning, looking at the full course of the black-machine relationship. My contemporary study turned into an historical study beginning in the 1930s when the Democratic machine was being launched, and when blacks were beginning their fateful switch from the "party of Lincoln" to the ascendant Democratic party. It proved to be an interesting trip; one thing after another kept cropping up that made remarkably little sense.

It finally occurred to me, after more stops and starts than I care to remember, that much of what seemed to be "out there" and what I thought should have been out there actually were the product of a particular set of assumptions and expectations rooted in an economic logic. The economic perspective I unwittingly held was filtering, magnifying, diminishing, hiding, and distorting various elements of the "pictures" I was looking at.

Take the machine. Understood in the economic perspective's familiar terms, it is a business firm, singlemindedly dedicated to maximizing profit. It wins as many elections as it can in order to secure as much wealth as it can, extracted in the form of patronage from the offices it controls. Yet I often found that machines were not the maximizers they were cracked up to be. Much hinged on the economic perspective's problematic assumptions about the structure of the machine, which bears on its "singlemindedness" and the relationship between organizational interests and elite interests, which in turn bears heavily on the goals machines actually pursue.

The same way with black voters. From the economic perspective, the bulk of them are understood to be consumers of the machine's favors and "friendship." Their dire socioeconomic need compels them into exchanging their votes for the party in power's resources. Yet, once again, I often found that this was not the case. Some poor black voters did behave some of the time as consumers, seeking to satisfy their own needs; yet at other times they behaved as citizens, seeking a collective measure of representation and even empowerment for their votes.

Ultimately, I resolved these puzzles and others by developing a multiple, interactive perspective, consisting of distinct economic, sociological, and political perspectives. Each perspective held different assumptions and expectations, and directed attention to distinctive dimensions of the black-machine relationship, which enabled me to systematically explain a much broader range of actions and outcomes. Thus, what was regarded as unusual and even deviant behavior by the terms of one perspective was viewed as typical and normal by the terms of one of the other perspectives. In turn, the broad historical framework I wound up using provided a rich and changing array of cases with which to assess the interactive perspective's utility.

Finally, I suppose a word of caution is in order. This is a scholarly study, as scholarly as I could make it; but it is not an arrid, journalistically balanced, or detached work. It is informed by a point of view. Chicago has been governed by political machines for all but a few of the past sixty years, and blacks, elite and mass alike, and whether they have supported the machines or opposed them, have derived only meager benefits from their governance. That is an empirical fact, and it is also a deplorable condition for which the machines and the elites running them should be held accountable and challenged.

Chicago's black communities have been treated as though they are islands: separate, unequal, and apart from the rest of the city. That is no way to run a city. The brilliant scholar and activist, W. E. B. DuBois, observed a good many years ago that "the problem of the Twentieth Century is the problem of the color-line." Little has changed in the interim. The color-line remains the great divide in Chicago's politics, and I hope this book helps knock it down.

Acknowledgments

Books such as this largely depend upon the kindness of strangers. I am deeply indebted to the many individuals on all sides who so generously shared their observations and thoughts with me, sometimes in formal interviews but more often simply in conversations. Many of you, goodness knows, will not agree with much of what I have written; nevertheless, I have shown my gratitude to all of you by only citing your assistance when I thought it would do you no harm.

I am grateful for the scholarly aid I received from various places. My Illinois Institute of Technology colleagues were wonderful critics: David Beam, Bob Davidson, Barbara Ferman (whose eye for the telling detail and energy for argumentation never cease to amaze me), and Joe Zikmund. My occasional colleagues at the University of Chicago were no less helpful: Terry Clark, the late David Greenstone, and Gary Orfield. Several of my original mentors at the University of Illinois–Urbana stayed with me over the long haul: Samuel Gove, Phil Monypenny (who helped me more than he knew when I was muddling through the problem at the outset), and Michael Preston. From afar, I was helped by Clarence Stone's always thoughtful and encouraging advice, and I was helped beyond measure by Norton Long, who steered me into urban politics in graduate school and has kept the lash on my back ever since; thanks for everything, friend. Critics employed by the University of Chicago Press were unfailingly generous with their criticism and advice. My students at IIT and the University of Chicago displayed extraordinary forbearance and good humor as I imposed various versions of the study on them.

Librarians at the Chicago Historical Society were helpful, and the librarians at that little gold mine, the City of Chicago's Municipal Reference Library, proved to be wonderful collaborators. It just goes to show that Vito Marzullo was right: good precinct captains make good public servants. (I'm only kidding, Debbie.)

Finally, my family. I am always astonished to read in acknowl-
edgments about remarkable families whose members, in aid of the
struggling scholar, stoke furnaces, cook meals, clean houses, feed
pets, and do all manner of helpful deeds. I did not lead that charmed
existence. All my wife seemed to do was drag me out into one campaign and political project after another. My daughter never tired of
inquiring, "What in the world is taking you so long?" My wily son
quickly learned how to exploit my love of procrastination. So a fair
share of our time was spent "hitting some on the Midway," "shoot-
ing hoops," and taking those wonderful camping trips to the go-kart
capital of North America, the Wisconsin Dells.

Part 1
Theoretical Perspective

1

A New Perspective on Machine Politics and Black Politics

What we profess and what we practice are sometimes badly at odds. The black political experience in America has long constituted a singular contradiction to our commitment to equality. The political machine similarly constitutes a contradiction to our commitment to democracy. When southern blacks began their great northern migration to the big cities shortly after the turn of the century, the two contradictions came together like star-crossed lovers and yielded some strange and bitter fruit.

Reality, moreover, often is at odds with supposition regarding what we know about the political machine, the black urban political experience, and the relationship between the two. This is certainly not because the subjects have suffered from any lack of attention. Yet our knowledge of them is confounded by dubious facts and glaring omissions, peculiar assumptions and misleading metaphors, and numerous inconsistencies.[1]

It may be that the "exotic" subjects are too peculiar to comprehend, and they are often painful to observe. Gaining access to them is another limiting factor. Class, cultural, and racial differences can also create a good deal of "distance" between students and subjects. In any event, we tend to view machine politics and black politics in unidimensional, mechanical, and alien terms. They are not like us, we seem to say, and we accentuate the differences.

Three Perspectives on Machine Politics and Black Politics
Maximizing and Exchange: The Economic Perspective

The perspective that has principally guided research on both machine politics and black urban politics[2] is rooted in economics. The political machine generally has been conceptualized as a structural monolith, an "apparatus" or an "instrument," driven by a single interest: winning elections for the purpose of extracting wealth from the offices it acquires, in the form of patronage contracts and jobs. Thus, students of machine politics have maintained that the machine is better understood as a profit-maximizing business firm than as a political party. "A political machine is a business organization in a particular field of business—getting votes and winning elections. . . . It is interested only in making and distributing income—mainly money—to those who run it and work for it" (Banfield and Wilson 1963, 115).

The electoral dimension of machine politics also generally has been understood in economic terms. Poor voters in general, and the bulk of black voters in particular, are said to engage in face-to-face exchanges with the machine's field agents. The agents "sell" various selective incentives, which the poor "purchase" with their ballots. Poor voters willingly enter into this exchange with the machine's agents, according to this view, because they possess a critical pair of deficits. They lack material and social resources, and they are devoid of political values. "The voter who is indifferent to issues, principles, and candidates puts little or no value on his vote and can be induced relatively easily (or cheaply) to put it at the machine's disposal" (ibid., 117).

Accordingly, the economic argument is complete and seamless. Along the organizational dimension, the machine is conceptualized as a profit-maximizing business firm rather than as a political party. Along the electoral dimension, the machine's supporters are conceptualized as consumers who exchange their votes for favors, rather than as citizens holding broader or higher values.

It is a simple matter to see how black urban politics seems to fit into the economic perspective's mold. Political machines thrived in the big northern cities to which blacks migrated from the south in the early 1900s, and although most migrating blacks lacked political experience, the machine's style of politics was not foreign to them. In his study *Machine Politics: Chicago Model* (1937, 4), Harold Gosnell found that machine politics was the province of "self-made men who had shown themselves more ruthless than their rivals. These men were not heir to any tradition which impressed upon them their responsibility to the general public."

This was something that the great bulk of black men who came north to the machine strongholds could understand. They arrived full of hunger, hope, and ambition, and nothing they had experienced in the south provided them with any impression that politics might be filled with high public purpose. The machines did nothing to disabuse them of such a notion. Thus, notwithstanding his high

Harvard education, Ferdinand Q. Morton, the black leader of New York City's Tammany machine during the 1920s, sounds as though he learned his politics at the same low school of hard knocks attended by the legendary George Washington Plunkitt (Riordan, 1963 [1905]). "We should treat it as an honest-to-goodness shopping trip. Politics . . . is a theoretical bargain counter, to buy wares and get the best deal we can in bargains" (Osofsky 1963, 173–74).

Things were no different in black Chicago during the 1920s and 1930s. The "black belt" was full of tough, talented, and ruthless men on the political make, as the chapter headings of Harold Gosnell's *Negro Politicians* (1935) indicate: "Edward Wright, The Iron Master," and "Oscar DePriest, The Militant Organizer." However, when the political machines established hegemony, the free-wheeling entrepreneurial days came to an end. The machine became the iron master, and strict limits were imposed on permissible behavior.

The term "black belt" refers to that area on the Near Southeast Side where many blacks lived within a narrow tract of land comprising the three community areas of Douglas, Grand Boulevard, and Washington Park. Blacks were compelled to live there through a combination of (a) threat of violence and (b) quasi-legal methods, the most notable of which were the racially restrictive housing covenants prohibiting the sale of rental of housing to blacks beyond the boundary of the black belt. Local courts generally upheld the restrictive covenants until 1948, when the U.S. Supreme Court ruled them unconstitutional in *Shelley v. Kraemer.*

The most powerful of Chicago's black political leaders, the legendary Congressman William "Boss" Dawson, used an engaging sporting analogy to describe the coercive character of the machine's compliance structure: "We must play the game according to the rules. I always play it that way and I play with my team. If you are on a baseball team you stick with your team or you may not be able to play much longer" (Clayton 1964, 73). Dawson, as ruthless, skilled, and ambitious as they came, actually did not want to play the game that way, as we shall see. Yet, ultimately he was compelled to, because nobody imposed stricter standards on what was permitted than Dawson's manager, Mayor Richard J. Daley.

Turning to the electoral dimension, the black voters who came north stood overwhelmingly at the bottom of the socioeconomic ladder, and most lacked any experience with politics. This appeared to make them natural fodder for the political machines. Chicago's "Boss" Dawson has described the harsh southern black backdrop against which machine politics was played out in northern black communities. "The plantation masters allowed them to build churches and conduct services as long as the Bible was the only subject of discussion. Politics was taboo. The Negro had no place to learn politics. It was not taught in the schools. It could not be discussed in the churches" (ibid., 70–71).

When blacks finally did acquire their first sweet taste of politics in the big northern cities, they learned that it often amounted to what Banfield and Wilson (1963, 125) called "a system of organized bribery." As the latest in a lengthy procession of impoverished, politically inexperienced immigrants to the cities, black voters became the focus of the machine's material blandishments. James Q. Wilson (1960, 54) explained how the relationship worked during the 1950s: "The machine can flourish in the Negro wards largely because of the status and needs of the Negro. The incentives it can offer are still attractive to many Negroes, whereas they have largely lost their appeal to other ethnic groups which have risen farther."

Coalition-Building and Representation: The Sociological Perspective

Although the economic perspective on machine politics and urban black politics has won wide acceptance, it has not gained universal favor. A small body of work has rendered some dissenting viewpoints. The early studies of Harold Gosnell (1935, 1937), for example, cast within a richly textured, eclectic descriptive framework, present some intriguing challenges to the economic perspective. So, too, do some recent studies that employ concrete, particularistic, and inductive logical frameworks and that challenge the more abstract and deductive logic underlying the economic perspective (Shefter 1976; Guterbock 1980; Bridges 1984; Erie 1988).

The countervailing perspective principally mounts what I want to call a sociological challenge to the prevailing economic perspective. Along the organizational dimension, it draws attention to the critical existence of sub-units holding some degree of discretion within the machine, which makes problematic the economic perspective's critical twin assumptions about the machine: its full articulation and governance by a unitary interest.

The sociological perspective is intuitively appealing. American government, after all, is structured at all levels along highly decentralized lines, and at the local level there usually is an array of special districts—schools, parks, pubic works, and the like—providing still more checks and balances. In the same way, the machine, with its numerous elected officials and usually a large number of ward leaders, presents a formidable challenge to those who would assemble its members into a comprehensive coalition and direct it toward a common purpose. Accordingly, from the sociological perspective, the principal task is not, as the economic perspective would have it, profit-maximizing; rather, it is coalition-building.

Readers familiar with the enduring debate among organizational theorists will recognize these clashing perspectives as the "rational" or "goal directed" model and the "natural systems" model of organizations (Gouldner 1959; Etzioni 1960; Wilson 1973). An essentially similar disagreement exists among students of urban development. Paul Peterson's widely influential *City Limits* (1981) launched the debate when he argued that cities, much like political machines and business firms, were guided by a unitary economic interest. In response, Stephen Elkins (1987), Clarence Stone (1989), and others (Stone and Sanders 1987) countered that cities actually held multiple, notably political and economic, interests. Therefore, cities could not be properly understood as being driven by an economic imperative.

The debate over a "structure-agency dialectic" that has emerged among Marxist students of urban politics is cut from similar cloth. This disagreement was initiated by Manuel Castells' seminal study *The Urban Question* (1977), which argued along much the same abstract and deterministic structural lines as Peterson did. In turn, Castells' critics contended, much as Elkins and Stone had responded to Peterson, that cities had to be understood as containing influential political and cultural spheres as well as an economic sphere, which is to say, cities are governed by multiple interests rather than a unitary interest (Smith 1984).

Along the electoral dimension, the sociological perspective draws attention to a different sort of articulation problem. The economic perspective itself actually points toward the problem, in that disagreement exists over just what induces the voter to support the machine. On the one hand, it is said that a material exchange occurs, in which the machine's agents provide "favors" for votes—ranging from patronage jobs and illegal fixes to garbage cans and tree trimming. The machine's agents, however, also are said to win support by providing "friendship"—an affectual exchange, as Thomas Guterbock (1980, 7–8) called it.

This amounts to an explanation of a radically different sort, because it introduces a collective ethnic-cultural interest, as opposed to an individual economic interest. The agent and the voter are said

to be enmeshed together within the intimate ties of an "ethnic village" or a "private-regarding ethos." (Banfield and Wilson 1963).
The distinction is an important one, although it is overdrawn. At
bottom, after all, there is a decidedly material basis to much of the
exchange of affection between agent and voter. The voter may regard the machine's agent as a "friend;" yet not because the agent
does things *with* him, but because he can do things *for* him. The relationship often is rooted in mutual exploitation.

Nevertheless, the cultural explanation does point toward the direction in which the sociological perspective takes us: conceptualiz-
ing voting behavior in collective terms. The sociological perspective
argues that voters cast ballots for the purpose of acquiring representation for some type of group interest: ethnic, racial, territorial, institutional, ideological belief, and so forth. In different ways, a number
of studies have addressed the electoral problem of individual economic gain versus collective representation in a machine setting,
and they have uncovered an array of collective attachments.

Thus, for example, Harold Gosnell (1935) explicitly rejected the
economic perspective's favors-for-votes explanation of black voting.
He did so after finding that blacks from the more affluent parts of
Chicago's black belt, not poorer blacks, were the first ones to shift
their support to the ascendant Democratic party in the 1930s (ibid.,
34–35). In general terms, Gosnell argued that black political behavior was culturally rooted in the unique experience of slavery and
emancipation. In this way, the Republican party was more akin to a
religious institution, as "the party of Lincoln, the emancipator,"
than a political party (ibid., 36). Accordingly, Gosnell was unsur-
prised that blacks alone among Chicago's voting blocs maintained an
abiding loyalty to the Republican party during the 1930s in the face
of the Great Depression's economic devastation and the Democratic
New Deal's sweeping political change.

Kristi Andersen's *The Creation of a Democratic Majority 1928–1936*
(1979) looked at the other side of the coin, as it were, " 'nonimmun-
ized' citizens—individuals without strong party identifications and
with little experience of political participation" (xiv). She, too,
formed an argument that cut sharply against the conventional economic grain, finding that the New Deal was not launched by a mass
conversion of Republicans into Democrats, as was assumed to be the
case, but rather that it succeeded by offering voters a novel ideological appeal, which had the effect of mobilizing large numbers of non-
voters into voters (23, 122). Many of the nonvoters mobilized by the
New Deal were poor immigrants who, according to the economic

perspective, should have been peddling their votes for favors in some local political market prior to the coming of the New Deal (40–42).

Thomas Guterbock's intensive study of a single Chicago ward, *Machine Politics in Transition* (1980), uncovered some remarkable evidence that countered the conventional economic explanation of low-income voting behavior. He found that although poor voters did, indeed, strongly support the Democratic machine, they actually received remarkably few services from it (143). This led Guterbock to conclude that the solid support of poor voters stemmed from their identification with the Democratic party as "the party of the little man" (169). They supported it on symbolic grounds rather than for material gain. In general, Guterbock found that the machine sought support by using a wide variety of symbolic appeals designed to display its commitment to the residents' community attachment (206–7).

Another Chicago community study, William Kornblum's *Blue Collar Community* (1974), found that the poor and working-class residents of his South Chicago steel mill neighborhoods held a range of collective attachments and that, in turn, the ward organization employed a range of electoral strategies that addressed them. The organization dispensed material inducements on an individual basis, although often by a community leader rather than a precinct captain in the poorest and most socially disorganized parts of the ward. However, the machine also appealed to collective racial and ethnic bonds, to class and community ties, and to the institutional attachment to the steel mills. The struggle for group recognition through representation was intense, dynamic, and ongoing in both the steel mill's union politics and in the ward's politics.

Elite Self-interest and Empowerment: The Political Perspective

As interesting and fruitful as the debate is between the profit-maximizers and the coalition-builders, a critical element bringing the political perspective to bear has been largely left out of the discussion. Incorporating this perspective yields a fuller and more realistic understanding of machine politics and the black urban political experience.

Along the organizational dimension, we need to take into account the self-interest of the machine's elite, as distinct from their organizational interest. In addition to maximizing the machine's effectiveness in winning elections and building coalitions among the machine's sub-units for the purpose of fostering cooperation and stability, the elite must look out for themselves. They hold a distinct interest in acquiring power, which is to say, gaining, maintaining, and enhancing their positions of command in the organization. This is accomplished by gaining control over the organization's internal decisionmaking centers. The elite cannot rely on the organization's success at the ballot box as a sufficient means of satisfying their needs. The critical fact is that what is good for the organization is not necessarily good for all its elites.

The distinction between an organizational interest and an elite interest has been given classical expression by Robert Michels' "iron law of oligarchy" (1962 [1911]). Although Michels' law has been widely criticized as overly deterministic, critics acknowledge that exceptions to the rule are hard to come by (Lipset, Trow, and Coleman 1962, 404; Lipset 1966, 32; Prewitt and Stone 1973, 20; Harmel 1989, 160–88). Thus, Kenneth Prewitt and Alan Stone in *The Ruling Elites: Elite Theory, Power, and American Democracy* (1973) conclude, "If one were to retitle Michels' discovery an 'aluminum tendency' rather than an 'iron law,' it would be remarkable how often it would empirically describe the nature of organizations. Few exceptions to this theory can be found."

The power of Michels' argument stems from his rejection of the economic perspective's assumption that organizations are rationally structured to achieve organizational goals. Instead, Michels showed in rich detail how the elite reconfigured organizational structures so that they actually served elite interests. The elite's capacity to accomplish this change in organizational direction rested on numerous advantages: superior knowledge of organizational affairs, control over formal communications with the membership, greater political skill, and the numerous deficiencies of the rank-and-file (Lipset 1966, 16–17).

Clarence Stone (1987, 10), although he generally works from a sociological perspective in which the principal elite objective is coalition-building, has used Michels' political perspective to draw attention to "the dual character of authority." As Stone says, elites may use their authority to "induce coordinated action on behalf of the common good." Yet at the same time, "those in authority inevitably possess a degree of discretion and that discretion may be used to fortify the power they have and perhaps even expand the privileges they and their allies enjoy. Political authority thus can be used to further personal or factional aims; this is the second face of authority."

Several studies have found that personal and factional aims can override organizational goals. Ironically, after Milton Rakove (1975, 35–39) painted the powerful Daley machine in the conventionally bright colors of economic rationality—being solely dedicated to maximizing electoral success—he poked a large hole in his canvas by showing that virtually all of the top political and government posts in the city and county were held by male Irish cronies of the mayor. Steven Erie's historical study of the political machine, *Rainbow's End* (1988), makes the same point on a grander scale. In examining a number of machines between the mid-nineteenth century to 1985, Erie found that ethnic factional rivalry between the Irish and their southern and eastern European competitors in the machine was pervasive and endemic. In his pathbreaking study, "The Emergence of the Political Machine: An Alternative View" (1976), Martin Shefter echoes Harold Gosnell's (1937) description of the early Chicago machine by richly detailing the lengthy prelude of elite and factional rivalry inside the New York City machine which preceded its emergence as a comprehensive, cohesive structure.

In each case, then, we find that what the economic perspective takes for granted, a highly articulated organization headed by an elite committed to the organization's interests is highly problematic and extraordinarily difficult to achieve. Moreover, even when the contentious elites and rival factions are assembled into a comprehensive coalition, no assurance is provided that the ruling elite will abandon its self-interest for the sake of the organization's common good. If statesmen are hard to come by in politics generally, it is all the harder to find them heading up political machines.

Along the electoral dimension, the political perspective similarly focuses on the acquisition of power as a prime consideration. Voters may behave as individual consumers, engaging in face-to-face transactions with the machine's agents. They also may express an interest in acquiring representation for some form of collective interest. Additionally, they may seek collective empowerment through the electoral process.

In their analyses of minority participation in governing coalitions, Rufus Browning, Dale Rogers Marshall, and David Tabb (1984, 1990) use the term "political incorporation" to describe a similar range of possibilities: "At the lower end, we have no minority representation; then some representation, but on a council dominated by a coalition resistant to minority interests; finally—the strongest form of incorporation—an equal or leading role in a dominant coalition that is strongly committed to minority interests. The higher levels of political incorporation are likely to afford substantial influence or control over policy" (1990, 9).

Distinguishing among exchange, representation, and empowerment is particularly important in studying machine politics. Machines seek to live off exchange. Small favors and friendships are the machine's stock in trade. It is the only form of relationship the machine willingly enters into with constituents, because it costs nothing in terms of power. It is at the point when groups start demanding collective representation that the machine begins experiencing difficulties.

Machines generally attempt to avoid the representation problem by providing only nominal recognition of collective interests rather than substantive representation. When a beleaguered Chicago machine committeeman, Alderman Vito Marzullo, began feeling the heat of Hispanic discontent in his ethnically changing ward during the 1980s, he candidly explained the strategy to a *Tribune* reporter: "If this ward ever elects a Mexican alderman, he's going to be my Mexican, not their Mexican."

Thomas Guterbock's insider's view of Mayor Daley's machine, *Machine Politics in Transition* (1980), found that the machine's aldermen were strongly discouraged from introducing any kind of substantive legislation in the city council. Inasmuch as the Daley machine was structured along strictly hierarchical lines, policy proposals were regarded as the mayor's prerogative (1980, 70). Reform aldermen in Daley's city council found themselves similarly constrained. Their proposals invariably were buried in committee. If it was determined that a buried proposal possessed some merit, it would be revived, reintroduced in modified form, and passed as the mayor's proposal (Despres interview, 1979).

Needless to say, if the machine looks unfavorably on demands for representation, it abhors any demand for empowerment. As Mayor Daley decreed, "There can be no organizations within The Organization" (Weisman and Whitehead 1974, 75). From the machine's viewpoint, its aldermen and other elected officials are expected to represent the machine's interests in the community, not the other way around. Accordingly, efforts to empower any interest other than the machine's interest are regarded as acts of disloyalty and are subject to severe sanction.

Thus, when a black machine alderman was being subjected to extreme pressure from his constituents at the height of the civil rights movement, he buckled and opposed one of Mayor Daley's nominees to the school board in a city council committee session.

He subsequently recanted and voted for the nominee in full council, but as far as Mayor Daley was concerned, the alderman's "treason" had placed him beyond the pale. The alderman was reslated, but his precinct captains were ordered to sit out the election, and he was defeated (Travis 1987, 252–53).

Yet despite the formidable barriers set up by the machine, demands for collective empowerment persistently recur. The sources of insurrection are numerous: the machine's unresponsiveness, rising expectations among groups, and external events which reshape the political landscape. Norman Nie, Sidney Verba, and their associates (1988, 17–22) described an instance of one such transformational external event. Prior to the civil rights movement, black rates of electoral participation were low, constrained principally by limited education levels. Then as the civil rights movement emerged, black group affiliations and collective beliefs increased, which served to significantly increase black electoral participation. However, when the movement subsided, participation subsided. Political man reverted to economic man, as it were, rising and falling on the strength of his collective commitment.

Creating an Interactive Perspective

To what extent can the three perspectives be integrated? They cannot be tightly assembled into an overarching new theory of machine politics and black politics, for the perspectives are too disparate, the phenomena too complex, and the tools of social science too limited for that. What we have to work with here are theoretical perspectives, each of which "directs attention persuasively to a few central processes that seem to explain (though not predict, in any scientific sense) a wide variety of phenomena" (Wilson 1973, 13).

Yet although we cannot precisely specify causal relations between processes and outcomes, there is much to be gained by assembling the perspectives into a broader interactive perspective instead of working within one particular perspective. Each of the perspectives offers advantages and deficits. Each raises pertinent questions of a particular sort, draws attention to certain details, and illuminates distinct patterns of relationships. At the same time, however, alternative questions and assumptions and other details and patterns are slighted or ignored.

It may be helpful to think of the three perspectives as painting different pictures. The economic perspective would render a painting in the chiaroscuro tradition, in which light is intensely magnified and narrowly focused on a single individual, while leaving the rest of the canvas obscured in dark shadows. Imagine, if you will, a painting of a powerful prince (although the Dutch painters in this tradition usually preferred portraying wealthy burghers), who stands there looking grim and resolute. He is in command and appears to know exactly where he is headed.

However, when the sociological perspective is used to cast additional light on the canvas, some shadows dissolve and more contextual detail can be seen. The prince is not alone. There are other lords of the realm standing behind him, and each of them appears to be tugging at him. Some are trying to draw him in one direction, and others seem to be urging him in other directions. On closer inspection, the prince now appears less resolute than before. He seems to be wondering in which direction he should head, and whether he can persuade the other lords to follow him.

Still more light is shed on the canvas by the political perspective, changing once again what the painting appears to reveal. Now we can see that both prince and lords are bearing knives, and looking far more dangerous than they did before. Several of the lords are not tugging at the prince; they appear to be slashing at him, seemingly eager to occupy the foreground themselves. When we examine the prince in this context, his grim resolution and concern now appear to be less over direction and more over whether he can retain his position of command amidst the slashing knives.

If we take up two practical and concrete cases from among those that we shall be looking at, we can further extend our sense of the interactive perspective's utility. One of the cases is the critical organizational problem of elite recruitment in the machine. Each of the three theoretical perspectives we have identified is driven by a logic that tends to explain elite recruitment in distinct terms.

From the economic perspective, elite recruitment usually is not regarded as a pressing problem requiring much attention. Elite qualifications are something that tend to be taken for granted, given the assumptions underlying the economic perspective. The organization is understood as being geared to maximizing efficiency and effectiveness. Accordingly, the elites who are recruited are measured on the basis of the expertise they possess. "Markets," as Robin Hogarth and Melvin Reder (1987, 6) have said, "are assumed to reflect actions taken by experienced decision makers seeking to maximize their own gains and, simultaneously, keeping the market efficient by exploiting the error of others."

However, the sociological perspective raises the prospect that elite recruitment may be conducted on any entirely different basis. Given the sociological perspective's focal concern with organizational stability, building coalitions among the organization's loosely articulated, often competitive subunits becomes the paramount goal. It follows, then, that loyalty to the organization may well take precedence over expertise as the basis for recruiting elites. As Alvin Gouldner (1959, 417) pointed out, because organizations are "social systems" as well as "rational systems," organizational survival actually may be threatened if elites are recruited solely on the basis of expertise.

The political perspective, in turn, views the objective of elite recruitment in still different terms. The political perspective takes the organization's elite as its basic unit of analysis, rather than the organization or its sub-units. Accordingly, it asks which of the organization's elites benefit from the recruitment of a particular elite, and which elites are disadvantaged by it. In the rough parlance of Chicago politics the question becomes, "Who's this guy's Chinaman?" Elites may well exploit the organization for their own narrow advantage, in which case elite recruitment serves the vital purpose of maintaining and enhancing the organizational control of particular elites.

In the real world, needless to say, these analytic distinctions are not always easily sorted out. Elites usually carry the whole mixed bag of traits, possessing varying degrees of skill, loyalty to the organization, and ties to particular sponsors. Nevertheless, as we shall see time and again in the cases that follow, elites do tend to come configured mainly in one form or another since the perceived interests and needs of the ruling elite and the organization change over time, and elites generally are recruited to satisfy these changing interests.[3]

If we take up the electoral problem of changing levels of support for the machine by its principal constituency (low-income voters), it can be seen once again that the three perspectives explain the behavior in significantly different ways. As we have seen, the economic perspective explains the relationship between the machine and poor voters in terms of an individual exchange of favors and friendship and votes. Accordingly, changes are explained by the machine's varying capacity to deliver benefits. Steven Erie's *Rainbow's End* (1988), for example, showed how the machine's ability to extract resources from higher levels of government changed over time, and that during periods of resource contraction machines were likely to suffer because they had fewer benefits to dispense.

The sociological perspective looks to varying levels of representation as its explanation of changing support for the machine. Machines, after all, do more than provide material and affectual rewards to voters on an individual basis. To the extent that voters hold some type of collective affiliation or belief, they are likely to hold an interest in seeing the collectivity recognized through representation in the governing coalition or in opposition to it. Thus, in an effort to address this symbolic collective interest, machines assemble "balanced tickets," containing a "rainbow" of representation from ethnic groups and other significant collectivities.

In turn, the political perspective uses critical issues, those which address collective empowerment, to explain changing levels of support for the machine. As Rufus Browning and his colleagues (1984, 1990) point out, in contending that "representation is not enough," there is a significant difference between being a member of a coalition and holding equal or dominant standing in it. This explains why machines tend to engage in an issue-free style of politics. As a wise old ward boss explained to Milton Rakove (1975), one of the twin secrets of the Chicago machine's success was adhering to the maxim: "Don't make no waves."

Sorting out these analytic distinctions in the messy real world of electoral politics is no simple task. Yet the distinctions are useful if only to sensitize the observer to the fact that electoral motivation and behavior are complex, changing, and subject to a range of influences. The machine's strength resides in its material resources and dense network of field agents, its willingness to concede symbolic representation to pertinent collectivities, and its capacity to avoid entanglement in volatile issues that may be used against it.

Yet, for a variety of reasons, the machine's leadership does not always use its considerable resources wisely. Its representatives, tightly constrained by their prior obligation to the machine, are usually allowed to provide only nominal representation to the groups outside the machine that they are supposed to be representing. Then there are times when powerful issues emerge over which the machine can muster only limited control. Consequently, as we shall see, over the span of more than a half-century, black voters in Chicago displayed an extraordinary range of behavior, notwithstanding the machine's virtual monopolistic control over resources along most of the route.

The Historical Dimension

A second interactive dimension can be incorporated into the analysis by placing the interactive perspective within an historical framework. All too often, political institutions and actions have been conceptualized in essentially constant and universal terms, so that, as Theda Skocpol (1984, 2) put it, "realities of the moment were naively treated out of context as proxies for all of human social life." Incorporating history into the analysis can serve as a useful corrective. In place of simplicity, we are confronted by complexity. Instead of constancy, we find variety and change. Rather than universality, we encounter richly textured patterns of particularity.

The utility of an historical perspective has been shown in several recent revisionist interpretations of machine politics. Amy Bridges' *City in the Republic* convincingly challenged the widely accepted "political ethos" explanation of the emergence of machine politics, which treats the machine as "a product of immigrant culture and ethnic conflict," by showing that machine politics actually emerged in the antebellum city well before there was "a strong immigrant presence" (1984, 4–5). Bridges goes on to explain the machine's emergence within the context of a conjunction of particular critical developments: "as the consequence of placing social conflicts attendent on industrialization in the context of widespread suffrage" (1984, 8).

Other revisionist studies of machine politics have pointed to the significance of a series of changing circumstances in altering the structures and interests of political machines. In his "Emergence of the Political Machine: An Alternative View" (1976), Martin Shefter challenged the "political ethos" explanation as well as similar arguments that explain the machine's emergence on the basis of relations between the machine and voters. In their place, Shefter provides a "natural history" of the machine's emergence, in which a changing array of interests held by particular political and business elites shape the machine, thereby moving it through an initial stage of "rapacious individualism" and into "party factionalism" before finally becoming a "dominant machine."

Alternatively, Steven Erie's *Rainbow's End* (1988) presents a "recurrent-problems" interpretation of machine politics. Looking at machine politics in eight cities over a 160-year period, Erie essentially explains both the rise and the fall of political machines in terms of their capacity to acquire resources. Over the course of a particular machine's "life cycle," it thrives when resources are abundant and suffers when resources become scarce. Erie also points to the reluctance of the Irish leadership of the machines to share resources with other ethnic groups, which exacerbates the resources problem, and during hard times inspires ethnic revolts against the Irish.

Finally, placing the interactive perspective within an historical framework is useful because, as Clarence Stone observed in *Regime Politics* (1989, 257–58), "The examination of a sequential process is a rough counterpart to laboratory control." Stone's historical analysis of Atlanta's politics demonstrates that "by following events sequentially, we gain some understanding of what remains constant, what changes, and what is associated with each. Given a significant degree of social inertia, a historical sequence holds some set of factors constant, but it allows for others (including the intentions of purposive actors) to change. . . . By observing the flow of events over time, we can see what combination of factors have recurring weight and what changing factors alter the course of events" (ibid.).

We can provide a taste of the richness of Chicago's machine politics and black politics and present an overview of some of the analysis that follows by tracing some of the critical features of Chicago's modern political history. Since the coming of the Democratic New Deal at the outset of the 1930s, Chicago until quite recently has been governed by a political machine. Yet the machine has undergone such a number of critical changes that it is far more useful to speak of distinct machine regimes than machine rule. The black political experience is best understood in the same terms. Racial considerations were present at the outset and persisted in various forms throughout the machine's long history, running like a red thread through the fabric of Chicago's politics.

The Kelly-Nash Immigrant Machine

During the first quarter-century of its existence, from the 1930s through the mid-1950s, the Chicago Democratic machine functioned in the electoral arena in virtually classic terms. The "river wards," housing the city's tide of poor Eastern and Southern European immigrants, provided the machine with the bulk of its support. The principal opposition to the machine came from the wards along the city's rim, where the city's heavily Protestant middle class resided. Thus, class reinforced by cultural and religious differences constituted the city's great political divide: poor against rich, Catholic against Protestant.

The great electoral anomaly was the black voter. Although the vast majority of black citizens were even poorer than the river ward immigrants, they gave the machine nowhere near the same level of support as the immigrants. Long after the machine had established undisputed citywide dominance—as late as the 1950s—the machine could muster only a bare majority of support in local elections in the black wards. Indeed, one of the three black wards was even headed by a reform-minded Republican alderman. Yet at the same time, the black wards were giving overwhelming support to the national Democratic party. As we shall see, the compelling issue of race played an instrumental role in creating this Democratic divergence in the black wards.

The Democratic machine deviated organizationally, from the classic economic model during this period. Although it was headed by capable and powerful mayors for the most part, first Anton Cermak (1931–33) and then Edward Kelly (1933–47), the machine was beset by factional rivalry. The principal opposition to Cermak and Kelly's leadership came from the so-called Southwest Side Irish bloc. The newspapers of the day viewed the conflict as between the mayor's "progressive wing" and the Irish bloc's "patronage and spoils faction." The basic problem confronting Cermak and Kelly was that they held only limited control over the machine's numerous centers of patronage and power (Gable 1953). Until wider control could be established, the machine would remain divided along factional lines.

Daley's Black Machine

Richard J. Daley was indisputably Chicago's most powerful machine mayor. Few mayors anywhere ever had more good fortune fall their way. Daley's principal piece of good fortune was the great Protestant, post–World War II exodus from the city to the suburbs in search of better housing. This left the already organizationally decimated Republican party without an electoral base. Without party competition to distract him, Daley was afforded the unprecedented luxury of being able to concentrate on eliminating rivals within the machine. As mayor, party chairman, and keeper of the budget, which he took away from the aldermanic "gray wolves" as a "reform" measure, Daley also had an unprecedented base of power from which to build, and within a short time the machine finally began to resemble the classic model found in urban government textbooks.[4]

Daley's other great piece of good fortune was provided by the

U.S. Supreme Court decision, *Shelley v. Kraemer*, which in 1948 overturned the racially restrictive housing covenants that had compelled
the vast majority of blacks to live within the narrow confines of a
black belt and generated a middle-class exodus in search of better
housing comparable to the white Protestant middle-class flight and
with similar political consequences. The more affluent blacks who
moved from the black belt left the poor behind to fend for themselves. Without the alternative leadership, resources, and all-
important choices the middle class had provided, the poor black
wards promptly fell to the machine. Beginning with Daley's first
election in 1955, the poor black wards emerged as the machine's
electoral stronghold, displacing the poor immigrant wards that had
carried the machine through the 1930s and 1940s. In short, the two
migrations transformed Chicago into a one-party city.

Daley's Middle-Class Ethnic Machine

Considering the way in which Daley's machine secured the black
wards—as a "gift" from the migrating middle class—its seemingly
solid black support actually rested on a shaky foundation. When the
civil rights movement swept into the city in the 1960s, the foundation collapsed. Voters in the poor black wards grew disillusioned
with the machine and withdrew from politics. The middle-class
black wards broke into open revolt, with nearly all of them electing
anti-machine aldermen during the latter half of Daley's mayoralty.
Running against a pair of liberal challengers, one white and one
black, in his final 1975 primary election, Daley failed to win a majority of the black vote. The classic class-cultural political divide had
been replaced by a racial divide.

With the shift to racial politics, the Daley machine acquired a
new electoral stronghold in the working-class and middle-class
white ethnic wards. Earlier, voters in these wards had given the machine only limited support, put off by the Democratic party's liberalism and by the "corruption tax" they had to pay to support the machine's excesses. However, these concerns paled in the face of racial
fears, and the Daley machine, in turn, abandoned virtually all pretense of being a liberal Democratic New Deal "party of the little
man" in the late 1960s.

In anger and fear as well as by calculation, the machine increasingly took on the character of a Democratic party of the old Deep
South, openly supporting a range of conservative and racist policies
and practices. Here is how one of the machine's shrewdest commit-

teemen, Michael Madigan, from the racially troubled South Side explained the shift. Responding to a news reporter's question, "What is the smartest political move you've witnessed," Madigan replied (1986, 114–15):

> Probably Mayor Daley's move from the left to the right as the country moved from the left to the right. When Daley was first elected he was a liberal. He enjoyed strong support from the black wards. As late as 1963, were it not for the black wards, he would have lost to Benjamin Adamowski for mayor. But in the mid-sixties there was a shift in public sentiment from the left to the right. He moved very adroitly to reflect that. The convention disorders [at the 1968 Democratic Convention in Chicago], and the position he took relative to the hippies and Yippies, clearly positioned Himself on the right. His statement on arsonists ["shoot to kill"] was reflective of his view that society was becoming less tolerant of criminality and lawlessness.

Daley's machine also began to crumble in its final years. After fending off in the courts for years a ruling that would abolish much of its huge forced-labor army of precinct captains, Daley finally was forced to capitulate in the 1970s. The so-called Shakman decree of 1972 (*Shakman v. Democratic Organization of Cook County, et al.*), which prohibited firing local government employees on political grounds, cut deeply into the machine's electoral advantage. (The ruling subsequently was extended in 1979 under Daley's successors to prohibit hiring on political grounds). Compelled to wage elections on a level playing field, the harsh effects on the machine showed up immediately. Throughout Daley's mayoralty, all or nearly all fifty of the city's wards generated a minimum of 10,000 votes for his candidacy. With the Shakman decree in effect in 1975, however, over half of the fifty wards failed to deliver their 10,000 votes. Two years later, when Daley's successor, Michael Bilandic, was elected, two-thirds of the wards produced less than 10,000 votes. Thus, the legacy Daley left his successors was a machine verging on collapse (Grimshaw 1982).

Post-Machine Politics

Since Mayor Daley's death in 1976, Chicago has had five mayors. Left without a machine to guide them, Chicagoans have found it difficult to settle on a new course. Setting aside the two part-term mayors (Michael Bilandic and Eugene Sawyer) each of Daley's successors, Jane Byrne, Harold Washington, and Richard M. Daley, has set a different course. Yet each mayor can be understood basically in the same terms: by the background he or she brought to the job and the knowledge acquired from observing his or her predecessor's political strategy (Ferman and Grimshaw 1991).

In Byrne's case experience and learning amounted to the same thing. Although it was hardly evident from her anti-machine campaign rhetoric, Byrne was a product of the machine, a protégée of no less than Daley himself. Thus after defeating the machine, she promptly abandoned her anti-machine coalition and reentered the fold. Her governing style amply reflected her tutelage under Daley, for she was as ruthless and dictatorial as Daley had been, and she openly exploited the racial issue in the same way Daley had at the end.

But what had worked for Daley did not work for Byrne. The machine was no longer a monolith she could command. A rival faction emerged around young Richard M. Daley, who regarded himself as the legitimate heir to the mayor's office as if by patrimonial right. Daley's faction contested Byrne at every turn, and in 1983 Daley presented himself as the candidate of restoration. At the same time, middle-class blacks, who had been Byrne's strongest backers, were furious over her betrayal of them. Then when she used blacks as pawns in her struggle to win white ethnic support away from Daley, Byrne wound up being challenged by Congressman Harold Washington in 1983. The initial taste of power Byrne had provided blacks only whetted their appetites for more of it.

By all accounts, Washington should not have won. Yet when Byrne and Daley split the white vote down the middle and Washington's mayoral campaign turned into a religious crusade, the miracle happened. Few seemed sure about what they would be getting with Washington. His white lakefront liberal and Hispanic backers hoped he was the liberal reformer he claimed to be. Blacks looked to him as a modern-day messiah who would lead them to the promised land of first-class citizenship. To white ethnic voters, steeped in racial fear and hatred, he was the raging embodiment of their worst nightmares.

Pledging himself to "fair and open government," Washington proved to be principally a reform mayor. Having been in the machine for years, though always at its fringes and occasionally risking all to fight it, and then abandoning it in 1980 for a successful congressional run, Washington was convinced that the machine was dead in the black community (Grimshaw 1987). The experience was reinforced by what he learned from Byrne. Looking at the anti-machine backing Byrne received from other parts of the city convinced Washington to run for mayor on the reform platform that Byrne had abandoned. Few besides Washington had believed it, but Chicago proved ready for reform. After his first term in office, the case for reform became all the more compelling. Washington's reform coalition expanded to the point where the last of the great machine cities became the nation's new vanguard of progressive reform.

Richard M. Daley, elected in 1989 to complete Washington's term, is caught in a dilemma. As "Son of Boss," he is by birth and experience steeped in the values and practices of machine politics, yet he is also entangled in the web of reform spun by Washington. Thus, where experience and learning were consonant for Byrne—pushing her toward the machine—and Washington—pushing him toward reform—, they are dissonant for Daley: he is torn between the two.

In trying to accomplish both objectives, Daley has created a novel "machine politics reform style" form of governance (Ferman and Grimshaw 1991). He has pledged himself to uphold Washington's reform standards of "fair and open" government, yet "fairness" is antithetical to the machine's style of "friends and enemies" governance, and "openness" stands in opposition to the "closed, insider" style of government practiced by machines. Thus, Daley is walking a tightrope. So far he has enjoyed remarkable success, aided by skillful press relations, highly favorable media coverage, and a divided and inept opposition that has mounted only weak and sporadic challenges to his contradictory course: saying one thing but doing another.

The Setting and Plan of the Book

In this study I will focus on machine politics and black politics in Chicago over the past half-century. The study begins during the Great Depression years, when the Democratic machine came to power and when black voters began making their realignment behind the ascendant Democratic party, and it culminates in the tumultuous 1980s and 1990s, a period in which the five mayors who headed Chicago were as distinct from one another as night from day. By the 1990s, blacks were back out in the cold again, embittered, divided, and lacking the leadership to reassemble the reform coalition Washington had constructed. The vast historical canvas provides a rich variety of cases, which enables us to assess the utility of the interactive perspective under a wide range of circumstances.

The introduction to the study is completed in chapter 2, where the interactive perspective is applied to some of the classical work on machine politics and black urban politics. Much of what we know about the two subjects stems from Harold Gosnell's two innovative studies, *Negro Politicians* (1935) and *Machine Politics: Chicago Model* (1937), and James Q. Wilson's widely influential *Negro Politics* (1960). The interesting thing, as we shall see, is that although the studies stand together as classic interpretations of machine and black politics, they sharply diverge at several critical theoretical junctures. Each holds a point of view that accentuates some features while slighting or ignoring others. The interactive perspective provides us with a more comprehensive understanding of the circumstances Gosnell and Wilson examined, thus forming the basis for constructing a more compelling explanation.

The next six chapters come in three pairs. Chapters 3 and 4 examine Chicago's Democratic machine, black Democratic politics, and relations between the two in their formative stages, a period running from the 1930s to the mid-1950s. Chapter 3 provides a new interpretation of the complex and contradictory course of the black Democratic realignment, and chapter 4 challenges the conventional view that a multi-ward machine, headed by Congressman William "Boss" Dawson, was formed during this period to govern the black wards.

Chapters 5 and 6 focus on the Richard J. Daley machine that dominated Chicago's politics for two decades, from the mid-1950s to the mid-1970s, with distinction being drawn between the first and second halves of Daley's long mayoralty. During the first period, Daley elevated the machine to the zenith of its power, and the black wards were transformed from marginal local Democratic status into the Daley machine's electoral stronghold. However, during the latter half of Daley's reign, the machine hit its nadir, as race replaced social class as the city's political divide. After the civil rights movement swept into Chicago, the poor black wards grew disillusioned with the machine, the middle-class black wards broke into open revolt, and the white ethnic wards set aside their fiscal concerns over the machine's excesses to embrace it on racial grounds.

Chapters 7 and 8 take up the complex politics of the post-machine period, covering the decade from 1977 to 1987. The first successful mayoral challenges to the machine were issued by minorities during this time, first by a woman, Jane Byrne, in 1979 and then by a black man, Harold Washington, in 1983, with black voters forming the nucleus for both successful challenges. The interactive perspective traces the Byrne machine's decline back to the waning Daley days, where he sought to contain rather than accommodate black interests. In turn, it traces much of Washington's success back to the racist excesses of Byrne's mayoralty. Thus, Byrne was not possible without Daley, nor Washington without Byrne.

In the final chapter, we take up the relationship that has emerged among machine, reform, and racial politics in the post-Washington period. Washington redefined reform in the novel redistributive terms of "fair and open" government, which stood in sharp opposition to the machine's "friends and enemies" and "closed" style of governance (Grimshaw 1984). At the same time, as Chicago's first black mayor, he provided the city's black populace with its first taste of first-class citizenship in a myriad of ways. Accordingly, reform and race stood in uneasy harness under Chicago's black reform mayor, while the machine suffered badly at his hands.

Neither of Washington's successors, Eugene Sawyer nor Richard M. Daley, has been able to hold race and reform together, and both of them, with deep roots in the machine, have attempted to reestablish a place for the machine in the city's politics. The development represents yet another variant of machine politics in Chicago—machine politics, reform style. How this latest in a long line of complex contradictions in the city's politics plays out will, for better or worse, shape the city's future in critical ways.

2

Revisiting the Classics

Much of what we know about machine politics and black politics rests upon some classic work done years ago in Chicago. During the 1930s, Harold F. Gosnell produced a pair of seminal studies, *Negro Politicians* (1935) and *Machine Politics: Chicago Model* (1937). *Machine Politics* focused on Chicago's Democratic machine just as it was getting off the ground under the leadership of Mayors Anton Cermak and Edward Kelly and party chairman Patrick Nash. *Negro Politicians* focused principally upon black politics during the waning heyday of Republican rule; with a few brilliant strokes, Gosnell also caught the first glimmering of the extraordinary party realignment in the offing—when black voters and politicians finally would forsake their deep and long-standing moral allegiance to the Republican "party of Lincoln, the emancipator" for the ascendant Democratic "party of the New Deal."

Some twenty-five years later, James Q. Wilson brought Chicago's black politics and machine politics up to date with his classic *Negro Politics* (1960). Wilson's study was made at the outset of Mayor Richard Daley's lengthy reign. It explored the tight interconnections between machine politics and black politics, arguing that black politics necessarily reflected the structure and style of a city's broader politics. Thus, the multiward "submachine" headed by Congressman William "Boss" Dawson essentially amounted to a black facsimile of the citywide machine lead by Mayor Richard "Boss" Daley.

These two bodies of classic work, along with Edward C. Banfield and Wilson's definitive summation "The Machine" in *City Politics* (1963), constituted the conventional wisdom about the basic organizational and electoral contours of machine politics and black urban politics. Much of the work that has followed largely amounts to jotting in the long shadows cast by these classical studies (eg., Rakove 1975; Gove and Masotti 1982; Holli and Green 1984).

Yet here is the paradoxical thing: although the works of Gosnell and Wilson stand together as classics, they clash at virtually every critical theoretical turn. In terms of the three perspectives we described in chapter 1, Gosnell essentially held, albeit in an unsystematic way, a political perspective, while Wilson used a more thoroughgoing economic perspective, and neither of them made much use of the sociological perspective. Thus, Wilson's *Negro Politics* introduced a fundamental theoretical shift by attempting to explain machine and black politics largely without reference to politics. The critical shift was obscured, however, by the vast differences in setting and in method that separated the works. I am going to focus on the critical shift of theoretical perspective; however, something must first be said about the differences of setting and method.

There is no question that machine politics and black politics during the 1920s and 1930s were vastly different, in some important as well as obvious ways, from those of the late 1950s. The political machine Gosnell described was just getting under way, and, in his view, it was riddled with competing centers of power revolving largely around intense ethnic rivalries.

The Irish factions were particularly distressed by the power acquired by Bohemian Mayor Cermak and his coalition of eastern and southern European factions, which diminished the traditional preeminence of the Irish in the Democratic party. When party chairman Pat Nash brought in the Irish party outsider Edward Kelly to replace Cermak—after Cermak was killed in 1933 by an assassin's bullet thought by some to have been poorly aimed at President Franklin Roosevelt—the Irish bosses were partially mollified. The Eastern European "outsider" was out, and the Irish were back in control. Yet ethnic representation was not sufficient to satisfy all the Irish ward bosses. Several of them remained bent on winning more control for themselves and their particular factions.[1] Accordingly, the machine remained divided by competing elites for some time.

Gosnell's black Chicagoans, political elite and voters alike, had little to do with Democratic machine politics. Indeed, black Democratic ward leaders were so few and obscure at that time that Gosnell even misidentified the lone black Democratic ward committeeman, Edward "Mike" Sneed, as "Michael Sneed," taking his nickname for his given name (1935, 90, 393). The black belt was solidly Republican throughout the 1920s and well into the 1930s. At the outset of the 1930s, when the great Democratic realignment took place, black voters were the only electoral bloc in the city that remained aboard the ill-fated Republican ships of Mayor William Hale Thompson and President Herbert Hoover, when economic storm and political sea change swept them under (Allswang 1971, 42).[2]

The machine politics and black politics James Q. Wilson encountered appeared to be poles apart in nearly every important respect. Richard Daley, as mayor, party chairman, and controller of the budget—which he had wrested from the city council's fierce pack of "gray wolves"—held near absolute control and headed a far more centrally directed and monolithic machine. The intense factional infighting and bitter ethnic rivalry that had been at the core of Gosnell's analysis were scarcely to be found in the 1950s. A solid consensus had formed, according to Wilson, around the organizational goals of efficiency and electoral success, replacing the conflict among rival elites that had characterized the machine during its formative years.

Black politics underwent a no-less-radical transformation between the 1930s and 1950s. An electorate that had been intensely Republican was solidly Democratic by the late 1950s. In place of highly contentious Republican ward leaders, a monolithic black Democratic "submachine" appeared to have emerged under the firm control of Congressman William "Boss" Dawson, who had been an inconsequential Republican alderman during Gosnell's time. "Boss" Dawson's lieutenants (five other black ward committeemen and aldermen) marched in lockstep to Dawson's commands, according to Wilson, just as Dawson toed the line laid down by his boss, Mayor Daley. All the way down the line, consensus replaced conflict. Gosnell's contentious and power-hungry elite had become complacent and well-oiled cogs in Daley's machine.

The methods used by Gosnell and Wilson were as distinct as the settings they described. Both men were operating at the cutting edge of their craft; but they were cutting in very different directions. Gosnell and others of the Chicago school of political science, notably Charles E. Merriam (Merriam and Gosnell 1924; Merriam, 1929), were self-consciously engaged in elevating the study of politics to a more detached and purely descriptive level. Political studies, of machine politics in particular, had previously tended toward a strong normative orientation, which the Chicago school believed prevented political science from achieving its proper place as an "exact science" (Ogburn 1935, xii).

For Gosnell and Merriam putting social science on a value-free footing represented an especially challenging task. Both men were deeply committed activists in Chicago's Democratic reform movement. Merriam had run as a mayoral candidate in 1911 and 1919, and Gosnell managed campaigns in the Fifth Ward, the great "mother ward" of reform politics that encompassed the University of Chicago.

Wilson was no less self-consciously attempting to elevate political science to a higher plane, to a more systematic, theoretically grounded, and deductive level of analysis. In doing so, he was reacting against the descriptive social science that Gosnell and members of the old Chicago school had been instrumental in establishing. In a foreword Wilson wrote for a revised edition of Gosnell's *Negro Politicians* in 1967, he implicitly spelled out the principal methodological differences between his own work and Gosnell's. *Negro Politicians* (1967, p. xii), Wilson said in his Introduction to that work, "lacks any explicit theoretical orientation and offers few large generalizations"; it "paid relatively little attention to the organization and tactics of Negro politics"; and it "reflects the relative disinterest of some of the older Chicago school of social scientists in questions of general social theory." Indeed, in *Negro Politics* (1960) Wilson found so little of value in Gosnell's work that Gosnell is only referred to twice in a general way in the endnotes and once in the text.

As important as the differences of setting and method are, however, their significance is actually overstated by the respective political and economic perspectives employed in Gosnell's and Wilson's work. Theoretical perspectives, after all, focus attention selectively, they rely upon particular assumptions, and they generate different expectations about "normal" behavior. Accordingly, some features of a situation will appear clearly in the foreground, leaving other features obscured in the background, and still other features will fall altogether outside the field of vision. So it is with the political and economic perspectives employed by Gosnell and Wilson.

Getting at Wilson's shift of perspective is complicated work, however, because Wilson never directly confronted Gosnell's radically different findings. He simply took what he found in the late 1950s as given, without devoting attention to how or why things had changed so profoundly in only the span of a generation. Thus, the two perspectives need to be brought together into a more direct and focused dialogue and placed within a broader historical context. By so doing, a diverse array of circumstances can be brought to bear on the two perspectives, when it will become apparent that there are significant similarities and continuities, as well as differences and discontinuities, between the two periods. Political and economic interests are present in both periods, although in different configurations, interactively shaping choice and other behavior. This is not to say that outcomes are altogether indeterminant. As the classic work by Gosnell and Wilson would lead us to believe, although not to the extent that they maintain, one or the other interest is likely to be prime. However, this depends upon the particular structures and concrete circumstances in which the interests are enmeshed, and it is these relationships and how they are reconfigured by changing historical circumstances that remain to be determined.

The Organizational Contradiction
Interests: Politics and Economics

Gosnell understood politics to be essentially a struggle by ambitious men for power, whether the struggle took place within a highly constrained machine setting or in a more conducive environment. That is how he characterized black politics within the highly factionalized Republican party. That is how he described politics within the much more centralized and monolithic Democratic machine. In his wideranging, richly descriptive fashion, Gosnell advanced several explanations for the primacy of an elite political interest. The principal factor he focused upon was a strong ethnic identification, a latent identity, that vied with the elites' manifest organizational identity. Together, the two contending identities pushed and pulled the machine in contradictory directions.

A prime example of the contradictory influence of elite interest and organizational interest involves William Dawson's first bid for public office as a Republican. Dawson chose to launch his career at the very top by taking on one of the most powerful men in his party when he challenged Martin Madden in 1928 for the congressional seat he had held since 1904. Madden sat in the inner circle of the local GOP and he headed the powerful House appropriations committee. Here is how Dawson framed his challenge: "By birth, training, and experience, I am better fitted to represent the district at Washington than any of the other candidates now in the field. Mr. Madden, the present congressman, does not even live in the district. He is a white man. Therefore, for those two reasons, if no others, he can hardly voice the hopes, ideals, and sentiments of the majority of the district" (Gosnell 1935, 79).

Rival elites within the Democratic machine generally displayed more prudence than Dawson. However, Gosnell provided abundant evidence that they, too, frequently pursued goals that pitted their personal political interests against the economic interests of the party. Thus, for example, in drawing ward boundary lines, although it would be in the machine's electoral interest to draw the lines so that they provided a broad range of ethnic representation, elites within the machine were no more willing than Dawson was to sacrifice their own interests for the organization's rational interests: "In drawing ward lines all the tricks of gerrymandering are also employed by the aldermen. . . . Nationality and racial groups were cut into small bits by the 1921 and 1931 ward lines. Ward committeemen of Irish extraction have been particularly active in splitting up their bailiwicks so as to prevent their defeat by Italian, Polish, or Jewish rivals" (1937, 32).

Wilson, in contradistinction, was far more inclined to interpret elite motivation and behavior in terms of an economistic organizational interest. Elite success in the machine was construed in rational terms; advancement resulted from meeting organizational needs, which yielded promotion over rivals who possessed less electoral expertise. Thus, here is Wilson's interpretation of William Dawson's rise to the top in the Democratic machine, to which he had shifted his allegiance in the late 1930s:

> In each case the Democratic leadership was confronted with a choice: shall we side with Dawson, who has given us certain support and produced results at elections and whose advice we have generally found to be reliable, or should we side with his challenger, who may be a man of untried prowess, or who has not been as successful, or who seems to be lacking in skill? In retrospect it is easy, and perhaps true, to say that building a single Negro machine was the most rational course to have followed, in terms of an economic calculation that judges the efficiency of patronage and money spent in terms of votes and elected officials produced. (1960, 80)

The interesting thing about Wilson's interpretation is that it altogether ignores the political dimension of the choice facing Dawson's superiors. The Democratic leadership appears to have acted without giving any consideration to how power relations within the machine would be affected by granting Dawson control over a five or six ward black empire. Wilson's assumption is all the more remarkable given Dawson's extraordinary ambition and, as Wilson says, his "superior skill in the political arts." Moreover, Dawson was black, which was no minor consideration then or now in Chicago's politics. It is there-

fore not unreasonable to suppose that the ruling elite did ask themselves what Dawson could be counted upon to do with all the power
they were being asked to place in his hands.

In fact, as we shall see, exactly that compelling political question
did enter into the calculations of at least one of the ruling elite who
was determining Dawson's fate. Even before he was elected mayor,
Richard Daley chose to curtail, rather than enhance, Dawson's
power. In choosing ward committeemen in 1952 and 1953 for three
of the wards (the Third, Fourth, and Twentieth) said to be part of
Dawson's multiward machine, Daley actually rejected all the candidates proposed by Dawson, selecting black elites loyal to him rather
than to Dawson. (The details of this development are discussed in
chap. 4.)

Moreover, as to the extent to which the expertise of the nominees entered into Daley's calculations—a prime consideration of the
economic perspective because of its vital impact on organizational
performance—two of the three black committeemen selected by Daley were political novices. Thus, Daley must have had more in mind
than electoral efficiency when he made his choices. In this instance,
as we shall see shortly, extending his control over the party in order
to acquire the party chairmanship dictated Daley's decision. Wilson's
economic perspective therefore limited his range of vision, hindered
him from taking some critical political considerations into account,
and badly skewed his interpretation.

Structure: The Sociological Dimension

Neither Gosnell nor Wilson devoted much attention to the central
issue addressed by the sociological perspective: the relationships between organizational structure and economic and political interests.
Wilson took it for granted that the machine was structured along
strictly hierarchical and monolithic lines, and therefore its organizational interest was secured as a matter of course. Gosnell's (1937)
nontheoretical, more detailed, and eclectic approach provided a
more complex and ambiguous account.

Mayor Cermak, for example, is said to have "ruled with an iron
hand, kept all the patronage under his thumb, and dealt ruthlessly
with those who furnished any opposition" (1937, 14). Yet Gosnell's
evidence shows that rival machine elites time and again issued
strong challenges to the mayoral leadership of both Cermak and his
successor, Kelly. However, the structural underpinning that enabled
either mayoral dominance or successful challenges by rival elites is

not provided, just the conflict itself: "During the term that Mayor Cermak controlled the organization, the Irish were jealous of the power exercised by the Slavic elements in the party. Since the coming to power of the Kelly-Nash machine, the German Jews and the native American elements have been struggling for power within the organization" (1937, 39).

A similarly intriguing structural problem exists with Gosnell's analysis of the relationship between the machine's ward organizations and its central administration. See, for example, Gosnell's complex description of the recruitment of ward committeemen and their role in the organization, where the process is explained in attenuated rational terms: "In order to become a ward committeeman in Chicago, the aspirant must begin political work at an early age. Long years of apprenticeship seem to be one of the qualifications. . . . Every important political faction in both the Democratic and Republican parties tries to select the best possible representative for each of the fifty wards" (1937, 28). Factional conflict was, of course, present; however, each faction was said to have sought skilled and experienced representation.

But after the committeemen were elected, the rational standards were largely set aside. The machine's vaunted standards of productivity actually turned out to be surprisingly modest: "Once elected, a ward boss who shows the ordinary amount of adroitness and party regularity is likely to be continued in office" (1937, 28). Unlike the central elite at the top of the machine, the ward committeemen tended to hold their posts for life. "Their superiors might change, but the ward bosses cling to their posts in spite of economic and political storms" (1937, 27).

A "gentlemen's agreement," a "club" culture, pervaded the machine. From the political perspective, this protected the incumbent ward elite from the rigor and shocks of competition. From the sociological perspective, the agreement provided the machine with a critical measure of stability. Despite the machine's reputation for cold-hearted efficiency and ruthless dedication to success, there was virtually no turnover of ward elite. The ward elite were shielded by a code of loyalty that protected them from the sharp sword of organizational rationality, and the central elite, also aided by the code, went along with the contradictory organizational standards of efficiency and loyalty.

Wilson, by contrast, worked at a more abstract and deductive level, not delving as deeply as did Gosnell into the particular and the concrete. Nor did he attempt to cast his analysis in comparative historical terms. This is unfortunate because if he had, he would have encountered some of the same complex structural problems that complicated Gosnell's analysis.

By looking more closely, for example, at the recruitment of black machine elites, he would have found that the so-called Boss Dawson machine was actually created and broken in the span of a few years by the shifting structural axis of power atop the machine. Dawson was created by one mayor, who used Dawson to advance his own interests. Dawson's fledgling empire later was destroyed by another mayor, who was similarly bent on advancing his own interests. (Again, the details are contained in the following chapters.)

Dawson's initial rise to power in the machine occurred under the most extraordinary circumstances. Having just been defeated in 1939 after two terms as the Republican alderman of the Second Ward, Dawson switched parties and threw his support to the Democratic candidate in a run-off election that was narrowly won by the Democrat. For his timely switch and efforts, and with the support of Mayor Kelly, Dawson was made the Democratic committeeman of the Second Ward, replacing a white incumbent who had become an embarrassing anachronism with the black Democratic shift.

Mayor Kelly's remarkable decision to slate Dawson was accomplished over howls of protest from party chairman Pat Nash. Yet Kelly was well served by his odd choice. Bringing Dawson back from the politically dead would provide Kelly with Dawson's undying gratitude. Dawson also would be Kelly's foil in the black wards against the other black Democratic committeeman, who had the backing of Kelly's principal rival, Thomas Nash. Tom Nash headed the Southwest Side Irish bloc, which the newspapers called the "patronage and spoils wing" of the machine, and it posed the chief opposition to Kelly's leadership. Thus, with Dawson's slating, the machine's two main factions had representation in the black wards, and Dawson could be counted upon to side with Kelly through thick and thin.

It took nearly a decade, however, before Dawson was able to extend his base of power beyond his own ward. A long overdue ward remapping in 1947 finally gave the ambitious Dawson the opportunity he was looking for. The remapping was controlled by new party chairman Jacob Arvey, a protégé of Kelly. (Pat Nash had died in 1943 and Kelly was persuaded by Arvey to step down as mayor in 1947.) Reflecting a balance of power favoring Arvey's West Side "river ward" bloc over Tom Nash's Southwest Side Irish bloc, the residence of Tom Nash's black committeeman in the Third Ward wound up outside the new boundaries drawn for the Third Ward, making him ineligible to serve as ward committeeman. In his place, Arvey installed Dawson's chief aide, making Dawson the de facto boss of a two-ward empire.

Dawson's empire, however, was neither complete nor did it remain stable for long. The 1947 remapping also created a third black ward, the Twentieth Ward, which remained beyond Dawson's control. Arvey turned it over to a black protégé of his law partner, Barnet Hodes, who served as committeeman of the Fifth Ward, from which the new Twentieth Ward had been carved. Then, within a short time, Dawson lost his control over the Third Ward. Dawson wanted to rule an empire, but his man in the Third Ward preferred to be his own man. As the battle between the two ward bosses escalated, Dawson wound up back where he had started, as just another ward committeeman.

But Dawson was nothing if not ambitious and determined. In 1952, when the committeemen were up for slating, Dawson advanced candidates for both the Third and the Twentieth wards, in a renewed effort to extend his control over all three black wards. Inasmuch as the Twentieth Ward committeeman was sponsored by Arvey's law partner, Hodes, it was hardly surprising that Dawson had no success there.

Dawson also was rebuffed in the Third Ward. His former aide was dropped, in accordance with Dawson's demand. However, Dawson's replacement candidate was passed over in favor of a candidate who had the backing of Arvey and a protégé Arvey was grooming to run for party chairman, one Richard J. Daley. Looking to acquire support for his run for the chairmanship, Daley wanted committeemen loyal to him in place. He simply did not trust Dawson, and for good reason. As a politician of the "old school," Dawson despised the machine's reform element, particularly Mayor Martin Kennelly. He was therefore not inclined toward Daley—who had the backing of the party's reform forces, notably Governor Adlai Stevenson and Mayor Kennelly—and leaned instead toward Daley's opponent from Tom Nash's "patronage and spoils wing" of the party.

Thus, during the course of his career in the machine, Dawson made a spectacular entry into it at the top with Mayor Kelly's support, he acquired a two-ward empire with party chairman Arvey's backing, and then his empire and his hopes for an even larger one were dashed by Daley's own empire-building aspirations. For all Dawson's ruthless ambition and exceptional political skill, then, his fate was fixed by the machine's shifting structural fault lines and the political interests of the machine's ruling elite.

The Electoral Contradiction

The historical differences between the 1930s and 1950s are even larger in the electoral arena. The most readily apparent difference involves the about-face of the black electorate. Within the span of a generation, die-hard Republicans were transformed into solid machine Democrats, or so it would seem from simply comparing election returns in the black wards during the two periods.

A related and interesting difference involves the character and intensity of black political involvement. During Gosnell's time, the black belt was a vibrant political community. It was not unusual to hear candidates giving political speeches on street corners or to find large halls packed with enthusiastic crowds for political rallies. A long and painful history of oppression as a group generated a collective political identity, and so black voters tended to perceive their political goals in collective terms. The black belt's compactness "facilitated economic, social, and political solidarity," and the solidarity was reinforced "by the persistent hostility of the white world" (Gosnell 1935, 19–20).

Few recognizable traces of this politically vibrant community could be found, however, in the 1950s. Organizational meetings of the Democratic machine's agents had taken the place of large, boisterous political rallies. The street corners were quiet, and politics was no longer a staple of daily conversation. An informant told Wilson (1960, 72): "What these people need is help in the little things. . . . There are very few interests that concern them." Black voters no longer conceived of politics as a hopeful enterprise for the "advancement of the race." In large part, this was because the machine had transformed politics into a cold, pragmatic business enterprise, as Wilson explained. "Politics, to the politicians, is the art of organizing a community for the purpose of electing men to office. It is not a vehicle for the public expression of grievances" (ibid.).

Yet once again it is important to recognize that the distinct perspectives employed by Gosnell and Wilson tended to magnify differences and discontinuities while obscuring similarities and continuities. Gosnell's political perspective accentuated the collective political element, and Wilson's economic perspective focused attention on the individual economic element. Moreover, neither study attended much to the problematic relationship between structure and interest in shaping electoral choice. Yet as we shall see, a pair of critical structural changes decisively altered black perceptions of the political machine.

Accordingly, we need to be mindful of the contrapuntal relationship between political and economic interests during both historical periods. We need to attend to the complex and changing sociological relationship between interests and structure. The interactive perspective supplies these missing elements and is therefore able to provide a more comprehensive and compelling explanation of electoral behavior during both periods, as it draws out the interconnections between them.

Interests: Politics and Economics

In an eloquent passage, Gosnell conveyed the centrality of politics in the black belt.

> The politicians have found that in the South Side area it is easy for them to reach a large proportion of the voters. . . . There may be many in the district who have had limited opportunities for schooling and some of the older ones may neither read nor write, but they are kept informed regarding political matters by a variety of face-to-face contacts. In church, at a lodge meeting, on the street corner, in their place of employment, at a restaurant, at home with their children who have just come home from school, or at a place of amusement, they learn about the political issues and the candidates of the day. (1967, 22–23)

Despite all of the discussions, however, the outcome on election day was cut-and-dried. The range of Republican support in the black wards ran between 70 and over 90 percent in both national and local elections, with the black belt representing the Chicago Republican party's electoral stronghold. Republican presidential candidate Herbert Hoover ran well through thick and thin, pulling 71 percent of the black-ward vote in 1928, and an ever larger 77 percent against Franklin Roosevelt in 1932. Republican Mayor Thompson received a phenomenal 91 percent in the black wards in 1927, and even with the Democratic handwriting clearly on the wall in 1931, 82 percent of the black voters in the Second and Third wards remained aboard the sinking Thompson ship.

Gosnell (1935) devoted a chapter to discussing Thompson's solid support among black voters. He found that Thompson conveyed a genuine affection and respect for black voters, that he worked hard at cultivating black support, and that his efforts were aided by the racist excesses of the Democratic party—using "Bye, Bye Blackbird" as a campaign song and referring to Mayor Thompson's administration as "Uncle Tom's Cabin," for example (1935, 47–55). In the final analysis, however, Gosnell returned to his basic political perspective in explaining the mayor's strong black support: a collective ideological reverence for "the party of Lincoln, the emancipator" (1935, 36). The utter magnitude of the emancipation experience reverberated through the years and bound blacks to the Republican party of liberation. Gosnell disposed of both Thompson's personal popularity and his adroit use of patronage by concluding: "It is probable that another man from his faction might have built up a similar reputation if he, rather than Thompson, had come into power at the proper time" (1935, 61).

Gosnell also provided a brief and provocative comparative analysis when he caught the glimmering of a Democratic shift in the black belt. First, he challenged the prevailing economic interpretation of the New Deal's appeal to black voters. Contrary to the conventional wisdom, Gosnell found that it was not the poorer black voters who shifted first, but rather the more well-to-do: "Greater gains were made by the Democratic party in 1934 in the outlying areas (Community 40) where unemployment was less and rents were higher than in depreciated areas (Community 35) where there were the largest number of relief cases" (1935, 34).

Then Gosnell drew upon his interviews to construct a generational explanation for the Democratic shift, presaging some of Kristi Anderson's brilliant analysis in *The Creation of a Democratic Majority 1928–1936* (1979). A critical distinction was drawn between older "traditionalists" and some emerging younger "realists." Among the "older generations the tradition of Abraham Lincoln as the emancipator, and the bitter disappointment at the collapse of the reconstruction regimes, have conditioned them against any association with the Democratic party" (Gosnell 1935, 36). However, "many in the younger generation are not moved by Republican traditions. They see a new Republicanism which cuts down the representation of the southern states in national conventions and they see the Democrats firmly in power" (1935, 36). Thus, the traditional solidarity of the black community, along with its collective ideological Republican orientation, were breaking down along the emerging lines of class and generations, and the ascendant Democratic party reaped the benefits.

By the time Wilson conducted his research in the late 1950s, the incipient party split had fully worked itself out, with the black wards having become as Democratic as they once had been Republican. Indeed, the party realignment proved so decisive that the black wards took the place of the poor white "river wards," which had been carrying the machine since its inception, as the machine's principal electoral stronghold.

Extrapolating Gosnell's political argument, we would expect to find that black voters had transferred their support to the Democratic party because it better represented collective black interests. Although the New Deal did not explicitly address racial discrimination until FDR's final campaign in 1944 (Drake and Cayton 1970, 359), the "party of the little man's" economic recovery programs certainly encompassed the interests of poor black voters. Thus, the New Deal's coattails would carry along the local machine, in the same way that Gosnell contended Mayor Thompson was carried by black attachment to the party of Lincoln.

Wilson, however, offered an individualistic economic argument in place of Gosnell's collective political argument. The machine was not understood as an extension of the national New Deal party, and it did not seek black support on collective ideological grounds. Rather, the machine won black support on its own distinctive material terms by meeting the socioeconomic needs of individual voters. Accordingly, Wilson argued, black voters provided the machine with high levels of support because they possessed high levels of need, which the machine satisfied. "The machine can flourish in the Negro wards largely because of the status and needs of the Negro. The incentives it can offer are still attractive to many Negroes, whereas they have largely lost their appeal to other ethnic groups which have risen farther. Low-paying jobs, political favors, and material assistance are still as important to many Negroes as they once were to foreign-born whites. The Negroes, unlike the Irish, have not priced themselves out of the market" (1965, 54).

Thus, we are left with a puzzle giving two distinctly different explanations of black electoral behavior: In the one case, black voters are said to be motivated by a collective ideology where the race issue looms large, and they support the party that best represents the aspirations of the black community. In the other case, the race issue is of far less significance, and socioeconomic need is identified as the source driving black voters individually toward the party best able to meet their needs.

Which explanation makes the most sense? Perhaps both answers are correct, and if so, then what produced the change from a collective political orientation to an individual economic orientation? Given what we have been told, we cannot say. However, if we extend the historical scope of the analysis and incorporate the contending perspectives into a broader analytic framework to create an interactive perspective, we can get to the beginning of an answer.

Structure: The Sociological Dimension

It is ironic that little attention has been paid to the intervening period between Gosnell's and Wilson's works, from the late 1930s to the early 1950s, given that era's theoretical and substantive importance, for it was at this time that the black Democratic realignment actually took place. It is therefore a fruitful place to assess the scope and utility of the contending political and economic paradigms.

From Gosnell's political perspective, we would have expected the black Democratic realignment to proceed along a slow, but steady course. The generational divide dictates such a path into the future. Older traditionalists who held deeply rooted ties to the party of Lincoln and an aversion to the Democratic party would gradually give way to a younger generation of realists who were less bound by the old ideology and therefore more receptive to the Democratic party's programs and power. The class divide Gosnell identified, where more affluent blacks were more receptive to the ascendant Democratic party, yields the same path forward, as more and more blacks improve their economic standing in the welfare state constructed by the New Deal.

Wilson's economic perspective generates a very different expectation. Here we would expect to find a prompt and substantial shift to the Democratic party, coming on the heels of its acquisition of power. It is the party in power that is able to confer the benefits required by those in need and, accordingly, the only rational course open to the great bulk of black voters was a realignment toward the new Democratic party of power.

As it turns out, neither the economic nor the political paradigm is able to adequately account for the changing behavior of the black electorate, and it is the sociological perspective's attention to the relationship between structure and interests that provides the missing link. Two contradictory patterns emerged during the 1940s: (1) Black voting in presidential elections followed one course, and (2) black voting in mayoral and aldermanic elections followed another as black voters began drawing a sophisticated and compelling distinction between the national Democratic party's New Deal and the local machine's "raw deal." (The details of the realignment are contained in chaps. 3–5.)

Black voting in presidential elections initially supports Gosnell's political interpretation as blacks retained their abiding faith in the "party of Lincoln" in face of the great Democratic sweep in 1932. However, in 1936 the black Democratic vote nearly doubled, rising from 25 percent to 49 percent, in line with Wilson's economic expectations that poor black voters would shift their support to the party in power. A second surge did not occur, however, until 1944, when the black Democratic vote jumped from 53 percent to 64 percent, at the time when FDR first spoke out against racial discrimination, addressing the issue in a campaign speech in Chicago (Drake and Cayton 1970, 359). This second surge lends support to Gosnell's collective-voting thesis.

Thus, the evidence is somewhat ambiguous, although the weight of it favors Gosnell's political interpretation. Clearly enough, black voting began and ended during this period on a collective ideological basis; yet the first great shift in 1936 could be interpreted in individual economic terms. Accordingly, we need to look at the local voting pattern for additional evidence, and when this is done, it becomes evident that black voting was predicated far more firmly on collective political grounds than on an individual exchange of favors for votes.

The local voting pattern in the black wards followed the same course at the outset. Democratic mayoral candidate Anton Cermak fared no better among black voters in 1931 than Roosevelt did a year later. Yet by 1939 Mayor Edward Kelly carried the black wards with a commanding 57 percent of the vote; 1939 was also the year in which the two black wards elected their first Democratic aldermen. Thus, local and national voting formed a single pattern.

Then, however, the local voting pattern set off on a novel course of its own. Mayor Kelly experienced his first slippage of black support in 1943, when he fell from 57 percent to 54 percent, putting him ten points below FDR's rising level of support in 1944. The Republicans also regained one of the two black aldermanic seats they had lost in 1939, and they narrowly failed to win back the other one by a few hundred votes in a run-off election. Local politics could no longer be understood as a reflection of national politics. Black voters were beginning to draw a sharp distinction between the national Democratic party and the Democratic machine.

Four years later the black Democratic contradiction became even more pronounced. The Chicago machine's new mayoral candidate,

Martin Kennelly, a party outsider with a reform orientation, pulled the largest vote in the city's history. However, he barely slipped by in the black wards. Kennelly even lost one of the black wards, but a win in the other one gave him an overall majority of less than 51 percent. A year later, by contrast, the Democratic presidential candidate, Harry Truman, won 75 percent of the black vote, marking an extraordinary spread of 24 points between local and national Democratic support. The Republicans also retained their aldermanic seat in the Third Ward, and "Boss" Dawson's candidate in the Second Ward was forced into yet another humiliating run-off election victory.

The vaunted Democratic machine's performance did not improve in 1951: Mayor Kennelly received another bare majority of less than 51 percent from the black wards and this time he failed to carry two of them. (A third black ward had been created in 1947 by ward redistricting.) The Third Ward also remained represented by a Republican in the city council. The only small sign of progress came in Dawson's ward, where his aldermanic candidate won for the first time without the necessity of a run-off election. Thus, after twenty uninterrupted years of citywide machine rule, the black wards were split down the middle in their evaluation of the machine.

Then in 1955 a second break in the electoral pattern occurred, in Richard Daley's first mayoral election. After producing only the barest of majorities in the preceding two elections, the black wards, which now numbered five wards, cast over 70 percent of their ballots for Daley. The machine also crushed its Republican opposition at the aldermanic level, including the Third Ward, where against all odds the Republicans had turned back the machine through three elections. The Democratic contradiction that had emerged in the 1940s and grown sharper with each election finally was resolved. Black voters finally were backing the machine as firmly as they had been supporting the national Democratic party for years.

Why? The long delayed local Democratic realignment was the result of a critical structural change accompanied by a particular campaign strategy that misfired. The one loaded the gun, and the other pulled the trigger. By the time of the 1955 mayoral election, the black community had been radically reconfigured by the U.S. Supreme Court decision in 1948, *Shelley v. Kraemer*. As mentioned above, the Court's decision enabled a large number of blacks with the economic means to secure housing beyond the black belt's boundaries for the first time.

The structural differentiation had a profound effect on the politics of the black wards. When blacks of all socioeconomic standing had been compelled to live together in the black belt, the black belt had comprised a unique community, and its unique social structure had provided the black wards with a unique political advantage. Poor blacks, who had made up the vast majority of the population, had possessed an exceptional political advantage in the form of a politically active middle class that had supplied role models, mentors, social and political organization, and financial resources and candidates. Thus, the residents of the black wards had a political choice rarely found in poor wards, and as a result the machine was fought to a virtual draw.

However, when the middle class began fleeing the black belt, the poor were left behind to fend for themselves. Under the new circumstances, no choice remained, and the machine finally was able to secure the wards in virtually uncontested fashion.[3] The black wards thus took on the political behavior of the poor white "river wards" in the 1950s because they now resembled them in social structural terms.

The takeover of the black wards by the machine was made all the easier by a campaign strategy used against the machine in the 1955 mayoral election. After he was dumped by the machine and replaced by Richard Daley, Mayor Martin Kennelly needed a strong issue in order to offset the machine's formidable organizational advantage. In the hope of generating a strong white backlash against the machine, the mayor seized the volatile race issue.

Kennelly linked the race issue to the classic anti-machine issue, its ties to organized crime—the "dictatorship from the dark," as an earlier mayoral opponent against the machine had put it. The mayor charged that his dumping had been engineered by black Congressman William Dawson, he brought up the widely reported allegations of Dawson's ties to organized crime, and he claimed that if Daley were elected, he would be controlled by the likes of Dawson and other powerful, corrupt inner-city ward bosses. The media, which generally supported Kennelly's reform candidacy against the machine, gave Kennelly's charges prominent and sympathetic coverage.

Kennelly's strategy failed to produce a sufficient white backlash against Daley. It did, however, generate an enormous backlash against Kennelly in the black wards. The *Chicago Defender*, the leading black newspaper, issued a passionate editorial on its front page. It defended Dawson, compared Kennelly's tactics to those of Hitler and Mussolini, and urged Kennelly's defeat as a matter of moral and civic obligation by all fairminded citizens (February 5, 1955). The machine's precinct captains in the black wards undoubtedly were the *Defender's* best newsboys for that particular issue.

Kennelly's strategy also effectively undermined the legitimacy of the anti-machine forces in the black wards. Since the black anti-machiners possessed little in the way of money or organizational resources, they always had relied heavily on moral suasion and the race issue in particular to carry the day against the machine. Kennelly's racist strategy thus took away the one leg they had to stand on. Attacking the machine or Daley's candidacy was widely perceived as aiding Kennelly's candidacy, and hardly anyone was prepared to support that course of action.

Accordingly, to borrow a Shakespearean distinction, Daley and the machine did not achieve success in the black wards so much as it was thrust upon them by Kennelly's racist campaign strategy. For a time, the Daley machine lived well off the good fortune that had been bestowed upon it. The black wards emerged as the machine's new electoral stronghold. However, when the race issue resurfaced again in the 1960s, during the civil rights period, the Daley machine revealed that it was no more prepared to respond to black interests than Kennelly had been. That launched the machine on its steady downward course of deterioration in the black wards, which culminated in the events of the 1980s.

Part 2
Formation
and Realignment

3

The Black Democratic
Realignment: Socioeconomic
Needs and Racial Values

Conventional wisdom, rooted in economic logic, contends that Chicago's black voters should have been among the first to shift their support to the ascendant Democratic party at the outset of the 1930s. Heaped at the bottom of the socioeconomic ladder, the great bulk of black voters required the benefits that only the party in power could provide. Accordingly, when the Democrats swept the Republicans out of office, locally as well as nationally, black voters should have had only a single rational course of action to follow.

Yet, in fact, the black electorate was the only group in Chicago that did not shift its allegiance, in either local or national elections, to the new Democratic party of power at the outset of the 1930s. All the city's white groups—Poles and Italians, Jews and Swedes, Germans and Czechs—switched. Blacks alone chose to remain outside what historian John Allswang has called *A House For All Peoples* (1971, 42).[1]

Moreover, when black voters did shift their allegiance to the Democratic party in 1936, a second peculiarity emerged. Kristi Andersen's study, *The Creation of a Democratic Majority, 1928–1936* (1979, 106), found that black voters shifted in a distinctive way. All the city's other groups formed Democratic majorities principally through the process of mobilization, in which non-voters were transformed into Democratic voters. Blacks alone forged a Democratic majority mainly through conversion—the transformation of Republicans into Democrats.

Ironically, inasmuch as her study overturned much of the conventional wisdom about the basis for the Democratic realignment, Andersen relied upon conventional economic logic to account for the peculiar black voting behavior. As she explained, "the social and economic position of most people in the [black] 2d ward was such that they could not easily afford political loyalties which no longer provided material benefits" (ibid.). Thus, while large numbers of whites dramatically changed their behavior in response to the new choice provided by the Democrat's "New Deal," most black voters remained locked into the same old economic style of politics: exchanging their votes for the favors provided by the party in power.

So it appears, at any rate, from Andersen's analysis. However, if we take the analysis farther, by looking at a wider range of black voting, including local as well as national elections, a vastly different picture emerges, which, in turn, requires a radically different explanation of black voting behavior. The new information supports a sociopolitical explanation, in which collective values play a critical role in shaping black electoral behavior. Black voters sought representation and empowerment as well as favors from the Democratic party.

The Democratic New Deal proceeded in two distinct stages among black voters. The first stage was economic, in which the collective class interest of the black electorate was addressed. Blacks were incorporated into the new Democratic party on the basis of their marginal economic standing, in essentially the same way that economically marginal white ethnic voters were brought into the New Deal.

Yet at the same time, black voters held a unique racial interest, and the strength of this status interest constrained their support for the New Deal. The New Deal revolution was incomplete, as far as blacks were concerned, because the Democratic party failed to address their marginal social status. It was for this reason that as late as 1940 only slightly more than half of Chicago's black voters were casting Democratic ballots.

The second stage of the New Deal revolution did not occur until 1944, when President Roosevelt finally chose to explicitly address the problem of racial discrimination. FDR took his stand on the discrimination issue in a campaign speech in Chicago, and St. Clair Drake and Horace Cayton, who were conducting research for their monumental *Black Metropolis* at the time, described the extraordinary tension and jubilation that attended the president's statement. "Negroes waited to see if the President would speak the Word. They were not disappointed. Four times within the speech, he struck the blow they were waiting for. He assailed the poll tax; he came out for a *permanent* FEPC [Fair Employment Practices Commission]; and twice he said that he believed in equal opportunity for all men regardless of race, creed, or *color*. Black Metropolis was jubilant. Roosevelt had waited until he came to the political capital of Negro America to make his pledge" (Drake and Cayton, 1962, 359; capitalization and italics in original).

Yet black electoral behavior in presidential elections only conveys half the story. In order to confirm the extent to which black voters were motivated by a collective interest in improving their class standing and racial status, we also need to look at local elections, where a remarkably different picture emerges. It was exactly at the point that President Roosevelt finally chose to take his stand on the racial question that Chicago's black voters began drawing a compelling distinction between the national Democratic party and the local Democratic machine.

Up until the mid-1940s, black voting in local mayoral and aldermanic elections was indistinguishable from presidential elections. The black Democratic realignment was proceeding on all fronts. However, when FDR committed the national Democratic party to the promise of racial equality, and the local Democratic machine failed to do so, two distinct black Democratic paths emerged. Support for the national Democratic party leaped to 64 percent in 1944, up from 53 percent in 1940, and it continued to rise to the point where 75 percent of the black electorate cast Democratic ballots in 1952.

At the same time, however, black support for the local Democratic machine began to collapse. Notwithstanding the machine's substantial citywide dominance and its abundant array of material resources, only the barest black Democratic majority, less than 51 percent, could be mustered in both the 1947 and 1951 mayoral elections. Moreover, one of the three black aldermanic seats remained in the hands of a Republican reformer. Notwithstanding their impoverished circumstances and the attendant need for material political "favors," many black voters drew a sharp distinction between the national Democratic party's New Deal and the local Democratic machine's "raw deal" on the race issue, and they voted accordingly.

It remains to be explained how this extraordinary Democratic contradiction was achieved. Although conventional wisdom places individual socioeconomic need well above collective racial values in determining black political behavior, the significance of racial status as a political factor is not difficult to comprehend. In a nation that upholds political equality as its ideal, the black political experience constitutes a profound contradiction. A brutal history in slavery; long, harsh years of deprivation and discrimination after entering "free" society; and an enduring position as a despised racial caste provided blacks with a distinctive political perspective. The social and economic yokes they were compelled to wear guided the political behavior of many blacks.

Yet values, however compelling, do not automatically serve as the basis for action. We need to identify the means by which the values were implemented into actions in order to comprehend the black Democratic contradiction that emerged midway through the 1940s. For this part of the development, we need to turn our attention to the unique social composition of the black community, to the prior-to-1948, heterogeneous black belt, which provided the overwhelmingly poor black wards with a distinctive political advantage in the form of a politically active middle class.

The National Black Democratic Realignment

The presidency represents the highest office in the land as far as the public is concerned, but members of the machine hold it in lower regard. "How many jobs does a president have, anyway?" Mayor Richard J. Daley reportedly once asked reporters in dismissing the office's importance. The machine also has less influence over voting in presidential elections than in local elections. The high estimate that voters place on the presidency generates high turnouts, which brings "uncontrolled" voters into the process—voters who are not obligated to the machine in some manner. The great issues often attending presidential campaigns—depression and prosperity, war and peace—also diminish the machine's hold over voters. Given the severity of the Great Depression in the 1930s, followed by World War II in the 1940s, such was certainly the case with the Roosevelt revolution and the Chicago Democratic machine's role in it.

Roosevelt's promise of a New Deal in 1932 had an enormous impact on Chicago's white voters, but it fell on deaf ears in the black wards. Black voters gave Roosevelt even fewer votes than they had Al Smith, the Democratic standard bearer in 1928—23 percent as opposed to 29 percent. Roosevelt's performance, however, turned the black wards around, and his vote more than doubled in 1936, rising to 49 percent, marking the first stage of the black Democratic realignment. Four years later, the black wards finally tipped over into the majority-Democratic column.

Black voters no longer were the outsiders in the city's politics. The tug of tradition finally gave way to the haul of modernity; the party of FDR's New Deal supplanted the party of Lincoln, the emancipator—yet only by a few percentage points. Black voters still lagged well behind white voters in support of Roosevelt's New Deal—53 percent to 59 percent.

The breakthrough year in the black wards was 1944—a second

stage of the black Democratic realignment. In response to Roosevelt's pledge in his 1944 campaign to deal with the racial discrimination issue, the black vote leaped to 64 percent, surpassing FDR's white vote by three points. However, no sooner had black and white voters finally come to a meeting of the minds on the New Deal than they parted company in the post-FDR era.

Roosevelt's successor, Harry Truman, groomed in the notorious Tom Pendergast machine in the southern border state of Missouri, nevertheless steadfastly supported Roosevelt's promise of racial equality. Despite the revolt of the southern "Dixiecrat" states at the Democratic convention, Truman maintained his commitment to a civil rights plank in the 1948 party platform.[2] His level of black support tipped the 70 percent mark; although turnout fell from the extraordinary heights it had reached in the FDR era. Four years later, in 1952, Illinois' Democratic Governor Adlai Stevenson, making the first of a pair of unsuccessful presidential bids, proved even more popular in the black wards, winning 75 percent of the vote.

However, as the city's black Democratic majority was expanding, its white Democratic majority was contracting. Truman's vote in 1948 in Chicago's white wards amounted to 58 percent, three points below FDR's vote in 1944. In 1952 Stevenson's level of white support fell four points below Truman's vote. The spread between black and white support for the Democratic presidential nominee thus exceeded twenty points. In the space of two decades, Chicago's black and white voters had traded places (see fig. 1).

Now we need to turn our attention to the source of black support for the new Democratic party of the New Deal. Following Kristi Andersen's study of the Democratic realignment, we need to ask whether the rise in black support came at the expense of the Republican party, in the form of conversion, or from voters newly mobilized into the electoral process. By examining the voting patterns in the Second Ward, one of the two black wards, between 1928 and 1940, Andersen makes the case that the great bulk of new black Democratic support came from converted Republicans. Then she goes on to explain the conversion in terms of (1) socioeconomic need—poor blacks could not "afford political loyalties which no longer provided material benefits"—and (2) the Chicago machine's dominance—"by 1936 the Kelly-Nash machine . . . was firmly in control of most of Chicago's patronage" (1979, 106).

However, when Andersen's analysis is extended in two ways—and in a third way in the next section—her economistic interpretation of black voting behavior is difficult to sustain. First, we need to

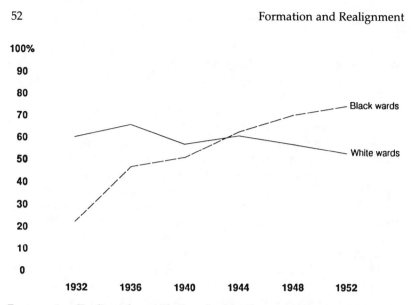

FIGURE 1. Trading places: Black and white Democratic voting in presidential elections, 1932–52. The black vote represents voting in the Second, Third, and, beginning in 1948, Twentieth wards. The white vote is the citywide vote minus these wards.

look at how the other black ward, the more affluent Third Ward, behaved. Two social surveys conducted during the 1920s and 1930s divided the black belt community encompassed by the Second and Third wards into three distinct socioeconomic areas on the basis of several indicators (cited in Drake and Cayton 1970, 384). The surveys found that the "best" area was located to the south of 47th Street in the Third Ward, and the "mixed" and "worst" areas were to the north of the 47th Street social class divide in the Second Ward.

Accordingly, if black voters were being motivated by socioeconomic need and were exchanging their votes for the machine's material favors, we would expect the rate of Republican to Democratic conversion to be higher in the poorer Second Ward than in the more affluent Third Ward. Yet that is not the case. In the critical realignment election of 1936, the rate of conversion actually was higher in the Third Ward. In the Second Ward, 62 percent of the Democratic increase can be accounted for by conversion, whereas 70 percent of the gain in the Third Ward can be attributed to conversion. (On the assumptions involved in the conversion versus mobilization calculations, see Andersen [1979] and Sundquist [1983, 229–39].)

Thus, the comparative analysis fails to support Andersen's economistic explanation. Rather, it is consistent with Harold Gosnell's finding that more affluent blacks, living at the south end of the black belt, were the first to shift their support to the Democrats. Gosnell used this finding to reject the individualistic favors-for-votes explanation in favor of a more complex explanation involving generational change—"many in the younger generation are not moved by Republican traditions"—and social class—the tendency of many middle class blacks to view "politics in a more realistic fashion" (1967, 33–36).

Next, if we extend Andersen's analysis by including presidential elections beyond 1936, a second critical piece of information can be brought to bear on the question of electoral motivation. The key election is the 1944 election, in which a second major black Democratic shift took place. Thus, the black Democratic realignment essentially came in two huge waves. Accordingly, unless one is willing to argue that the machine poured exceptionally large amounts of resources into these two particular elections, it is difficult to sustain the economistic favors-for-votes explanation.

In the 1944 election, black turnout increased by 4 percent, from an already extraordinarily high 91 percent in 1940 to a phenomenal 95 percent; yet the Democratic share of the vote rose 13 points. Thus, as in the 1936 shift, the bulk of the Democratic gain apparently came from conversion. What produced this second distinctive stage of the black Democratic realignment? We have argued, drawing on the field research of Gosnell as well as Drake and Cayton, that many black voters held a strong interest in racial status, apart from the class interest that was addressed early in the New Deal. Accordingly, it was only when Roosevelt extended the terms of his New Deal in 1944 by addressing the issue of racial discrimination, that the Democratic realignment was completed in the black wards.

There were two distinctive stages of the black Democratic realignment (see fig. 2). The first stage occurred in 1936, when blacks were incorporated into the New Deal Democratic party on the basis of their social class, and the second stage came in 1944, when blacks were incorporated on the basis of their racial status. In the end, black political loyalties were the mirror image of what they had been two decades earlier.

The Local Black Democratic Realignment

For a number of reasons, the local Democratic machine's candidates should have outperformed the national Democratic party's candi-

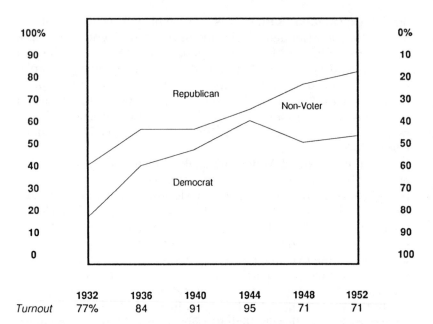

	1932	1936	1940	1944	1948	1952
Turnout	77%	84	91	95	71	71

FIGURE 2.   The two stages of Chicago's black Democratic realignment: Presidential elections, 1932–52. Turnout here is based on actual registered voters, not on the estimated voting-age population used in Kristi Andersen's (1979) analysis.

dates in the poor black wards. The machine deals with a more controlled electorate in local elections. Fewer voters turn out, many of them are obligated to the machine in some manner, and the great issues that sway voters in presidential elections play much less of a role in local elections. Indeed, the machine is well known for avoiding controversial issues. If you "don't make no waves and don't back no losers," as one of Chicago's ward bosses put it, you are less likely to get swept out of office (Rakove 1975).

"Housekeeping" services—patching potholes, collecting garbage, trimming trees, and the like—and the "friendship" that well-connected agents of the machine provide are the stuff of local elections, and this provides the machine with a second critical advantage as it redefines public services as private "favors" dispensed on a quid pro quo basis. "You take care of me, I'll take care of you; that's the way it works between friends." Chicagoans tend to understand this style of politics because it is the modus operandi of the local political culture. Thus, in this context, politics is reduced to economics, citizens become consumers, and the machine holds near monopolistic control over the public economy.

The machine also invests a greater share of its resources in key local elections, particularly mayoral elections, the unparalleled prize of local politics. The basis for the investment decision is straightforward. Local offices yield a higher return, in the form of patronage contracts and jobs. From the machine's viewpoint, then, mayors are far more important than governors, not to mention mere presidents. The main value presidents can provide is their coattails, which the machine's candidates can cling to and ride into some rich local office.

The Democratic machine's several advantages were further magnified during the realignment period by the utter impotence of the local Republican party. As Gosnell (1937) reports, shortly after Democratic Mayor Anton Cermak was elected in 1931, ending a long reign of Republican control of the mayor's office, the Democrats acquired a virtual monopoly over city and county offices. Without patronage to sustain it, the Republican party was transformed into an amateur enterprise.

Yet for all its advantages, the Democratic machine benefited most at the outset from the wrenching impact of the Great Depression, which thoroughly discredited the Republican party. Voters across the nation as well as in Chicago chose to "throw the rascals out," giving the Democrats the opportunity they had unsuccessfully sought for years. The economic storm was strong enough to even drive out of office Republicans as formidable as Mayor William Hale Thompson, who had served with but a single scandal-induced interruption since 1915. All but one of the city's voting blocs abandoned Thompson. Blacks alone, whose blind faith in the party of Lincoln, the emancipator, prevented them from reading the new Democratic handwriting on the wall, stayed by Thompson's side in 1931.

No election better testifies to the rapidity with which the Democrats seized control of the local political apparatus than the 1935 mayoral election. Emil Whetten, the Republican's candidate against Democratic Mayor Edward Kelly, was actually recruited by the Democrats. When the newspapers got hold of the deal, Whetten's stock plummeted among Republican voters (Gosnell 1937, 19), and he lost the support of the Republican ward bosses as well. Announcing that his campaign was short of funds, he asked the bosses to purchase the campaign literature they would be distributing on his behalf (*Chicago Tribune*, April 1, 1935).

Furious and humiliated, the GOP ward bosses informed Whet-

ten that he was on his own (Ibid, April 2, 1935), and the election
returns reveal the woes that can befall a candidate in Chicago when
the polling places are left unprotected. Mayor Kelly wound up with
80 percent of the black vote, a stunning increase of 62 points over
what Cermak had received four years earlier. Yet, on the other hand,
the Republican aldermanic candidates won handily in both of the
black wards. Either black voters had learned to split their ballots in
remarkably sophisticated fashion or the Republican ward bosses
had used remarkably "short pencils" in counting the ballots.[3]

The 1939 election confirms the short-pencils interpretation. The
Republicans fielded a genuine candidate, and most of the black Republican ballots that had vanished in 1935 reappeared in 1939.
Nevertheless, a strong registration drive by the Democrats accompanied by a high turnout put Mayor Kelly well over the top. Black
registration rose by over 25,000 voters, an increase of 44 percent,
and turnout reached a local realignment period high of 79 percent.
Mayor Kelly's margin of 57 percent exceeded President Roosevelt's
vote in the following year by four points.

Indeed, 1939 stands as the critical local Democratic realignment
election in the black wards. Not only did Kelly win handily and do
better than FDR, but both the black wards elected Democratic aldermen for the first time. The black Democratic realignment was proceeding along all fronts, or so it appeared at the time.

Four years later, however, a Democratic divergence between
support for the national and the local Democratic parties began to
emerge, and it grew progressively wider over the remainder of the
realignment period. Black support for the national Democratic party's main standard bearer continued on its upward course. The
Democratic machine's mayoral candidates, on the other hand, began
losing support in the black wards.

On the surface, the first sign of slippage did not appear to be
serious. Mayor Kelly's black support fell from 57 percent to 53 percent in 1943. However, according to Drake and Cayton's *Black Metropolis* (1962, 357–58), Kelly might well have lost the election in the
black wards had it not been for an unusual development. A coalition
of progressive trade unionists, who ordinarily despised "corrupt
machine politics," agreed to help Mayor Kelly in order to preserve
black support for the Democratic party at the national level. Thus,
in their determination to "checkmate the isolationist Republicans,"
the trade unionists went all out for Kelly.

The unionists' strategy did not, however, encompass the Democratic aldermanic candidates in the black wards, and they accord-

ingly fared far less well than Mayor Kelly. The Republicans, seemingly against all odds, recaptured the Third Ward. They brought out
the aged, but still popular, Oscar DePriest, former congressman, for
one more contest, and in a close runoff election, the old war horse
prevailed. Much the same thing occurred in the Second Ward,
where Congressman William "Boss" Dawson held sway. Dawson's
candidate was forced into a runoff election, from which he emerged
victorious, but only by a few hundred votes. This was hardly an indication of a politically indifferent black electorate willingly exchanging its votes for the machine's friendship and material favors.

The machine's position continued to deteriorate in 1947. Once
again, a look behind the public surface provides an insight into the
machine's problem in the black wards. The problem, in a word, was
race. While the national Democratic party was steering toward a
progressive position, by pushing for an end to racial discrimination,
the Democratic machine was moving in the opposite direction, by
pulling back from Mayor Kelly's modest anti-discrimination measures in public housing and in the public schools.

Kelly took the position that the city's small supply of public
housing should be made available to returning war veterans and
their families on a nondiscriminatory basis, regardless of the racial
composition of the community in which the public housing was located. This meant that some black families would be housed in
white communities (Meyerson and Banfield 1955, 124–25). Kelly
also intervened in a heated racial controversy at Morgan Park High
School, and once again came down on the side of racial integration
(Biles 1984, 92–94). Given the city's extraordinary levels of segregation and discrimination, as shown, for example, in Dianne Pinderhughes' *Race and Ethnicity in Chicago Politics* (1987), Kelly's modest
measures amounted to pathbreaking public policy.

According to the party chairman at the time, Jacob Arvey, an
intense white backlash generated by Kelly's actions made the three-
term mayor unelectable. Armed with the dismal results of a private
straw poll, Arvey approached Kelly with the bad news: he would
have to step down for the good of the party. "Ed, you're being hurt
by something that I believe in, and I believe you were right in.
But . . . we owe it to the party to disclose to you what our straw poll
indicates" (Rakove 1979, 12). Chicago was not ready for racial progress, even in small increments.

Kelly was replaced by Martin Kennelly, a prominent businessman and civic leader, who was cast as a blue-ribbon reform candidate. Kennelly, running as a reformer with the machine's backing,

received the largest vote in the city's history—922,967 votes, or 59 percent. But in the black wards, where Kennelly's reform credentials were scrutinized closely to determine where he stood on the race issue, the popular mayor secured only a bare majority of less than 51 percent.

Kennelly actually lost in the Third Ward, where the Republicans also retained the aldermanic post they had won back in 1943. A somewhat better showing in Congressman Dawson's Second Ward provided Kennelly with enough of an edge to secure a bare majority of the black vote. The Second Ward Democratic organization also held onto the aldermanic seat, although it had to endure another humiliating runoff election.

Thus, at a time when Democratic presidential candidate Harry Truman had the backing of 70 percent of the black electorate, Kennelly was barely getting by, and one of the two black aldermanic seats remained in Republican hands. The race issue was tipping the scales to create a black Democratic divergence, notwithstanding the great socioeconomic need of the black electorate and the machine's formidable organizational and material edge.

It should not be surprising, in light of the circumstances under which Kennelly secured the machine's backing, that he proved unsympathetic to black interests as mayor. At times, Kennelly even went well out of his way to alienate black voters. Thus, when the reform-minded black Republican alderman of the Third Ward, Archibald Carey, Jr., introduced an open-occupancy housing bill in the city council, a bill which, needless to say, stood no chance whatsoever of passing, Kennelly nevertheless took the floor for the only time in his term to speak out against it (Meyerson and Banfield 1955, 137).

The reform mayor's efforts to enforce the letter of the law also often worked to the disadvantage of a substantial black "underground economy," which blacks were compelled to operate because of racial discrimination. Thus, Kennelly ordered a crackdown on "jitney cabs," unlicensed—and illegal—cabs that served the black community (*Chicago Defender*, June 19, 1948). Yet since white cabs generally would not serve the black community, and white cab companies would not hire black drivers, the police, under Mayor Kelly, had turned a blind eye to the activity. The political "contributions" jitney owners provided to their protectors in the machine added a political dimension to Kennelly's changing of the rules of the game (Davis interview, 1979).

The same thing occurred with the popular, but illegal, "policy wheels" (Chicago's term for what is commonly known as the numbers game) that flourished in the black community,. Here the racial twist was even more compelling. According to the *Chicago Defender*, the police crackdown on the policy wheels was carried out on a discriminatory basis. Wheels run by the white crime syndicate were allowed to keep spinning. Only wheels operated by blacks unaffiliated with the syndicate were shut down by the police. In the *Defender*'s view, then, Mayor Kennelly's police department was spearheading the crime syndicate's takeover of what had been a lucrative and exclusive black enterprise (*Chicago Defender*, May 29, 1948; June 5, 1948). The policy wheels, too, needless to say, had been a rich revenue stream for the black machine ward organizations.

Although it had come to take a highly partisan Democratic stance during the New Deal era, the *Chicago Defender* ran several stories that were highly critical of Kennelly, reflecting the distinction black voters were drawing between the national and local Democratic parties. Kennelly was blasted for failing to take a stand on the racial conflict in which several public housing developments were embroiled (*Chicago Defender*, February 13, 1954; September 11, 1954) as well as for racial discrimination in the city's hiring and promotion practices (August 28, 1954).

In view of Kennelly's abysmal record, it is not surprising that Congressman Dawson strenuously opposed his reslating in 1951. At the slating session, the usually taciturn congressman lashed out at Kennelly. Dawson's concern, however, was not racial discrimination but political discrimination. Dawson wanted his patronage and his protection back (Royko 1971, 61–63). The other ward bosses were sympathetic—they also had suffered under the reform mayor's zeal for civil service reforms—but the machine was in the throes of an intense, uncertain power struggle, and Kennelly had to be reslated.

With the assistance this time of a vote-withholding scheme organized by the black ward leaders, intended, in part, to display their bitter dissatisfaction with Kennelly, the mayor once again secured only a bare majority of black support. Kennelly lost the election in two of the three black wards, the Third and Twentieth (a new black ward created in 1947) wards. However, Dawson's Second Ward came through again with a modest majority of 2,000 votes, providing Kennelly with an overall black margin of less than 51 percent. (The details of the vote-withholding scheme and Dawson's double-dealing role in it are contained in the next chapter.) Once again, as well, the

Third Ward retained its Republican alderman. However, for the first time, a Democratic alderman was easily elected in the Second Ward, and the Democrats also prevailed handily in the new Twentieth Ward.

Thus, after two decades of Democratic dominance, locally and nationally, the Democratic divergence that emerged in the mid-1940s had reached extraordinary proportions by the 1950s. Despite the Democratic machine's two decades of nearly absolute dominance, it was being fought to a virtual draw in the black wards in mayoral elections, and one of the black wards was even in a Republican alderman's hands, and a reform-minded Republican at that.

These difficulties, coupled with the fact that there was solid black support for the Democratic presidential ticket, reflect the critical role that a collective black interest in racial status played. Notwithstanding the machine's near monopolistic control over the favors and friendship needed by an overwhelmingly poor community, until the machine redressed itself on the racial issue, it would continue to fare poorly in the black wards. Figure 3 indicates the widening magnitude of the black Democratic divergence.

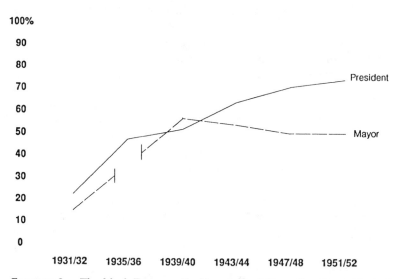

FIGURE 3. The black Democratic divergence: Mayoral and presidential elections, 1931–52. The figures are for the Second and Third wards between 1931 and 1947, after which the Twentieth Ward is included. The 1935 mayoral election was excluded because it was "rigged" in Kelly's favor and yielded highly distorted results (see Gosnell 1937, 19).

Table 1   **Machine Support in the Black and White Inner City Wards:
Mayoral Elections, 1939–51**

Wards	Principal Ethnicity	Median Income/ Median Schooling	Democratic Mayoral Majorities			
			1939	1943	1947	1951
2	Black	$2,168/8.2	4,416	1,134	1,325	2,110
3	Black	$2,527/8.5	4,450	2,803	−35	−248
14	Polish	$3,727/8.6	12,647	10,527	12,589	9,869
24	Jewish	$3,474/8.7	21,446	19,638	22,901	18,275
31	Italian/ Polish	$3,577/8.5 $4,144/8.9	9,678	9,623	12,652	8,630

Source: Ethnicity, income, and schooling figures are from Philip M. Hauser and Evelyn M. Kitagawa, eds., *Local Community Fact Book* (1953), and apply to the community areas comprising the wards.

Social Structure and Electoral Behavior

In order to gain a better appreciation of just how unusual the behavior of the black wards was in local elections, we can compare their voting to that of the poor white inner-city wards. Throughout the period from 1931 to 1952, the Democratic machine secured its largest margins in the poor white inner-city wards. Their support was so consistent and strong that one study of the Chicago machine referred to them as the "Automatic Eleven" (O'Connor 1975). All of the eastern and southern European immigrant groups were represented in the machine's electoral stronghold wards: Russian and Polish Jews, Italians, Poles, Czechs, and Lithuanians. Table 1 compares the performance of three of these poor white wards, selected because their boundaries were not altered much by the 1947 ward remap, with the black Second and Third wards.

What produced the poor black wards' unusual electoral behavior? Two factors bear on the question. First, there was the unique social composition of the black wards, creating the black belt, in which the vast majority of blacks lived within a narrow tract of land on the Near Southeast Side until restrictive housing covenants were declared unconstitutional in 1948 in *Shelley v. Kraemer*. The violence and restrictive covenants produced a city within the city. Blacks of all social classes lived within the boundaries of "Bronzeville." While more affluent blacks tended to live along the southern end of the district, and the poor congregated at the northern end, Drake and Cayton point out that "instead of middle-class areas, Bronzeville tends to have middle-class buildings in all areas, or a few middle-class blocks here and there" (1970, 660). Drake and Cayton captured the class-integrated character of Bronzeville with this observation: "Stand in the center of the black belt—at Chicago's 47th St. and South Parkway . . . On a spring or summer day this spot, '47th and South Park,' is the urban equivalent of a village square. In fact, Black Metropolis has a saying, 'If you're trying to find a certain Negro in Chicago, stand on the corner of 47th and South Park long enough and you're bound to see him' " (1970, 379–80).

The second factor bearing on the electoral behavior of the black wards is that the conventional analysis of social class, which assigns standing on the basis of occupation, does not uncover the actual social composition of the black wards. In conventional economic terms, the composition of the black wards appears to be overwhelmingly lower class. On the basis of occupation, the vast majority of blacks occupied the lower rungs of the social ladder. Drake and Cayton provided a black and white comparison of the city's occupational structure in the 1930s (see table 2).

As Drake and Cayton go on to explain, however, this represents a misleading conception of the actual social composition of the black community for two reasons. To begin with, racial discrimination imposed an artificially low "ceiling" on employment opportunities, which produced a considerable amount of underemployment, as well as unemployment. Thus, even though many blacks had the education, talent, and ambition for higher levels of employment, they were limited to unskilled and service-level jobs.

The classic instance of black underemployment was the Red Cap job—handling baggage at train, bus, and plane stations. For whites, this was a low-prestige, dead-end service job, attracting men of limited education and little drive. Not so for blacks, however. Drake

Table 2   **The Occupational Structure of Black and White Chicago, 1935**

	Whites	Blacks
Professional, managerial	20% (223,000)	6% (5,900)
Clerical	21% (230,000)	4% (4,000)
Skilled	19% (216,000)	8% (7,000)
Clerical semi-skilled	22% (247,000)	20% (18,000)
Unskilled	10% (116,000)	24% (22,000)
Service	7% (78,000)	38% (34,000)

Source: Adapted from Drake and Cayton, *Black Metropolis* (1962, 217). The figures are estimates derived from several sources. Drake and Cayton's data indicate that the black and white occupational structures were essentially the same in 1930 and 1935.

and Cayton found that the majority of black Red Caps were high school graduates, and many even had college training (1962, 237–42). Accordingly, "hidden" among the unskilled and service jobs at the bottom of the occupational ladder—baggage handlers, train porters, post office clerks, and the like—was a substantial black middle class, in terms of education, values, and behavior.

The second thing about the social composition of the black community is that a moral class structure, rooted mainly in the church, cut across the economic class structure. The moral values inculcated by the numerous churches in the black community—Drake and Cayton found 500 of them within the black belt's eight square miles (1970, 611)—as well as the secular values of "respectability" and "striving" created a substantial "poor but middle-class" element. These were individuals who "display some actual effort to 'better [their] condition—which means anything from joining the right club or church to getting a better job" (ibid., 662).

The distinctive political role performed by the black church merits particular emphasis. Its reach was far more comprehensive than that of the typical white church because it was expected to perform as a political institution as well as a religious institution. The church had historically been the sole institution to which blacks had had access during the long and difficult period of segregation and oppression. After the great northern migration, its secular outlook became even more pronounced. As a leading student of the black church put it: "The regularly established Negro churches placed less emphasis upon salvation after death and directed their activities increasingly to the economic, social, and political problems of Negroes in this world" (Frazier 1964, 84).

Moreover, the church was relatively free of the white controls that severely constrained other black institutions, and this had significant implications for the kind of political role the church was expected to play. Black politicians were understood to be limited by the white political machine's restrictions. Black civic leaders generally had to operate within the confines imposed by white philanthropy. The black press was dependent upon white advertisers. Black ministers, on the other hand, were principally dependent upon their own black congregations. Accordingly, the church was in a far better position to play a leading role in "advancing the Race," by serving as a "protest institution," speaking out against the injustices imposed by a "hostile white world" (Drake and Cayton 1970, p. 412–29).[4] Needless to say, not all black ministers played such a role. Reverend Archibald Carey, to take a notable example, turned his church into a "political machine," as Ira Katznelson put it, dispensing patronage for Mayor Thompson (1976, p. 93–100).

Thus, the class heterogeneity of the black community, the presence of a substantial middle class "hidden" among its lower class occupational structure, and the moral class structure constructed by a politically oriented black church had profound political implications. Unlike the class homogeneous poor white wards, the black wards possessed a sizable middle class which had the capacity to provide strong opposition against the machine. The middle class possessed the resources needed to construct political organizations, recruit candidates, and finance their campaigns.

The countervailing campaigns led by the middle class had a larger constituency to appeal to than would appear from viewing the black community solely in occupational class terms. The "hidden" middle class, individuals who were "in but not of the lower class," would, on the basis of values and education, be far more receptive to normative political appeals than would a typical working-class constituency.

Finally, the black community's distinctive moral structure, rooted in the church, with its secular political values of protest and "advancing the Race," vastly improved the prospects of countervailing political organizations working against the machine. In an important sense, the black church, rather than the Republican party, was the machine's principal opponent in the black wards. Its collective moral appeal constituted a profound challenge to the machine's individual material appeal. Thus, the two competing institutions worked to present black voters with a compelling choice rarely found in poor communities.

The black Democratic divergence, then, was produced by a countervailing middle class that generally supported the national Democratic party, but strongly opposed the local Democratic machine. At the mayoral level, the machine had a difficult time in the black wards because the positive appeal of its material favors was offset by its racist public policies. The evidence was everywhere: restrictive housing covenants, "double-shift" public schools, segregated and second-class health care, severe employment discrimination, and on down the line. Accordingly, the poor white wards gave the machine massive margins of support, but the machine barely got by in the poor black wards.

At the aldermanic level, the black candidates who opposed the machine generally were men of high social standing, closely affiliated with the church, with a history of involvement in the protest movement against racial discrimination. Even within the machine's ward organizations, and generating a great deal of tension, the conflict could be found.

The most successful of the countervailing candidates was the Reverend Archibald Carey, Jr., who defeated the machine twice, in 1947 and 1951, in the Third Ward. Carey was the pastor of Woodlawn AME Church, located at the far southern end of the black belt, a church that played a prominent role in the protest movement. Carey's church, for example, hosted CORE's (Congress of Racial Equality) first national convention in 1943 (Travis 1987, 305). In addition, Carey was an attorney with a citywide reputation as a reformer. The city's most prominent reform organizations, the IVI (Independent Voters of Illinois), a local affiliate of the Americans for Democratic Action, and the BGA (Better Government Association) endorsed Carey's candidacy. Carey also benefited from the political prominence of his father, who had been one of Republican Mayor William Thompson's key black political advisors and supporters. (Logsdon, 1961; Katznelson, 1976)

Carey's counterpart in the other black ward, the Second, was Mack Atkins, a prominent businessman who also was active in the church, as chairman of the board of directors of Ebenezer Baptist Church. Atkins was a funeral home director, and this naturally put him into a broad network of churches, lodges, and club organizations. Although he never defeated "Boss" Dawson's Second Ward machine, Atkins came very close on two occasions: in 1943 he forced Dawson's candidate, former fireman William Harvey, into a runoff election, which Harvey won by only a few hundred votes, and in 1947 Atkins forced Harvey into another closely fought runoff election.

However, in 1951, when Atkins' place was taken by a young social worker, William Robinson, who lacked Atkins' wide array of religious and social ties and high standing in the community, the machine finally swept to victory with ease. The breakdown of the black belt in 1948 also substantially aided the machine. As the middle class fled the black belt, the poor increasingly were left to fend for themselves.

Within the machine, the most notable countervailing candidate was Earl Dickerson. Dickerson initially was elected with the machine's support in 1939. By defeating incumbent Republican Alderman William Dawson, Dickerson became the ward's first black Democratic alderman.[5] However, when Dawson changed parties and with Mayor Kelly's support became Second Ward Democratic committeeman, Dickerson promptly lost his machine backing.

Dawson and Dickerson stood poles apart, and conflict was all but inevitable. Part of the problem involved power; who would run the ward? But the larger part of the problem was purpose. Dickerson was an outspoken "race man," active in a range of protest organizations and activities (Travis 1987, 155). Dawson was the quintessential machine man, whose public silence on the race issue reached legendary heights.

When Dawson dumped Dickerson in 1943, the maverick turned to religious, labor, and reform organizations for help but to no avail. Dawson denounced him as a "silk stocking"—a graduate of the University of Chicago's prestigious law school, Dickerson served as a director of Supreme Liberty Life Insurance Company, the largest black insurance firm in the nation—who "could not relate to the ward's poor residents." Years later Dickerson (interview, 1979) acknowledged the partial truth of Dawson's charge. Although he was morally bound to the community and devoted a lifetime to "advancing the Race," a deep class cultural divide separated Dickerson from the ward's poor residents. He was not one of them in a social sense; he acknowledged it and many voters recognized it, and Dickerson paid dearly for his inability to bridge the divide.

Another maverick of sorts worked in the machine's Third Ward organization. Roy Washington, whose son Harold would become the city's first black mayor, was a complex man, who had a foot planted in both of the institutions—machine and church—that fought for sway in the community. He was a ward leader, an attorney employed by the city, and a prosperous businessman in real estate. On Sundays, however, he made the rounds of the ward's churches as an itinerant African Methodist Episcopal minister. Harold Washington described how the peculiar political-moral polarity pulled at his father: "Politics was a centerpiece around our house. . . . My father discussed politics at the dinner table almost every night. . . . William L. Dawson, Oscar DePriest, Mike Sneed, Arthur W. Mitchell and C. C. Wimbush were frequent visitors in our home. . . . The only subject that superseded politics in our home was religion" (Travis 1987, 468).

When Roy Washington finally chose to run for alderman, his situation became even more complex. He ran as the candidate of a "new breed" coalition of businessmen and professionals which was bent on "elevating the organization's image." The ward's "old school" committeeman, Edward "Mike" Sneed, a janitor before the machine slated him for committeeman, reluctantly went along with Washington's candidacy. Sneed realized that the new breeders viewed him as the principal impediment to progress and that they had enough influence in the organization to force him to endorse Washington. After some second thoughts, however, Sneed decided to get the new breeders before they could get him. He discreetly threw his support to Washington's Republican opponent, and this provided the deciding margin over Washington (Davis, Love interviews, 1979).

Even the most secular and powerful of the black ward bosses, Congressman William Dawson, who would admit to no particular faith, acknowledged the peculiar and powerful role that religion played in his community's politics. He closed each one of his ward organization's meetings by "preaching" to his precinct captains in the same ritualistic way. Dawson, however, did not advocate protest, of course, or even speak of racial advancement. Rather, he preached the need for resignation and finding salvation in the next world, perhaps in recognition of the hopeless place of blacks within the white machine: "Walk together, children, and don't get weary, for there's a great camp meeting in the Promised Land" (Davis interview, 1979).

In Perspective

The economic perspective's favors-for-votes explanation of black voting behavior constitutes the conventional wisdom. Yet in the several cases we examined, its explanatory power proved to be quite limited for in order to explain black voting in any of the elections we looked at—at the presidential, mayoral, and aldermanic levels—the sociological and political perspectives had to be applied as well.

Thus, at the outset of the Democratic realignment in the early 1930s, the economic perspective led us to expect a massive black shift to the ascendant Democratic party. Yet in both the presidential and mayoral elections, black voters were the only ones who failed to provide the Democratic candidates with substantial support. We also found that the rate of conversion from Republican to Democrat was somewhat higher in the more well-to-do Third Ward than in the poorer Second Ward. Accordingly, something more than socioeconomic need was driving black voting behavior.

That something proved to be, as the political perspective would lead us to expect, a commitment to collective racial advancement.

Time and again, we saw that a substantial proportion of black voting could only be understood as the expression of collective political values. The national black Democratic realignment, for example, was not completed until President Roosevelt finally addressed the issue of racial equality in his 1944 campaign. Conversely, the Democratic machine began losing black support at the same time because it failed to follow the national Democratic party's lead. The modest steps Mayor Kelly took to reduce racial segregation generated such a strong white backlash that he was compelled to step down as mayor.

The sociological perspective was instrumental in uncovering the basis for the black community's divided political views. The unique social composition of the black wards explained their unique political behavior. With the vast majority of blacks confined within a black belt, the overwhelmingly poor black wards contained a novel middle-class element, and the countervailing political activity of the middle class provided voters in the black wards with a political choice rarely found in the more class-homogeneous poor white wards. The political strength of the middle class was reinforced by the church, the black community's historic institution of racial advancement and political protest.

A Democratic divergence emerged in the black wards during the 1940s. Following the completion of the black national Democratic realignment in 1944, more and more blacks poured into the Democratic party. However, at the local level, blacks were moving in the opposite direction. Mayor Kelly fared poorly in 1943, and Mayor Kennelly could muster only the barest majority of black votes in his two elections. The machine could do no better in aldermanic elections. Thus, despite the machine's two decades of citywide dominance and the dire socioeconomic need of most blacks, a substantial proportion of the black electorate was determined to chose its own representation rather than settle for what the machine was willing to provide.

4

Structure and Power: The "Boss" Dawson Myth

At the same time that large numbers of black voters were fighting the machine and creating an electoral contradiction, the machine's black elite were fighting among themselves, generating an organizational contradiction. Both developments defied the conventional wisdom rooted in economic logic. The applicability of the economic perspective to organizational behavior, after all, is premised on the presence of expert practitioners in the organization (Hogarth and Reder 1986, 6), and, as it happened, that is exactly what the machine's recruitment of black elites provided.

The black ward committeemen recruited by the machine early in the realignment process were nearly all highly skilled, experienced political practitioners (Love and Partee interviews, in Rakove 1979). Yet the anticipated high level of electoral productivity, commensurate with the high skill level of the black elite, did not materialize. Instead of serving the organization's electoral interest, the black elite devoted much of their attention to fighting each other, thereby damaging the organizational interest in the process. Thus, political self-interest, along with organizational fault lines that facilitated elite rivalry and conflict, fractured the logical economic nexus between expertise and productivity.

The intense elite rivalry in the black wards was anything but a deviant case. As Harold Gosnell (1937, chaps. 1–2) found in his study of the Chicago machine, elite rivalry was no less intense and pervasive atop the machine during its formative years. The pervasive conflict indicates the need to reexamine the bold assumptions made by the economic perspective. We need to determine whether the machine was actually structured along strictly hierarchical lines, which the economic perspective takes for granted. We also need to determine the extent to which the machine's ruling elite dispensed rewards on the basis of electoral productivity in order to assure compliance with organizational goals.

As it turns out, neither assumption squares with the actual conditions that prevailed throughout the lengthy realignment period, from the 1930s to the mid-1950s. The machine was cracked structurally, along two critical fault lines. One fault line ran horizontally. Instead of a single chain of command, there were several competing chains of command, with each command post anchored to a particular patronage center. As a result, the machine's compliance structure was highly particularistic and controlled by rival elites, with loyalty being directed to particular factions rather than to the organization as a whole (Gable 1953; O'Connor 1975).

Mayor Kelly certainly held the lion's share of patronage, and, for the most part, worked closely with party chairman Patrick Nash, hence the designation "Kelly-Nash machine." However, the Kelly-Nash machine was neither fully centralized nor unified, and this had critical consequences for the way in which the machine was managed. The chairmanship of the city council's powerful finance committee, for example, which held budgetary authority and thus controlled a substantial amount of patronage, often was held by a rival to Kelly and Nash's leadership, as were several other committee chairs. The president of the Cook County board—often referred to as "the second mayor"—also wielded considerable power on a more or less autonomous basis. The county assessor's office, which regulated commercial property tax rates and therefore had access to numerous wealthy campaign contributors, represented another independent fiefdom. A number of special districts—schools, parks, sanitation—held thousands of patronage jobs. Several other sizable centers of patronage, notably in the judiciary, operated largely beyond Kelly and Nash's purview.

By and large, the machine was structured along one overarching factional line throughout the realignment period. The Kelly-Nash faction, aided by the skillful and energetic Jacob Arvey, who served for years as Nash's informal party co-chairman before taking Nash's place, was principally rooted in the West Side "river wards." These were the historical port-of-entry wards for the city's eastern and southern European immigrants. The other principal faction was headed by Thomas Nash, distantly related to party chairman Nash, who led a group of wards the newspapers referred to as the "Southwest Side Irish bloc." Tom Nash was a prominent and wealthy criminal attorney, who also served as the committeeman of the Nineteenth Ward, one of the wealthiest wards in the city and a bastion of WASP Republican strength.

Ironically, the generally more well-to-do wards in Tom Nash's faction constituted the machine's "patronage and spoils wing." The Kelly-Nash faction, based in the poor river wards, was more allied to the "New Deal," and represented what the newspapers often characterized as the machine's "progressive wing," particularly under Arvey's leadership (*Chicago Daily News*, November 4, 1946). At the close of the realignment period, when the machine was poised to select a new party chairman, informed sources were divided over which of the two factions would prevail in the showdown (Gable 1953, p. 108).

During this period, the machine also was fractured along vertical lines, reflecting the inherent structural tension between a centralized authority and a large number of ward organizations—fifty in the city and an additional thirty in the suburban townships— which represented a diverse and competing array of class, ethnic, territorial, and other interests. Under a fully centralized structure, the ward organizations would constitute so many "administrative outposts" under the control of the central elite. However, many of the ward bosses yearned for, and frequently achieved, more autonomy than that. From the ward bosses' perspective, the ideal arrangement amounted to autonomous fiefdoms, in which the local barons merely paid nominal fealty to the ruling elite and ran their wards as they saw fit.[1]

The machine's numerous patronage centers, the horizontal fault line, facilitated a high degree of ward autonomy, thereby widening the vertical gap. Because the ward bosses were able to acquire patronage from a variety of competing sources, they were able to chart relatively independent courses of action by negotiating with the rival ruling elites. Thus, the Kelly-Nash machine did not proceed simply by issuing orders down a unitary chain of command but also by issuing "bribes" to secure the cooperation of rival elites. The ethnically balanced slate, then, was not so much an electoral strategy; it was primarily an internal political strategy, designed to secure the support of rival factions within the organization.[2] Since neither of the main factions possessed sufficient resources to acquire the compliance of much more than a bare majority of the ward leaders, the machine remained split down the middle.

The structural divisions and rivalry among the ruling elite yielded critical consequences for the black political elite. Politics in the black wards reflected the division and conflict at the top of the machine. As the competing factions sought allies in their struggle for dominance, the black elite acquired divided loyalties, lining up with one faction against the other. They were not so much members of the machine serving organizational goals, as the economic perspective would have it, but associates of particular factions, which were bent on acquiring control of the machine's command posts.

Thus, the interactive paradigm, which takes into account an internally focused elite interest in the acquisition of power as well as an externally focused organizational interest in the acquisition of electoral profits, sheds new light on this poorly examined formative period of Chicago's machine and black politics. The prevailing view holds that through support from above and because of his own exceptional political skill, Congressman William Dawson was able to put together a sub-machine that ruled the black wards during the realignment period (Wilson 1960). However, as we shall see, for all his skill, determination, and ruthless cunning, Dawson's fortunes rose and fell in the turbulent backwash of elite rivalry atop the factionalized machine. He rose to the top when it served the political interest of a particular ruling elite, and then he fell from power when that course of action served the political interest of yet another ruling elite.

The Emergence of the Black Machine Elite

The route to the top in the machine's ward organizations ordinarily is a long and gradual process. As Harold Gosnell (1937, 28) found, "In order to become a ward committeeman in Chicago, the aspirant must begin political work at an early age. Long years of apprenticeship seem to be one of the qualifications." An individual typically starts out as an assistant precinct captain, and only after a successful probationary period, is he or she given a patronage job. Then comes a long, slow climb up the organizational ladder. With further success, more challenging assignments are provided and better patronage jobs are acquired.

The most reliable captains enter the ward organization's inner circle, with reliability being measured in terms of trustworthiness as well as productivity. Thus, four of the six criteria Gosnell (1937, 66) found that ward bosses used in evaluating their precinct captains involved loyalty: "gives absolute obedience," "satisfied with a subordinate role," "not too demanding for himself," and "does not ask too many questions." Only two criteria pertained to productivity: "makes friends easily" and "works hard and steadily." Those who enter the inner circle become privy to many of the organization's secrets, and it is from this vantage point that some individuals make the great leap to the top and become a ward boss.

The interesting thing about this conventional scenario is that only one of the five black machine ward bosses recruited during the realignment period conformed to it. The first black machine ward boss, Edward "Mike" Sneed, elected in 1932, has been largely lost to history. In a chronological history of the Third Ward Democratic organization issued by the ward organization in the 1980s, Sneed went unmentioned. Even though Sneed served as the ward's committeeman from 1932 to 1948, his successor, Christopher Wimbish, was identified as the organization's first head. By all accounts, Sneed was entitled to the obscure status he achieved. No one I spoke with could recall anything noteworthy that Sneed had accomplished, and all offered negative assessments of his leadership and his personal qualities. He was known, in the parlance of the times, as a "muscle," a crude, barely literate, and blustery man who used the authority of his position to have his way (Caldwell, Jones, Washington interviews, 1982).

Sneed was recruited by the outgoing white committeeman of the Third Ward, Thomas Nash, when the ward changed racially. Nash moved over to the Nineteenth Ward, where he assembled the Southwest Side Irish bloc, the faction that constituted the chief impediment to the leadership of Mayor Kelly and party chairman Patrick Nash. One of the principal reasons that Sneed failed to accomplish much of anything on his own was that he never moved outside of Nash's large shadow. The *Chicago Defender* made this point by characterizing Sneed not merely as a Democrat but as a "Tom Nash Democrat" (October 4, 1947).

Sneed's selection caused quite a stir at the time but it reflected the balance of Democratic power in the black wards at the time. For his own part, Sneed possessed few personal or organizational qualifications for the high post. A man of limited formal education, he was employed as a janitor in a downtown building that housed the law offices of the attorney who challenged him for the committeemanship. Further, his lack of a decent patronage job reflected his minor status in the ward organization.

According to Sneed's challenger, Earl Dickerson (interview 1979), Sneed's chief claim on the committeeman post was his brother's involvement in the policy racket. Sneed was selected as a "front" for the policy wheel operators—and, of course, for Nash as well. The policy operators at the time possessed considerable political influence because they provided the weak black Democratic ward organizations with much of their patronage (Drake and Cayton 1970, 470–94).[3] Nash's own ties to the white crime syndicate—one of the

city's leading criminal defense attorneys, he had served as counsel
to Al Capone (O'Connor 1975, 65)—cemented the three-way relationship. Thus, despite his departure, Nash retained firm control
over the Third Ward organization.

Sneed was not joined by a second black machine committeeman
until 1940, when William Dawson was elected in the Second Ward,
one year after the ward elected its first black Democratic alderman.
As Sneed had done, Dawson replaced a white committeeman who
had been holding the office even though the ward had been predominantly black for over 20 years. (The first black alderman, Oscar
DePriest, had been elected in 1915.) Beyond this formal similarity,
however, Dawson and Sneed were as different as night and day.
Sneed essentially fell into a political career through his brother's ties
to the policy racketeers. Dawson lived for politics. Drawing again on
Earl Dickerson's (1979) recollections: "Power was Bill's passion. In all
my years in politics, I have never heard anyone talk on the subject of
power with the passion and eloquence of Bill Dawson. It was all he
cared about and lived for, really. He had a lovely wife and family that
he almost never saw. Money? Sure, he made enough of that. They
were all hoodlums back then, or tied in with the hoodlums. But, it
wasn't the money that Bill was after. It was that damned passion for
power that drove Bill."[4]

Oddly enough, despite his passion for politics, Dawson did not
run for elective office until the advanced age of forty-two. Yet true to
the form he would establish, when he finally did start, he tried start-
ing at the top. It is conventionally understood about Dawson during
this period in the Republican "wilderness" that he was a maverick.
He made his way with a volunteer band of "army buddies," and he
used inflammatory racial appeals to win electoral support. In turn,
it is said, once Dawson entered the machine, he became strictly an
organization man, working within the machine's narrow confines to
achieve limited, concrete goals. His public silence on the race issue
became nearly absolute (Wilson 1960, 50, 78). The evidence, however, suggests otherwise, as Dawson appears to have undergone a
far less radical transformation than is commonly supposed.

Dawson entered the political arena like a violent explosion in
1928, when he assembled his band of "army buddies" to challenge
long-term, powerful white incumbent Martin Madden for his
congressional seat. Racial representation was, indeed, at the heart
of Dawson's claim on the seat: "By birth, training and experience I
am better fitted to represent the district at Washington than any
of the candidates now in the field. Mr. Madden, the present con-

gressman, does not even live in the district. He is a white man. Therefore, for those two reasons, if no others, he can hardly voice the hopes,
ideals and sentiment of the majority of the district" (Gosnell
1967, 79).

What is questionable, however, is the extent to which Dawson
was acting on his own, as a maverick. More likely he was working
on behalf of his mentor, the powerful Oscar DePriest, by "softening
up" the elderly Madden for DePriest, who was closely allied with
Mayor Thompson and regarded himself as the heir apparent to the
congressional seat. Dawson's early admiration for and deep commitment to DePriest are unquestionable. Dawson recalled in the 1960s
"what great admiration I had for Oscar DePriest as a man who really
had 'guts' " (Clayton 1964, 70). Indeed, Dawson had been so impressed with DePriest that he pledged to him in 1919 in a letter that
"he could always depend upon me for support in anything he would
undertake in the future and that I was ready to stand by him" (ibid.).
Moreover, when Congressman Madden suddenly died shortly after
defeating Dawson in the primary (Dawson received only 28 percent
of the vote), it was DePriest who was selected by Mayor Thompson
to take Madden's place on the ticket.

A few years later, when DePriest, the Third Ward committeeman, consolidated his control over the black wards by taking over
the Second Ward, he sent over his two top aides to effect the takeover, and one of them was none other than the reputed maverick
William Dawson. It is, of course, possible that DePriest recruited
Dawson only after he had issued the bold challenge to Madden on
his own. Yet, given the virtual certainty that Dawson would be severely punished for taking on the powerful Madden, particularly in
view of the audacious way in which he issued the challenge, it is
reasonable to suppose that Dawson would have secured the protection that DePriest could provide against the high risk he was under-
taking. Thus, it may plausibly be argued that Dawson was not the
independent maverick he was cracked up to be. He was working his
way up DePriest's organizational ladder by helping DePriest remove
Madden from the path, and Dawson was rewarded for his efforts
when DePriest set him up as the alderman of the Second Ward.

To DePriest's dismay, however, the Second Ward Republican organization he put together turned into a battleground. Dawson,
ever ambitious, wanted the committeeman position held by De-
Priest's other lieutenant, William King, and the two men were at
each other's throats on a continuous basis. Dawson, enticed by the
Democratic shift that was in the air or simply going along in order to

get along, frequently crossed party lines to support Mayor Kelly in the city council. As a result, Dawson was endorsed by Kelly for re-election in 1935; however King withheld his endorsement until DePriest's pressure forced him to capitulate. (*Chicago Defender*, February 23, March 2, 1935) Then Dawson raised the stakes the following year by challenging King for committeeman. This time DePriest intervened on King's behalf, and, with his backing, King handily defeated Dawson by a 2:1 margin.

In part because of the strife in the Second Ward, DePriest lost his congressional seat in 1934, and, as the conflict continued, he failed to regain the seat in 1936. Then in 1938 Dawson turned his burning ambition on his old mentor by challenging DePriest in the Republican congressional primary, and the pupil wound up mastering his mentor. Dawson failed, however, to defeat the Democratic incumbent. Yet that turned out to be the least of Dawson's problems. By turning on DePriest, Dawson was left without the protection he needed against his nemesis, King, and King promptly took advantage of Dawson's vulnerability.

With the circle of opportunity for the Republicans steadily drawing smaller, competition for office grew ever fiercer, and in 1939, King dumped Dawson and declared his own candidacy for alderman. Dawson was not left entirely on his own, for once again Mayor Kelly crossed party lines to endorse him over the Democratic candidate. However, Kelly ran into difficulty when he attempted to get the Second Ward Democratic organization to go along with his endorsement of the Republican Dawson. The Democratic ward organization was fielding a strong black candidate—Earl Dickerson—for the first time, and many of the precinct captains resisted Kelly's pressure to dump Dickerson. Mayor Kelly's magnanimous response to the captain's reluctance doomed Dawson. The mayor informed the captains, according to Dickerson (1979), that they would be allowed to make their own choice of candidates in the election. Enough of them stayed with Dickerson to put him into a runoff election with King. Dawson wound up running a close third against the two organization-backed candidates.

The wily Dawson remained out in the cold for only a short while, however. He assembled his band of volunteers, informed them that he was switching parties, and urged them to join him in backing Dickerson against his old Republican rival King. Dawson's timely switch spelled the difference for Dickerson. He defeated King by only 2,370 votes, which, arguably, were produced by Dawson's volunteer force. (Dawson had received 8,575 votes in his third place finish.) At any rate, that is undoubtedly how Dawson must have explained the breakthrough Democratic victory to Mayor Kelly when he went downtown seeking Mayor Kelly's support for Democratic committeeman of the Second Ward. Oh, to have been a fly on the wall to have observed Kelly's reaction. Even by Chicago's low standards, the audacious move reeked of rank opportunism.

In light of the Second Ward precinct captains' reluctance to back Dawson over Dickerson in the aldermanic election, the mayor advised Dawson that he would have to secure Dickerson's support for the move. So, arriving in an old jalopy and wearing a rumpled, patched suit, Dawson invited Dickerson to take a ride with him down to the lakefront at 31st Street to discuss the proposition. In Dickerson's estimation, Dawson had nothing working in his favor. It was obvious to Dickerson that Dawson could not be trusted. He had battled with King for years, then he had turned on his mentor De-Priest, and now he was abandoning his party. Thus, what was to prevent him from turning on Dickerson?

The political values of the two men were poles apart. Dickerson was an idealistic New Dealer, he had the backing of the ward's reform forces, and he was determined to steer an independent course inside the Kelly-Nash machine. In Dawson, Dickerson saw only one aspiration: power. Dawson's close ties to Mayor Kelly represented another ominous source of conflict. How far could Dickerson safety stray from the Kelly-Nash line with Dawson breathing down his neck?

Yet the deal was struck. Dawson, who once said of himself, "God gave me the key to understand men and to know them. If you learn to handle men, the right ones—all men for that matter—you can get what you want" (Clayton 1964, 73)—knew his man. He promised Dickerson that if he supported him for committeeman, then Dawson would back Dickerson for Congress (Dickerson interview, 1979). Dickerson was, of course, well aware that Dawson had twice thrown his own hat into the congressional ring; thus, there was a serious question as to whether Dawson would honor his pledge. But passionate ambition got the better of Dickerson's judgment. Above all else, Dickerson yearned to walk the congressional stage, where the New Deal was being crafted and the great issues of the day were being debated. The cut-and-dried city council run by the Kelly-Nash machine was no place for a man of Dickerson's talent and high ideals.

Party chairman Pat Nash was stunned by Mayor Kelly's decision to slate Dawson, and he voiced strenuous objections to it (Dickerson, Davis interviews 1979). He argued that there were several black Democrats in the ward who were far more entitled to the ward committeemanship, men who had paid their dues, and that putting such a recent convert into the top position made a mockery of party loyalty. Many of the Second Ward precinct captains shared Nash's reservations, according to Dickerson (interview, 1979). They understandably feared that Dawson would replace them with his own Republican friends and volunteer workers.

Yet there was shrewd political method to the mayor's apparent madness. He undoubtedly understood that by breathing life back into the politically dead Dawson, he secured Dawson's undying gratitude and loyalty. At the same time, Mayor Kelly acquired a skilled ally in the black wards to combat his rival Tom Nash's man, "Mike" Sneed. Given Dawson's long experience and political skill along with the mayor's backing, it would not be long before Kelly's voice would prevail in the black wards. Indeed, it was not long before Dawson emerged as the ranking machine man in the black wards. But the ambitious Dawson wanted still more than that.

The Emergence of "Boss" Dawson

Before he could get more, however, Dawson had to consolidate his control over the Second Ward organization. When Alderman Dickerson approached Dawson in 1940 about replacing Arthur Mitchell in Congress, Dawson informed Dickerson that he would have to wait; Dawson needed to get the organization under firmer control before he moved on Mitchell (Davis, Dickerson, interviews, 1979). However, when Dickerson raised the issue again in 1942, the alderman's worst nightmare came true: Dawson had persuaded Mitchell to step down without a fight, and Dawson was claiming the seat for himself.

The proud and ambitious Dickerson refused to give up without a fight, and he threw his hat into the Democratic primary ring. But as the organization's candidate, Dawson won handily. He also got a sweet taste of revenge against old rival, William King, when he defeated him in the general election. King carried the black Second Ward, as the Republican congressional candidate invariably did.[5] However, a strong Democratic vote from the white wards in the First Congressional District carried Dawson to victory.

All that remained was for Dawson to finish off the intrepid Dickerson, and he accomplished this in 1943 by dumping him as the organization's aldermanic candidate, replacing him with Dawson's secretary, William Harvey, an ex-fireman. Dickerson learned of his dumping before the organization's slating session was held, and although he knew that the cards were stacked against him, he chose to go before the precinct captains to appeal for their support. However, the ward organization's leadership vilified him. He was castigated for failing to support Mayor Kelly in the city council. He was denounced for failing to be a team player in the ward organization. He was rebuked for abandoning his aldermanic seat midway through his first term when he ran for Congress. He was damned as a silk stocking who could not relate to the ward's poor residents (Davis, Dickerson, Love, interviews, 1979).

The charges were damaging and the last one was personally painful, because as Dickerson (interview, 1979) acknowledged years later, all of them were essentially accurate. He was an idealistic New Deal Democrat, and this inevitably put him at odds with Mayor Kelly and Congressman Dawson's conservative machine style of politics. He resisted the harsh constraints imposed on the machine's city council, often clashed with the party line, and openly yearned for a congressional role. He felt awkward and uncomfortable with many of the ward's residents and precinct captains. Well educated, affluent, a prominent businessman, and reform minded, a wide social and cultural gap separated Dickerson from most of his constituency and the organization's precinct captains. The personal touch, so vital at the ward level, was sorely lacking.

The aldermanic election wound up as a runoff between the organization candidates, William Harvey and Mack Atkins. This provided Dickerson with a golden opportunity to get even with Dawson by taking a page from Dawson's book of tricks: switching parties and throwing his support to Atkins. However, according to Dickerson, his commitment to the New Deal prevented him from crossing over to the Republican side. Instead, he sat out the runoff election, refusing to endorse either candidate, and Dawson's Harvey won by 600 votes. A nod from Dickerson toward Atkins very likely would have reversed the outcome. In any event, Dickerson wound up in Washington shortly after the election, heading President Roosevelt's Fair Employment Practices Commission.

The aldermanic victory fully consolidated Dawson's control over the Second Ward organization. He held the two top posts of committeeman and congressman. His former secretary was the alderman. One of his oldest and closest friends, Corneal Davis, was one of the organization's state representatives. Another old friend, Christopher Wimbish, said to be Dawson's only peer in the organization in terms of talent and ambition, was the organization's president and he held the sole black state senate seat. The organization's rank and file was filled with many ex-Republican regulars and volunteers, who had switched with Dawson to the ascendant Democratic party.

The consolidation enabled Dawson to train his sights on constructing a vaster empire. His first opportunity came in 1947, when he received an enticing request from his beleaguered colleague in the Third Ward, "Mike" Sneed. While Dawson was effectively consolidating his control, Sneed had been hanging on for dear life. Conflict within Sneed's organization had enabled the Republicans to regain the aldermanic seat in 1943. In 1947 Sneed was again beset by organizational strife. A group of businessmen and professionals affiliated with the organization had prevailed upon Sneed to slate attorney Roy Washington for alderman. Sneed very reluctantly acceded to the request.

Sneed's reluctance stemmed from the division and conflict between him and Washington's backers. They had styled themselves as the organization's "new breed," young professionals and businessmen who wanted to broaden the organization's appeal by upgrading its image. In their estimation, Sneed represented an "old school" style of politics. Poorly educated, rough and gruff, fronting for Tom Nash and the policy racketeers, Sneed had no capacity to articulate the aspirations of the middle class. Yet for all of his limitations, Sneed undoubtedly understood that if Washington won, the new breeders would be coming after his committeeman post next.

Which was what prompted Sneed to approach Dawson after Washington won a place in a runoff election. Sneed wanted Dawson's help in discreetly undermining Washington's campaign. Sneed had enlisted the support of several policy racketeers, and he needed Dawson to send over some top precinct captains to work on behalf of Washington's Republican opponent, Archibald Carey, Jr. According to sources in both the Second and Third wards, policy racketeers, Dawson's captains, and some of Sneed's own men wound up working quietly for Carey in the runoff, which Carey won by over 2,000 votes (Love interview, 1979; Washington interview, 1982).

However, Sneed wound up losing the war after he won the battle. The new breeders took their case of Sneed's treachery downtown to party chairman Jacob Arvey. (According to Harold Washington later [1982], his father, Roy, was so furious that, armed with a gun, he spent several weeks looking for Sneed.) When the ward boundary lines were redrawn in late 1947, Sneed's residence was placed outside the new Third Ward boundary lines, which prevented him from seeking reelection as committeeman.

The *Chicago Defender* named new breeder Roy Washington as one of the leading candidates to take Sneed's place (October 4, 1947). However, when the downtown slatemakers emerged, they named State Senator Christopher Wimbish, Dawson's top aide in the Second Ward organization, as their choice for the Third Ward committeemanship. Dawson apparently had persuaded the slatemakers that the best way to end the Third Ward's debilitating organizational strife was by importing a strong man from outside the ward, and Senator Wimbish clearly fit the bill. The move effectively made Dawson the de facto boss of a two-ward black empire, or so it seemed at the time.

Dawson's star also began rising at the national level in the late 1940s. As one of only two blacks in Congress (Adam Clayton Powell, Jr., had been elected from New York in 1944, but he had a strained relationship with President Truman), Dawson played a critical role in Harry Truman's 1948 presidential campaign. He was placed on the Democratic National Committee, and he traveled across the country campaigning for Truman. He was particularly effective in the southern states, where he rallied black voters, many of whom were still deeply attached to the party of Lincoln and appalled by the racist excesses of the southern white Democratic party. Dawson also helped himself in the Congress by campaigning for several white Democratic congressmen while stumping for the president (Davis interview, 1979).

Truman wound up carrying Illinois by only 38,000 votes, and, with a winning margin in Chicago's three black wards of 50,000 votes, Dawson could claim ample credit for the victory. The *Chicago Defender*, which had a broad black readership across the southern states, also took a lion's share of the credit: after the election it published a letter from President Truman on its front page, thanking the paper for its support. Proudly running a bold banner over the letter, the *Defender* proclaimed, "Results Speak" (November 27, 1948).

The *Defender* (April 4, 1948) also reported an extraordinary local development that was said to be in the works. If party chairman Jacob Arvey decided to step down, the machine would be run by a triumvirate. Al Horan, an old and powerful West Side ward boss closely tied to Arvey, would be one member of the leadership team. Joseph Gill, another influential old timer from the Northeast Side, would aid Horan. The third member of the troika would be none

other than "Boss" Dawson. Dawson's strides seemed to be those of
a colossus. Never before had a black politician held so much power.

The Fall of "Boss" Dawson and the Black Ward Organizations

Yet at the same time that Dawson's political fortunes were soaring,
the economic lifeline of the black ward organizations' was being sev-
ered. The multimillion-dollar policy racket, controlled by a black cartel that contributed huge sums of money and provided numerous
jobs to the black ward organizations, was being taken over by the
city's powerful white crime syndicate. Although there are no accurate figures indicating the racket's income, a newspaper account in
the 1930s indicated that the payoff to the machine central headquarters alone amounted to nearly half a million dollars a year (*Chicago
Daily News*, February 13, 1939). "Every Friday, Ily Kelly, representing
the policy wheel syndicate, visits Skidmore's scrap iron yard at 2840
S. Kedzie Avenue. Upon arriving there, Kelly hands Skidmore, representing two 'big shot' politicians, $9,500 in cash. Kelly is guarded
by two gunmen on these trips."[6]

Dawson always denied that he benefited personally from the
racket. However, he did acknowledge (*Chicago Sun-Times*, February
3, 1955) that he accepted campaign contributions from the policy operators. He also admitted (*Chicago Tribune*, December 12, 1950) that
he used his political influence to protect the black cartel against en-
croachments by the white crime syndicate, maintaining that "if anybody is going to make money out of the frailties of my people, it's
going to be my own people."[7] While Kelly was mayor, Dawson had
been able to remove any police officers who harassed the protected
wheels. In a rare interview, Dawson expressed his contempt for
Mayor Martin Kennelly while he lavished praise on former Mayor
Kelly as a man who was "willing and ready to assume responsibili-
ties" (Chicago Crime Commission 1954, 10).

Within only days of Kelly's announcement in May 1946 that he
was relinquishing the party chairmanship to Jacob Arvey, the white
crime syndicate moved in on the black policy cartel, thus signifying
the decisive importance of Mayor Kelly's sponsorship of Dawson.
The head of the black cartel, Edward Jones, was kidnapped and held
for $100,000 ransom. Using a more casual and colorful prose than
can be found in today's news accounts, the *Chicago Tribune* reported
the development this way: "Police, politicians, bartenders, barbers,
bootblacks, and newsstand operators in the Negro section of the

south side agreed yesterday that Edward Jones is the Boss of Bronze-ville, the Negro Santa Claus, the colored Robin Hood, as well as the policy boss who was kidnapped for ransom" (May 13, 1946).

After paying the ransom, Jones and his brother left Chicago to take up residence in Mexico. Not long after that, the home of Julius Benevenuti, one of three whites allowed into the black syndicate, was bombed, and he promptly fled to Italy (*Chicago Defender*, April 26, 1947). In 1950 James "Big Jim" Martin, the major black policy operator on the West Side was shot, and he departed for South America (*Chicago Defender*, November 18, 1950). By the time U.S. Senator Estes Kefauver brought his celebrated interstate organized crime commission to Chicago in December 1950 to hold hearings, only one major black policy operator, Theodore Roe, remained, and he was murdered in 1952 (*Chicago Daily News*, August 5, 1952).

The Kefauver Committee's files indicated the inroads that had been made by the white syndicate. The records of the new white operators of Julius Benevenuti's policy wheel reflected a payment of $278,000 to Anthony Accardo and Jacob Guzik, the heads of the city's crime syndicate, for what was only described as "special ser-vices" (Chicago Crime Commission 1953). The records also indi-cated that the Accardo-Guzik wheel's income had expanded at a staggering rate, as other wheels were being squeezed out of the lu-crative business.

Congressman Dawson appealed for help. However party chair-man Arvey, whose ties to the white crime syndicate ran long and deep (O'Connor 1975, 42), was unwilling or unable to help Dawson in the way Mayor Kelly had. Then when Dawson showed the temer-ity to approach Mayor Kennelly, the outraged reform mayor ordered Dawson out of his office as soon as he broached the subject (Royko 1971, 61–62; Davis interview, 1979). In an extraordinarily bold move, the *Chicago Defender* attempted to resist the syndicate's takeover by running a series of exposés that even named the dangerous names involved in the coup. The series prudently was authored by an anonymous "insider." The following account reflects the *Defender*'s rare daring: "There is buzzing in underworld circles that the lucra-tive field of 'policy' and handbooks is getting frequent visits from remnants of the old Capone mob. According to latest reports, Jack Guzik has established his 'gestapo' headquarters at 6258 Cottage Grove, with 'Golf Bags' Hunt handling matters. . . . Of course, the police are 'active' against policy joints, provided they are run by col-ored. . . . the big white ones are immune. . . . The move is growing to take the 'racket' out of the hands of Negroes and put it under the control of the 'mob' and to 'syndicate' it, assessing each wheel $250 a month" (May 29, 1948).

Another article in the series was entitled, "Insider Finds 'Golf Bag' Hunt Runs District, Not Cops" (June 5, 1948). Mayor Kennelly undoubtedly was humiliated by the series. However, as the Kefauver Committee's hearings brought out, the mayor and police commissioner actually had remarkably little control over the police department's activities. The police commissioner's central staff consisted of merely two aides, and despite the mayor's urgent pleading, the city council refused to rectify the imbalance (Investigation of Organized Crime in Interstate Commerce 1950, 123, 125). The aldermen preferred a decentralized operation, in which district commanders held power, who were in turn subject to the influence of the ward bosses in their districts. The police department thus was effectively administered by the ward committeemen.

The Kefauver Commission ultimately solved the problem by passing a new federal gambling tax requiring gamblers to provide addresses when applying for a gambling license, which enabled local authorities to locate and arrest them. The requirement promptly transformed the lucrative policy racket into a small fly-by-night enterprise (*Chicago Defender*, January 12, 1952). The Chicago crime syndicate shifted much of its gambling activity to Nevada, and the once well endowed black ward organizations were left without an economic base upon which to draw financial support.

By the time the 1952 elections rolled around, the black ward organizations were in difficult straits, as the *Chicago Defender* (February 2, 1952) candidly observed: "Campaign money is short this time, as the gamblers are largely shut down." Writing a few years later, unaware of the devastating change of fortune created by the crime syndicate's takeover and the subsequent closing down of the policy racket by the federal government, James Q. Wilson described the utter dependency of the impoverished black ward organizations on funds from central machine headquarters: "It is important to emphasize the role money plays in the Negro wards. The only factor which interests many captains and committeemen is how much money will be put into those areas on election day . . . If the organization has half a million to spend, the big boys are likely to put half of it in the Negro wards" (1965, 54).

The devastating economic takeover of Dawson's empire was followed by an equally devastating political takeover. The first public sign of Dawson's new plight came during the 1951 aldermanic elections. By then Dawson and Christopher Wimbish, the chief aide he had set up as the committeeman of the Third Ward in 1948, had fallen out. Dawson wanted to rule an empire, but Wimbish insisted on dealing directly with the downtown bosses, instead of taking orders from Dawson. Accordingly, Dawson urged the slatemakers to field Aaron Payne, Dawson's campaign manager in 1948, as the Third Ward aldermanic candidate (*Chicago Tribune*, December 8, 1950). However, the slatemakers deferred to Wimbish, allowing him to select his own aldermanic candidate.

Dawson also attempted to move in on the Twentieth Ward, a third black ward created by the 1947 remap, by urging the slatemakers to select Robert Miller, a businessman and recent Republican convert who served as one of Dawson's principal fundraisers. He had no success there either. The committeeman of the Twentieth Ward, Kenneth Campbell, was a protégé of Barnet Hodes, the committeeman of the Fifth Ward from which the new black ward had been carved. Hodes was the law partner of none other than party chairman Jacob Arvey, and so it is unsurprising that Dawson's efforts against Campbell were thwarted. However, Campbell did feel sufficiently threatened by Dawson's treachery to give up his more lucrative position with the state commerce commission and run for alderman himself (*Chicago Daily News*, December 22, 1950).

Despite the setbacks, Dawson persisted in his quest for a multiward empire. During the 1951 mayoral election, he somehow convinced his two colleagues, Wimbish and Campbell, to join him in a bold demonstration of disfavor with Mayor Kennelly's antipatronage policies and failure to protect the black policy cartel. The black ward leaders would show their dissatisfaction by withholding electoral support from Kennelly (Wilson 1960, 82). Given the mayor's unpopularity in the black wards, Wimbish and Campbell may well have been glad to forgo the uphill struggle of pulling out votes for him.

In any event, black turnout dropped dramatically and Kennelly was defeated in the Third and Twentieth wards. However, Dawson's Second Ward carried the mayor by over 2,000 votes. The front page of the *Chicago Defender* promptly spelled out the dire implications of the vote withholding scheme: "Demos Face Shake-Up As District Leaders Flop" (April 7, 1951). If Wimbish and Campbell retained any doubts about the trap into which they had been led, Dawson disabused them at the slating session for ward committeemen the following year. Once again Dawson put up the names of Aaron Payne and Robert Miller as his candidates for the Third and Twentieth ward posts.

However, once again, the slatemakers rejected Dawson's empire-building scheme. Campbell, backed by Hodes and the powerful Arvey, was slated in the Twentieth Ward. Wimbish was dumped in the Third Ward. However, he was replaced by a political novice, Ralph Metcalfe, a decision that Dawson had strenuously resisted behind the scenes, according to Dawson's aide Corneal Davis (interview, 1979). Dawson proved to be no match, though, for Metcalfe's sponsor atop the machine.

Richard Daley, gearing up for a run for party chairman, was determined to slate committeemen committed to him, and Daley did not trust Dawson. Daley was the candidate of the old Kelly-Nash-Arvey West Side faction, and he also had the backing of the machine's reform element, notably Governor Adlai Stevenson and Mayor Kennelly. He would be opposed by Clarence Wagner, who was being supported by the machine's Southwest Side Irish patronage and spoils wing, and that was the direction in which Dawson, bitterly opposed to the reformers backing Daley, clearly was leaning (Caldwell, Korshak interviews 1982).

The lines between the two factions ran right down the center of the machine, and the outcome was regarded as a toss up (Gable 1953). Thus, every vote counted, and so, from Daley's point of view, it was essential that Dawson's power be curtailed, not increased. Dawson's standing in the machine accordingly hinged on the outcome of the party chairman contest. If Wagner prevailed, he could once again muster his resources for still another empire-building effort. However, if Daley prevailed, Dawson would be out in the cold.

In Perspective

Notwithstanding the widespread acceptance of the economic perspective's conception of the political machine as a monolithic, single-minded organization, we found that the sociological perspective provided a more apt and useful conception of it. The sociological perspective's concern for the discretionary power of organizational sub-units directed attention to the machine's disarticulated structure.

Mayor Kelly and party chairman Patrick Nash reigned supreme throughout most of the realignment period, from 1931–1951. However, rival factions continuously challenged Kelly and Nash's lead-

ership, and the machine's disarticulated structure facilitated the factional rivalry. Kelly and Nash held the lion's share of the machine's
patronage, yet several centers of patronage and power remained
largely beyond their control, and it was these centers that supplied
the resources which enabled the challenges. The principal opposition bloc, the so-called Southwest Side Irish bloc, was headed by
Thomas Nash.

Accordingly, the ruling elite had to conduct their affairs with two
goals in mind. They held an economic interest in the machine's well-
being, and they also held a political interest in their own well-being.
Winning elections and securing wealth for the organization certainly
were important considerations, as the economic perspective leads
us to believe. Yet the considerations were conditioned by a deeper
understanding on the part of the elites. Offices were not won by the
machine, but by particular factions within the machine. Thus, the
resources extracted from the office could be used to advance and
retard the well-being of particular factions.

The position and behavior of the black ward elites reflected the
structural disarticulation and elite rivalry atop the machine. The
black elites were not members of the machine so much as they were
associates of particular factions in the machine. Thus, as we saw,
"Mike" Sneed was, as the *Chicago Defender* called him, a "Tom Nash
Democrat." William Dawson was the protégé of Mayor Kelly, and
therefore Sneed's rival. Christopher Wimbish and Kenneth Campbell owed their principal allegiance to party chairman Jacob Arvey,
who sponsored their rise to the top, and protected them, at least for
a time, from Dawson's empire-building designs.

Contrary to Harold Gosnell's finding, that "You Can't Lick a
Ward Boss," we found life was precarious for the black ward bosses.
Their fortunes rose and fell in conjunction with their sponsors' fortunes. Sneed was displaced by Wimbish, who in turn was ousted by
Metcalfe, as power at the top shifted from Tom Nash to Jacob Arvey
and then to Arvey's protégé, Richard Daley. The legendary "Boss"
Dawson, who had few peers as a politician of ruthless cunning and
burning ambition, climbed and collapsed in the same fashion. What
Mayor Kelly had created—the most powerful black politician in the
country—Mayor Daley destroyed, and for the same reason: to advance his own political interest.

Part 3

Maturation
and Decline

5

Daley's Black Machine:
The Productivity-Patronage
Contradiction

During the post–World War II era, a series of upheavals profoundly altered the political landscape of the city and machine. The sum of the changes yielded a radically different machine politics and black politics. After a quarter-century of rule, the machine finally began to resemble the classic centrally directed and monolithic machine found in urban politics textbooks. Voters in the poor black wards finally began to behave as the economic perspective assumes they must behave: providing the machine with massive majorities across the board.

Yet when we look beyond surface impressions, it is clear that although the new behavior finally began conforming to conventional expectations, its emergence depended upon highly fortuitous circumstances and unusual decisions by the machine's new elite. The new politics was not driven by economic imperatives but by a complex array of environmental shifts, structural changes, and political choices.

The most decisive and fortuitous of these changes came on the eve of the long-awaited showdown for party chairman between Richard Daley and Clarence Wagner. Both candidates brought formidable resources to the contest. Daley had the backing of Acting Chairman Joseph Gill and the West Side faction, headed by former chairman Jacob Arvey. The machine's small, but prominent reform element, notably Governor Adlai Stevenson and Mayor Martin Kennelly, also was backing Daley.

The media generally portrayed Daley in highly favorable terms. One newspaper identified him as one of the machine's "brightest stars. Together with County Chairman J. M. Arvey, Alderman George D. Kells (28th) and others, he represented the younger pro-Roosevelt element upon which the Democrats hoped to rebuild as their elder members fell by the wayside" (*Chicago Daily News*, November 4, 1946). Daley encouraged this perception during the chairman's race by telling reporters that "the younger committeemen want me" (*Chicago Daily News*, July 17, 1953).

Clarence Wagner was the candidate of the patronage-oriented old guard faction, headed by Tom Nash's Southwest Side Irish bloc. The same newspaper that characterized Daley as the candidate of progressive change, portrayed Wagner in negative retrograde terms. His candidacy "is interpreted as meaning old-timers are through with 'reform candidates' and want machine politicians back in office" (ibid.).

By all accounts, Wagner's resources were a match for Daley's. He was the chairman of the city council's powerful Finance Committee, which controlled the budget and thus countless patronage jobs and contracts. He served as Mayor Kennelly's floor leader, and so strong was his influence in the administration that the media often referred to him as the "second mayor." His principal backers, Tom Nash's Southwest Side bloc, had been growing stronger during the 1950s. When Daley had attempted to get slated for the coveted county board presidency in 1950, for example, he was passed over in favor of John Duffy, the alderman from Tom Nash's Nineteenth Ward (*Chicago Tribune*, January 6, 1950).

As fortune would have it, however, the committeemen never had to cast their perilous ballots. Wagner was killed in an auto accident a few days before the election. The Southwest Side bloc scrambled desperately to come up with an alternative candidate, and then it threw in the towel. It could not cope with Wagner's death and a critical rules change engineered by the Daley faction. "Normally, each committeeman casts one vote, but under the seldom used Primary Act [a state law], each committeeman would cast the number of votes the party received in the primary" (*Chicago Daily News*, July 17, 1953). Since Daley was backed by the committeemen from the West Side wards, the machine's electoral stronghold, the rules change gave him a decisive edge in the voting.

Daley actually wound up winning much more than the party chairmanship. With Wagner's death, the Finance Committee chairman was open, and Daley was able to fill it with an influential Northwest Side ward leader, P. J. "Parky" Cullerton. Moreover, several of the machine's most powerful old war-horses indicated that they would be stepping down. In particular, Joseph Gill and Albert Horan, two Daley backers who controlled large patronage centers in the local courts, were retiring, and Daley used their patronage centers to further extend his control over the organization (ibid., July 18, 1953). The powerful county assessor's office remained under the control of a Kennelly man; however, he had only weak backing in the party, and so that lucrative patronage center was an obvious candidate for takeover by the new party chairman.

Finally, State Senator William Lynch, Daley's oldest and most trusted ally, steered a bill through the state legislature that shifted budgetary authority from the city council to the mayor's office (*Chicago Sun-Times*, January 26, 1955). Provided Daley could move Kennelly out of the mayor's office, a move that clearly was in the offing, he would control still another substantial patronage center. Thus, when Daley was elected mayor in 1955, he entered office with far more patronage under his control than any of his predecessors had possessed, and he adroitly parlayed it into an increasingly broader sphere of organizational control.

Concurrently, the city landscape was undergoing a pivotal series of changes. The affluent Protestants residing in the outlying wards, who made up the electoral backbone of the Republican opposition— in 1951 Republican aldermen held sixteen of the city council's fifty seats—began fleeing the city for the suburbs in the post-war years. The Protestant exodus set off an explosive chain of demographic shifts that transformed Chicago into a one-party city.

Poles and Italians living in and along the fringes of the inner city began pouring into the far Northwest Side wards, taking the place of the departing Germans and Scandinavians. The great symbolic changing of the ethnic-religious guard on the Northwest Side came in 1958. A four-term Republican congressman, Timothy Sheehan, was defeated by a Polish Democrat, Roman Pucinski. Sheehan turned out to be Chicago's last Republican congressman.

Droves of eastern European Jews from the West Side crossed the city to the Northeast lakefront wards, replacing more suburban bound Germans and Swedes. Scores of Irish from the near South Side wards made the great leap to Beverly and Morgan Park on the far Southwest Side, long the places of the city's most prosperous Protestant residents.

The most dramatic of the population transformations took place on the West Side and the Southeast Side. The shift here was racial. To the west, a rapidly growing black population entered the poor river wards, the traditional port of entry for successive waves of eastern and southern European immigrants. To the south, blacks fled the old black belt, moving into Jewish communities to the east and into Swedish-Irish communities to the south. A double fulcrum of racial fear and realtor avarice transformed the color of these communities with breathtaking rapidity. So even after the U.S. Supreme

Court knocked down the walls of the black belt, Chicago retained its infamous status as the nation's most racially segregated big city (Hirsch 1983).

The end result of the manifold population shifts was the elimination of the Republican party as a serious factor in local politics. It had managed to survive for two decades without any organizational resources to speak of, save the modest sums of patronage that Republican governors were willing to put into the city. But there was simply no way for the city's Republicans to overcome the great Protestant exodus to the new post-war suburbs.[1] Many of the Republican party leaders who remained in the city began flying under false colors, calling themselves Republicans, but behaving as "Republicrats," collaborating with the machine in order to survive and occasionally prosper (O'Connor 1975; Rakove 1975). Reflecting its inability to cope, the Republican party would resort to slating a liberal Democrat, Alderman Robert Merriam from Hyde Park, as its mayoral candidate against Daley in 1955.

Against this backdrop of critical developments, we can begin our analysis of the Daley machine. Daley's first mayoral election in 1955 represents a watershed in the city's black politics because it resolved the long-standing electoral contradiction running through the black wards. Indeed, the long overdue black local Democratic realignment was so decisive that the black wards displaced the poor white immigrant wards as the machine's main electoral stronghold.

Yet the massive new black democratic majorities did not result in any increased black power within the machine. Instead, a new black contradiction emerged, an organizational contradiction. Daley's decided political preference for organizational control meant that few non-Irish in the machine, and virtually no blacks in particular, benefited in significant ways from his leadership. Daley's political standard of decision making, which revolved around maintaining and enhancing his organizational control and power, overrode the machine's economic standard of decision making, which involved rewarding electoral performance in order to maintain high standards of productivity. With the opposition in the suburbs resulting from the Protestant departure, there was simply far less need to maintain the machine at peak performance.

Personal "fealty" to the mayor supplanted the organizational "contract" to the machine. Top party and government positions became a preserve for the mayor's male Irish loyalists (Rakove 1975, 35–40). If they were competent, that was a bonus; but above all they had to be faithful. This meant that although the black wards emerged as the machine's most productive electoral units under Daley, the black wards leaders received scant rewards for their efforts.

Nevertheless, they still were expected to be utterly faithful, and they were. For the black ward leaders, the machine was not the benign economic enterprise we find in the literature, where compliance is secured by material rewards. It was primarily a paramilitary organization, in which compliance was compelled through coercion.

In order to cut down on the high costs ordinarily associated with coercive compliance systems (Etzioni 1961), Daley instituted a novel system of elite recruitment, elevating men of high standing in the black community, but men who possessed little of the political experience or demonstrated skill of their predecessors. This virtually assured Daley that his black elite would make few demands on the organization's resources. Thus, when the civil rights movement swept into Chicago in the 1960s, Daley's black aldermen came to be known as the "silent six" for the unswerving loyalty they gave the mayor under the crushing pressure of the political rebellion and upheaval sweeping across their communities.

Resolving the Black Electoral Contradiction

During the heyday of Republican rule in the 1920s, the small black electorate played a critical role in local elections. In 1927, for example, the three South Side black wards provided over 70 percent of Mayor William Thompson's winning margin. In general, the black wards represented the Republican party's electoral stronghold. The role provided the black ward leaders with a substantial claim on Mayor Thompson's resources.

By the 1930s, however, the black wards had lost their political influence. In 1939, the same three wards that had supplied Mayor Thompson with 70 percent of his winning margin gave Mayor Kelly a mere 7 percent of his victory margin, and the situation grew worse in the 1940s. By the early 1950s the black wards could barely muster a Democratic majority in mayor elections. Thus, the Democratic machine was constructed and acquired its hegemony with scant black support. Accordingly, the early black Democratic ward leaders could lay little claim to the machine's resources, and little was just what they received.

The black Democratic ward leaders by and large were a highly skilled and experienced lot. Yet they were up against formidable odds. The machine's racism, encompassing every facet of black life, was a severe problem that became all the worse after the national Democratic party began embracing racial reforms during the 1940s. The new progressive national standard made the local party appear that much more retrograde and racist by comparison. The black ward leaders also had to cope with a strong countervailing middle class that provided voters with a genuine choice of candidates in ward elections. Capitalizing on the racism confronting the black community, middle-class candidates mounted one strong challenge after another against the machine. Finally, elite rivalry and conflict within the machine weakened the machine's electoral performance.

In the mid-1950s, all three obstacles to the local Democratic party's success finally were removed. This enabled the black wards to resume the critical role they earlier had played in local politics. Indeed, the black wards became so overwhelmingly Democratic that Daley's new machine was above all else a black machine in electoral terms. In turn, the new status conferred on the black ward leaders a legitimate claim on a substantial share of the machine's resources.

Population Dispersal and Class Differentiation

Until the U.S. Supreme Court finally struck down the use of restrictive housing covenants in *Shelley v. Kraemer* in 1948, over 70 percent of the city's black population were compelled to live in just three contiguous community areas—Douglas, Grand Boulevard, and Washington Park—that made up the bulk of the black belt. The remaining black population resided in small isolated clusters spread across the South Side and the West Side. In 1940 the black population numbered 277,731, which constituted 8 percent of the city's population.

When the Supreme Court announced its residential desegregation decision in 1948, thousands of black families poured out of the black belt in search of better housing. The decision defused a situation that had reached explosive proportions. Drawn by the city's booming war industry, blacks had poured into Chicago in the 1940s. Thus, an already densely packed black belt, full of dilapidated housing, was bursting at the seams (Hirsch 1983). Table 3 indicates the magnitude of the black population explosion as well as the extraordinary dispersal resulting from the 1948 court decision.[2]

The critical electoral realignment that followed the population shift resulted in large part from the class-distinctive character of the dispersal. Arnold Hirsch (1983) and others (Mikva 1951; Fishbein 1962) who studied the dispersal have pointed out that a combination

Table 3   **Black Population Growth and Dispersal from Black Belt,
1930–60**

Year	Black Population Growth	Proportion of City Population	Proportion in Black Belt
1930	—	6.9%	71.6%
1940	18.7%	8.2%	72.9%
1950	77.2%	13.6%	50.0%
1960	65.1%	22.9%	21.0%

The Black Belt is defined here as the three community areas of Douglas, Grand Boulevard, and Washington Park. *Source:* The data are drawn from The Local Community Fact Book series.

of high demand, limited supply, and unscrupulous realtors drove up
housing prices to exceptionally high and often exorbitant levels. Accordingly, most of the scarce new housing was acquired by the
middle class. The dispersal thus created two class-distinctive black
communities. The old southern boundary of the black belt became a
new class divide. The middle class increasingly lived to the south of
63rd Street, while the poor remained behind in the old black belt
wards and on the West Side.[3]

The class differentiation carried profound electoral implications.
The poor residents of the old black belt wards, bereft of their countervailing middle class leadership, became far more susceptible to
the machine's influence. The electorate no longer was afforded the
kind of choices that had stymied the machine in local elections.
Thus, if only by default, the machine very likely would take over the
poor black wards. The machine's problem would come from the new
black areas housing the middle class. Until the machine came successfully to grips with the racial problem, the hostility of the middle
class toward it would very likely persist in the new areas.

The 1955 Mayoral Election and the Resolution of the Race Issue

The exodus of the middle class from the black belt wards loaded the
gun of local Democratic realignment. The race issue that surfaced in
the 1955 mayoral election provided the gun with a trigger. The
smouldering race issue burst into flames after the machine's central
elite decided to dump its two-term mayor, Martin Kennelly, in favor
of party chairman Richard Daley's candidacy. Kennelly's relationship
with the black community was such that blacks generally perceived

the coup as a positive response to their plight. Daley's political move thus produced powerful unintended electoral consequences.

Despite its usually strong Democratic ties, the *Chicago Defender* had torn into Mayor Kennelly during his second term over a broad range of racial issues. Criticism of Kennelly's handling of racial conflict in public housing appeared frequently in its pages. Trumbull Park, a public housing complex on the far south side, was the scene of a running race riot since the first black family had moved there in 1953. As the *Defender* (February 13, 1954) reported, "Bombs exploded almost nightly." A harsh denunciation of the mayor's "complacent attitude toward the racial outbursts" by the head of the local NAACP was reported (March 13, 1954). A statement issued by two trade unions with large black membership was carried in the paper, pointedly asking of Kennelly: "Mr. Mayor, could a 13-month-long race riot take place in Chicago if the law were being enforced?" (September 11, 1954). When the executive director of the public housing authority, Elizabeth Woods, a staunch advocate of racial integration, was fired, the *Defender* (September 4, 1954) blasted Kennelly for her dismissal.

The mayor also came in for a large share of the blame for the city's urban renewal program. Even the normally mute black machine aldermen were quoted in the *Defender* vigorously denouncing the program. Congressman Dawson's Alderman Harvey lashed out at the University of Chicago's Julian Levi, who helped plan a large portion of the city's program, calling him "a fascist . . . He struts around just like Hitler and Mussolini in their day. Chicago and the nation can do without men of his ilk" (December 11, 1954).

Kennelly's police department received the *Defender's* wrath for its racially discriminatory practices. The department had no black officers, and only 8 of its 530 sergeants were black. The *Defender* (August 28, 1954) accused the department of using biased efficiency ratings, which accounted for 30 percent of the examination grade, to hold down blacks.

Thus, it undoubtedly came as little surprise to the black community that when Kennelly was dumped by the machine, the mayor accused Congressman Dawson of engineering the move. Recognizing a volatile issue when they saw one, and generally siding with the reform-minded mayor, the media gave extensive coverage to Kennelly's charges. In a blistering editorial entitled "Policy, Narcotics, and Mayoral Politics," the *Chicago Sun-Times* (February 1, 1955) denounced Dawson's alleged role in the dumping: "While Dawson did not singlehandedly execute the coup, there is no doubt that he wielded more influence than any other man in the organization's decision to deny Kennelly the Democratic machine's support in the February 22 mayoral primary. Dawson has long been a force for evil within the local Democratic organization. He is a political overlord of a district where policy rackets and narcotics peddling flourish as they do nowhere else in the city."

Not to be outdone, the *Chicago Tribune* reported an interview with a convicted black confidence swindler, Claude Murphy, who was testifying before a grand jury convened to look into organized crime activity. Murphy claimed that he had been a "bagman" for the crime syndicate, collecting $58,000 per month from the black policy wheels, and that "40 percent of the collections went to the secretary of a prominent politician for the latter's benefit" (cited in Final Report of Emergency Committee on Crime, Chicago City Council, December 30, 1955, 8). Murphy steadfastly refused to actually name Dawson, but few readers could have concluded that he was fingering anyone else. The mayor's strategy thus linked the volatile race issue to the classic anti-machine issue, the machine's ties to organized crime—the "dictatorship from the dark," as an earlier machine opponent, Thomas Courtney, had called it (*Chicago Daily News*, February 18, 1939).

Daley, the man the media had hailed as the "rising star" of the machine's "progressive wing," was treated mainly as a naive dupe in the affair, who had inexplicably turned his back on reform. An editorial described him as one who had once "represented the 'better element' within the Democratic party." But "Now he is running as a candidate of the crowd that dumped Kennelly because they didn't like his City Hall reforms" (*Chicago Sun-Times*, February 21, 1955).

For his part, Daley campaigned as a populist candidate, representing the neighborhoods against the powerful downtown business interests who were mainly backing Kennelly. Commenting on a series the *Chicago Sun-Times* (February 11, 1955) had run denouncing the venal ward bosses behind Daley's candidacy, Daley replied: "There are worse bosses than bosses in politics. They are the bosses of big business and big influence." Describing his supporters to reporters, he declared: "These people don't belong to State Street or LaSalle Street. They belong to the heart of the melting pot of Chicago. They represented the neighborhoods." To his supporters, Daley pledged: "I'm a kid from the stockyards, and I will remain with you" (ibid., February 15, 1955). Before a crowd of black supporters two days before the election, Daley praised Dawson and defended him: "Why is it that when a man becomes successful in politics he becomes a boss? I say Bill Dawson is a real leader. Never in my 15 years in political life has he asked me to do anything that wasn't right" (ibid., February 21, 1955).

The down side of Kennelly's strategy showed up in the front pages of the *Chicago Defender*. The anticipated white backlash the mayor was counting on never materialized. However, a powerful black backlash did. The *Defender* characterized Kennelly's attack on Dawson as a thinly veiled racist assault on the black community. In a long and passionate front page editorial, the *Defender* (February 5, 1955) defended Dawson, compared Kennelly to Hitler, and urged the mayor's defeat as "the responsibility of all decent citizens of both races to make certain that race baiting will produce no victories in Chicago. . . . Kennelly's strategy is clearly designed to arouse the indignation of whites against a powerful Negro leader and influence them to vote their prejudices rather than their well-founded convictions." The black Democratic precinct captains undoubtedly proved to be the *Defender's* best newsboys for that particular edition of the paper.

Kennelly's strategy could not overcome Daley's organizational edge. The party chairman carried twenty-six of the city's fifty wards, defeating the mayor by over 100,000 votes. The election proved to be a classic referendum on reform versus machine rule. Kennelly's vote came from the more affluent outlying wards, the traditional source of anti-machine opposition. Daley's strength was located in the inner city, the machine's electoral stronghold.

The bulk of Daley's winning margin, 60 percent of it, came out of the five black wards on the South Side. Two wards with substantial black populations on the West Side were similarly productive. Only two white wards provided Daley with comparable levels of support: his own Eleventh Ward and the First Ward, the so-called headquarters of the crime syndicate's political fiefdom. Given the dismal performance of the black wards in prior mayoral elections, the 1955 primary marked a critical turning point.

The *Chicago Defender* (February 26, 1955) was exultant, spelling out on its front page, in wildly optimistic terms, what it saw as the lessons to be drawn from the performance of the black electorate. "On Tuesday, the people of Chicago, and not the bosses, dumped Mayor Martin H. Kennelly. His defeat brought two of the most important realities of Chicago politics into sharp focus. They are: 1. No candidate can violate the rules of decency and fair play by permitting race baiting to become a factor in his campaign. . . . 2. The Negro voter has become enormously powerful and politically mature. He has learned to reward friends and punish enemies."

In its political column, "Political Pot," the *Defender* (March 19, 1955) pointed to the apparent critical flaw in Kennelly's campaign strategy: "But the master minds of the smear Dawson campaign have not taken the psychology of the Negro into account. . . . The inescapable fact is that Dawson is a symbol to his people. He is the most powerful Negro politician the country has produced. . . . As a result, smears by suggestion and attacks without evidence have boomeranged, particularly when there is a suggestion that the entire community which Dawson represents, tolerates or even welcomes lawlessness."

The 1955 breakthrough led to a realignment of the black wards. The wards that had been a hotly contested battleground between the machine and a countervailing middle class became progressively more machine oriented during the first half of Daley's lengthy mayorality (see table 4).

In broader terms, the black wards displaced the poor white immigrant wards as the Daley machine's electoral stronghold. On the West Side, some of the immigrant wards simply acquired poor black voters in place of poor white voters, and they remained as strong as ever. On the South Side, a new group of black wards emerged, collectively identified as the "Dawson machine," to take its place atop the machine (see table 5).

The Democratic divergence between local and national patterns of support that had characterized the black wards during the 1940s and early 1950s also was resolved under Daley. Black support for Democratic mayors and presidents exceeded 65 percent, and during Daley's first two elections, he secured a greater proportion of black support than presidential candidates Adlai Stevenson and John Kennedy did. Not until 1964, when the Republican party provided

Table 4   **Machine Majorities in the Black Belt Wards: Mayoral Elections, 1943–63**

Ward	1943	1947	1951	1955	1959	1963
2	1,134	1,325	2,110	13,416	13,733	12,890
3	2,804	− 35	− 248	11,860	12,739	18,852
20	—	—	− 795	10,459	12,652	15,020
Total	3,938	1,290	1,067	35,735	39,124	46,762

Source: Chicago Board of Election Commissioners

Table 5   **White Immigrant and Black Machines: Democratic Mayoral Support, 1939–63**

Composite Ranking	White Immigrant Machine (1939–51)		Daley's Black Machine (1955–63)	
	Ward	Principal Ethnicity	Ward	Principal Ethnicity
1	24	Jewish	24	Black
2	29	Italian/Jewish	11	Polish/Lithuanian
3	14	Polish	29	Black/Italian
4	26	Polish	2	Black
5	27	Italian/Black	1	Italian/Black
6	32	Polish	3	Black
7	31	Italian/Polish	27	Black/Italian
8	23	Jewish/Czech	20	Black
9	11	Polish/Lithuanian	25	Heterogenous
10	22	Czech/Polish	4	Black

Source: Composite ranking is based upon Democratic majorities in mayoral elections between 1939 and 1951 and between 1955 and 1963. Ethnic composition was estimated by plotting community areas on to ward boundaries, using the 1947 and 1961 ward maps.

a "choice instead of an echo" in the form of arch-conservative Barry Goldwater, did Daley's black vote run behind the Democratic presidential candidate's black vote. Indeed, Goldwater's candidacy put the final nail in the black Republican coffin. He won less than 4 percent of the black vote, an average of only 1,140 votes per ward. Figure 4 shows the shift from divergence to convergence in the black wards.[4]

The only dark cloud on the machine's horizon during these halcyon days in the black wards was the middle class. The Daley machine was able to capitalize everywhere in the black community on the decisive advantage Kennelly's racist campaign strategy had supplied. However, the middle class electorate, to the south of the 63rd Street class divide, never was as supportive as the lower income wards in the old black belt area.

The two poorest wards, the second and third wards, invariably ranked among the machine's ten most productive wards between 1955 to 1963, the first half of Daley's mayoralty. However, the more affluent Sixth Ward, the only one of the so-called Dawson wards located south of the class divide, reached this lofty plateau only once, when the black community came together as never before during the Polish Democratic renegade Benjamin Adamowski's challenge to Daley in 1963.

The machine's problem with the black middle class surfaced in a far more pronounced and dramatic way in 1963, as the first half of Daley's mayoralty came to a close. In the rapidly racially changing Seventeenth Ward on the Far South Side, the black community elected its first anti-machine alderman under the Daley machine. A flamboyant Charles Chew, campaigning against the machine's "plantation style" of politics and promising that "A Vote for Chew is a Vote for You," defeated a white incumbent, whom the machine had left in office even though the ward had become predominantly black. A large number of independents from across the South Side, attracted by Chew's daring rhetoric and the prospect of beating the machine, worked in his campaign (Matthewson 1974).

Chew's breakthrough victory against the vaunted Daley machine gave heart to the black anti-machine middle class forces that were beginning to regroup in the new territories. As more wards south of the class divide acquired majority black populations, the Daley machine would find itself with much more trouble on its hands. As the civil rights movement gained momentum and the machine responded with only token symbolic gestures of accommodation, the borrowed goodwill that the machine had been living off of—acquired from Mayor Kennelly's racist assault—would run out. During the second half of Daley's mayoralty, the middle class wards would break out in open revolt against the machine, while the productivity of the poor black wards would collapse under the weight of their disillusion with the machine.

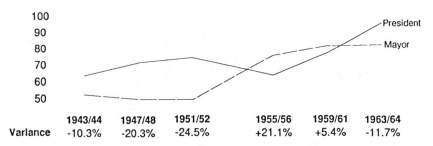

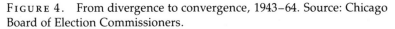

FIGURE 4. From divergence to convergence, 1943–64. Source: Chicago Board of Election Commissioners.

The New Organizational Contradiction

We saw during the realignment period that rivalry among the black ward leaders created an organizational contradiction. When the black elite turned their expertise on one another, the conflict broke the nexus that is presumed to exist between expert practitioners and organizational productivity. An organizational contradiction of a different kind emerged under Mayor Daley. It involved a disjunction between productivity and rewards. As the black wards emerged as the machine's most productive units, the black ward leaders acquired a strong claim on a greater share of the organization's resources. Yet the rewards never materialized. The black ward organizations wound up little better off when they were productive than they had been when they were not.

The situation became all the more contradictory when, with but a single exception, the black ward leaders failed to lay claim to additional rewards, or at least failed to raise any objections to the disparity. As we shall see, the silence of the black ward leaders in the face of the inequity was the product of two critical organizational changes instituted by the new mayor. Mayor Daley initiated the recruitment of a new type of ward elite, an elite who possessed little claim on the office, and who therefore was unlikely to lay any claim to greater rewards. The mayor also encouraged a fierce rivalry among the black ward leaders, instituting a divide-and-conquer strategy that effectively prevented them from banding together in any common cause. The combination of new strategies reduced the black elite to political impotence inside the machine, despite their productivity in the electoral arena.

As conflict between the black community and the machine heightened during the tumultuous 1960s, the black ward leaders were subjected to severe criticism for their silence and subservience to the machine. The normally supportive *Chicago Defender*, deeply attached, and, according to several sources, deeply indebted financially to the Democratic machine, began carrying stories about "the silent six," a term coined by the sole independent black alderman, Charlie Chew. Yet, the ward leaders persisted in their vows of silence and obedience to the organization in the face of the assaults.

The Productivity-Rewards Contradiction

During the difficult realignment years, when the black ward organizations had been barely able to muster a majority vote out of their wards for the machine, they possessed little by way of a legitimate claim on the machine's resources, and little is just what they received.[5] In the executive branch of city and county government, there were no black commissioners. In the legislative branch, a black alderman was not appointed to a committee chairmanship in the city council until 1953, and that apparently was extracted as a political reward by Congressman Dawson. After Dawson shifted his support to Daley in the contest for party chairman, his alderman, William Harvey, was appointed chairman of the Health Committee two weeks after Daley's election (*Chicago Defender,* August 9, 1953). It amounted to only a minor reward in material terms, but it represented a great symbolic breakthrough for the black ward organizations.

The main black gains came in the judiciary. However, once again the progress came as a result of political considerations, rather than as a reward to the ward organizations for their productivity. The first black Democratic judge actually was a Republican from one of the white ward organizations. Wendell Green initially was selected by Mayor Kelly to serve as the sole Republican minority party member, as required by law, on a three-person Civil Service Commission. After years of faithful service in that capacity—he "made no waves"—Green was asked to formally switch parties, and Kelly slated him for the bench in 1942.

A second black judge was not slated until a storm of protest swept over both parties during the mid-1940s for failing to give any consideration to the nomination of more black judges. Both party chairmen, Jacob Arvey and John "Bunny" East, the Republican county chairman, were urged by the *Chicago Defender* to break the color line by slating a black for the Superior Court. The *Defender's* (August 30, 1947) breakdown by ethicity revealed that the lion's share of judicial seats on the superior and circuit courts was held by the Irish. When neither party slated any additional black candidates, the *Defender* (September 13, 1947) issued a stinging editorial. Taking their readers behind the scenes, both parties were castigated for failing to even give any consideration to a black candidate during their deliberations.

The second wave of the protest crashed down when a group of three prominent black independent attorneys assembled themselves under the banner of the Progressive party to run for the bench in 1947. The slate was headed by the distinguished Richard Westbrooks, founder of the black Cook County Bar Association, created in 1913 when the white Chicago Bar Association refused to admit black attorneys to its membership. Westbrooks was joined by Earl Dickerson, a prominent businessman and the former Second Ward Democratic alderman who had been ousted by Dawson, and Sidney Jones, who would go on to become Democratic alderman of the Sixth Ward in the 1950s. With the explosive restrictive housing covenant issue pending before the federal Supreme Court, the Progressive judicial slate focused its campaign on the race issue by pledging to "Wipe Out Jim Crow From the Courts," (*Chicago Defender*, November 1, 1947).

Needless to say, the black Progressive party slate failed to carry. It performed well enough in the black wards, however, to extract a concession from the machine a few months later. A second black judge, Fred "Duke" Slater, was added to the ticket, and, not to be outdone, the Republican party also put up a pair of black judicial candidates. Thus, this time it was outside pressure rather than electoral productivity that produced the reward. Yet along with the reward, the Democratic slatemakers sent a message to the black ward organizations. Instead of giving them the judicial plum, the slatemakers reached into a white ward organization, Tom Nash's Nineteenth Ward, to find the second black judge. Slater had lived for several years in the Nineteenth Ward's small, affluent black community, and he served as Nash's supervisor for the ward's eighteen black precincts (*Chicago Defender*, March 6, 1948).

A third black judge, Henry Ferguson, was added in 1950, and he represented the first judge to come out of a black ward organization, the Twentieth Ward. Yet again, productivity had little to do with the reward. The Twentieth Ward had only been created in 1947, formed largely out of the black precincts of the Fifth Ward, and it had not had any time to establish an electoral record. The slating of Ferguson thus amounted to a personal favor by party chairman Arvey to his law partner Barnet Hodes' black protégé, Kenneth Campbell, the new committeeman of the Twentieth Ward. Campbell had worked for many years supervising Hodes' black precincts in the Fifth Ward.

Under Mayor Daley, despite the vastly increased productivity of the black ward organizations, nothing changed until the very end of the first half of his mayoralty. The change followed the extraordinary performance of the black wards in the 1963 mayoralty, when Daley was strongly challenged by Benjamin Adamowski. Daley defeated the former Democratic renegade Pole by almost 138,000 votes. However, Daley very likely lost the white vote. The seven wards headed by black aldermen supplied 70 percent, or nearly 96,000 votes, of

Daley's winning margin. When wards with substantial black populations but headed by white aldermen are taken into account, Daley
very likely owed his reelection to black voters.

Daley responded by providing the black ward organizations
with their first rewards under his leadership. A black, Deton Brooks,
was appointed in 1964 to head the new federal anti-poverty program, The Chicago Committee on Urban Opportunity. Brooks was
the first black commissioner in the city's history, and as the federal
bounty swelled under President Lyndon Johnson, the CCUO became a major source of patronage for the black ward organizations.
The black ward organizations had not had it so good since the lucrative policy racket swelled their coffers in the 1940s.

Blacks also acquired three additional chairmanships in the city
council. Two of the chairs were minor, the Utilities Committee and
the Judiciary Committee. However, Daley's favorite among the black
alderman, Ralph Metcalfe, whose ward had produced the largest
vote for Daley in the 1963 mayoral election, received a genuine
plum, the Buildings and Zoning Committee, a rich source of patronage second only to the Finance Committee.

Three additional black appointments were made to the judiciary
as well in 1963. All three judges came out of black ward organizations, presumably for services rendered in the 1963 mayoral election. Thus, 1963 represented a breakthrough year in two respects. It
marked the largest amount of patronage ever bestowed upon the
black ward organizations. It also marked the first time that the machine had honored its organizational obligation to reward electoral
productivity. During the Kelly-Arvey era, patronage had been dispensed on a personal political basis or in response to community
pressure. During Daley's first two mayoral terms, no patronage of a
substantial kind had been provided, despite the high standing of the
black ward organizations in the electoral arena.

Yet viewed in broader terms, at no time did the black ward organizations acquire rewards commensurate with either their population size or their productivity. In table 6 the distribution pattern for
the realignment period and the first half of Daley's mayoralty can be
seen.[6]

The Basis for the Contradiction

At the end of a lengthy interview with one of the late Congressman
Dawson's closest aides, I asked why Dawson and the other black
ward leaders had not fought back against Daley and demanded a

Table 6   **The Black Productivity-Patronage Contradiction**

	1945	1950	1955	1960	1965
Population	11%	14%	19%	23%	27%
Production	54%	51%	72%	86%	84%
Wards	4% (2)	6% (3)	10% (5)	12% (6)	14% (7)
Council chairman	0%	0%	7% (1)	7% (1)	27% (4)
Judgeships	2% (1)	4% (2)	5% (3)	5% (4)	6% (8)
City commissioners	0%	0%	0%	0%	5% (1)

Population percentages in off-census years are straight-line estimates. Productivity is measured by Democratic support in mayoral elections. Judgeships are for the municipal and circuit courts. Parenthetical figures are actual numbers of units.

fairer share of rewards. After a long silence, his hesitant, murmured reply was simply: "How? What could we have done?" (Davis, interview, 1979).

In fact, Dawson, although in his seventies but still ambitious and determined, had made an effort to fight back, after Daley's re-election in 1959. The congressman approached a "leading Polish politician in Chicago and proposed a black/Polish alliance to take the city and the machine away from Daley and Irish politicians" (Rakove 1982, 223). Dawson's desperate proposition, however, came to naught. When Benjamin Adamowski challenged Daley in 1963, the black wards wound up providing the vote that saved Daley's mayoralty. Following the election, Dawson took up full-time residency in Washington, D.C., and devoted his attention to congressional affairs, leaving his aides in charge of the ward organization and local politics (Davis, Love, interviews, 1979). Dawson's self-exile from the city reflected the absolute magnitude of Daley's control over the black wards.

Daley's destruction of Dawson actually began back in 1952, with the slating of Ralph Metcalfe for Third Ward committeeman over Dawson's strenuous objections (Davis interview, 1979). The following year, Daley furthered Dawson's isolation and demise by appointing black interim committeeman Claude Holman, who also was not a Dawson man, to head the Fourth Ward. Holman, a prominent attorney who had migrated to Chicago from Kansas rather than from the south, regarded himself as a breed apart and a cut above the likes of machine "hacks" such as Dawson (Martin interview, 1982; Melas interview, 1985). His ward was racially integrated, it included some of the city's most influential citizens, many affiliated with the University of Chicago, and Holman took pride in the fact that his was not just another black ward organization. Although Holman "wore his race defiantly, like a chip on his shoulder," he kept as many white precinct captains as he could—many of them had bolted the organization upon his appointment—and he selected a white president for the ward organization (Melas interview, 1985).

Within a short time, Dawson and Holman were at one another's throats. Ostensibly, the fight was over an open-occupancy housing ordinance Holman was cosponsoring with the white liberal, anti-machine alderman from the Fifth Ward, Leon Despres. Dawson, whose silence on the race issue had reached legendary proportions, was furious over Holman's breaking of the code of silence. It represented an open challenge to his preeminence among the black ward leaders, and so he set out to destroy Holman. Dawson retaliated by sending over one of his top aides, State Senator Fred Smith, to take up residency in Holman's ward, and word was conveyed to Holman that Smith would be taking over his committeemanship (Davis, Love, interviews, 1979). When the Cook County Central Democratic Committee met, Dawson attempted to seal Holman's fate. He demanded that Holman be stripped of his patronage. Daley, however, responded by decreeing that Holman's patronage "be freezed" (Korshak, interview, 1982).

Daley's fateful decision to side with Holman against Dawson sent a clear message to the black committeemen: they now were Dawson's peers; he no longer had to be feared or followed. Thus by gambling with the mayor, Dawson lost what remained of his power. Yet an often-unacknowledged part of Daley's political brilliance was the discretion he used in keeping Dawson's destruction hidden from public view. Dawson was allowed to retain his congressional seat, he continued to be lauded in the *Chicago Defender* as the undisputed leader of the black wards, and none of the black ward leaders was permitted to publicly challenge Dawson's ceremonial leadership role.

Inside the black ward organizations, however, it was a different thing. Holman's hatred of Dawson knew almost no bounds. After the mayor sided with Holman against Dawson, he admonished Holman about any further fighting with Dawson (Korshak, interview, 1982). Holman responded to the injunction by transforming Dawson into a non-person. Ward officers and precinct captains were ordered to never again mention Dawson's name in Holman's presence or inside the ward office, according to an aide.

As for relations between Holman and Metcalfe, an officer in Holman's organization at the time described it as "the kind of a thing you often find between two sons; they were always competing with one another for a greater share of 'father' Daley's affection. Nobody ever worked harder for the 'old man' than those two guys did" (Melas interview, 1985). Needless to say, Daley did not discourage the affection, competition, or conflict. As the conflict grew more heated, Holman transformed Metcalfe into another non-person, banishing from his hearing and from Fourth Ward headquarters the use of Metcalfe's name along with Dawson's. As long as the bitterness and rivalry persisted among the black committeemen, the mayor could rest assured that no collaboration for common political ends would occur.

In addition to crushing the collective will of the black elite through his destruction of Dawson and the divide-and-conquer strategy, the mayor also instituted a novel elite recruitment strategy, which assured that the individual demands of the black elite would remain modest. Ordinarily, as in the case of all but one of the black elite recruited during the Kelly-Nash-Arvey period, only highly skilled and experienced practitioners were elevated to the machine's top ranks. As Gosnell (1937, 28) found, "long years of apprenticeship," during which time expertise was acquired and demonstrated, was the principal standard of elite recruitment in the machine.

Mayor Daley introduced a novel standard for the recruitment of black elites. Daley's black elite possessed neither experience nor demonstrated skill. They were political neophytes, compared to the likes of Dawson, Wimbish, and Campbell. Ralph Metcalfe, the first of Daley's elites, had played virtually no role in the Third Ward organization he came to head (Caldwell, Washington, interviews, 1982).[7] Claude Holman had been more active, but only in a marginal way, in the Fourth Ward organization. In the speculation over who would acquire the ward's committeemanship, Holman's name never surfaced as a potential candidate. The ward organization's leaders with whom I spoke agreed that Daley's selection of Holman "just came out of the blue," as one put it (Martin, interview, 1982; Melas, interview, 1985).

Robert Miller, who was recruited by Mayor Daley to head the Sixth Ward in 1956, was a recent Republican convert. Miller had remained in the Republican party as late as 1948, angrily bolting only after he had been passed over by party chairman John "Bunny" East for committeeman of the newly created Twentieth Ward (East, interview, 1979). He promptly became active in the Twentieth Ward for the Democrats, and he did not move over to the Sixth Ward he came to head until 1955, after a black alderman, Sidney Jones, had been elected (Jones interview, 1985). As the owner of a string of funeral parlors, Miller's chief political skill was fundraising, which insiders assumed was the reason the financially strapped Dawson had promptly adopted him as a protégé (Caldwell, interview, 1982). As we saw, Dawson had unsuccessfully put Miller forward as his candidate for Twentieth Ward alderman in 1951 and again in 1952 for committeeman.

In all three cases, then, Mayor Daley conferred what amounted to a political "gift" upon undeserving novices, selecting them over more experienced rivals. As Daley undoubtedly understood, this generated an exceptional measure of gratitude from the recipients of the gift. Moreover, since the mayor's novices lacked roots in the ward organizations they were appointed to head, Daley did not have to contend with the community and ward organizational ties that generated conflicting loyalties among committeemen. These black elite owed their loyalty strictly to Daley. In turn, as the recipients of such a rich and undeserved blessing, Daley's black elite could not be expected to press for many more rewards. Their lack of political experience further constrained their ability to make demands.

Thus, from a political point of view, namely, Daley's ability to extend his control over the organization, the new black elites were ideally suited to his needs. They would make few demands on the organization's resources, and they would be utterly loyal to the mayor. Just how effective they would be in the electoral arena, given their limited political experience, was another matter. Yet it is reasonable to conclude that that was a secondary consideration for Daley.

It is important to recognize, however, that Daley's political novices were not altogether lacking in merit from an organizational point of view. What they lacked in political experience, they possessed in social prestige. In contrast to the earlier black machine elite, who, because of their rich political experience and expertise, we can call "politicians," the new black elite were "civic notables." They were deficient in political experience; but they possessed high standing in the community, in part because they were not regarded as political "hacks" in the earlier Dawson mold. Thus, unlike the earlier machines, Daley's machine provided the black middle class with political representation. Yet, of course, because Daley maintained such a tight rein on his elite, the measure of representation never would be more than nominal.

Ralph Metcalfe, as a former Olympic champion, was a widely aclaimed hero in the black community. As committeeman, he capi-

talized on his Olympic background by holding annual "junior olym-
pics" contests in his ward, which were enormously popular and
helped to legitimize his ward organization (Patch, Washington, interviews, 1982). Claude Holman was a prominent attorney, and one
of the city's few black attorneys with a law practice that cut across
racial lines. As evidence of his exceptional stature, Holman was the
first black trustee of John Marshall Law School. A common explanation offered for his selection as ward committeeman was that "he
had enough class to get along with all the white 'big shots' living in
his ward" (Martin, interview, 1982; Melas, interview, 1985). Robert
Miller, Daley's third black committeeman, was a prominent businessman, owning a string of funeral parlors on the South Side.
Miller was nowhere nearly as polished as Metcalfe and Holman
were, and he never displayed the political skill his two colleagues
acquired. Yet as a prosperous businessman, he was regarded as a
successful man who had made it on his own (Caldwell, interview,
1982; Jones, interview, 1985).

Because of their social prominence, Daley's black elite also had
access to a wider range of financial resources than the earlier black
elite possessed. Many black businessmen and members of the
middle class in general looked unfavorably on politics as a "filthy
business," and they looked down on the machine in particular (Wilson, 1965, 57–59). However, because Daley's black elite had acquired
their initial prestige outside the machine, they were better able to
solicit support in these frequently hostile quarters. Given the black
ward organizations' paucity of financial backing since the demise of
the policy racket and their consequent dependence on the machine
for money, the ability of Daley's black elite to raise some funds on
their own was no minor virtue.

As it turned out, however, when the civil rights movement
swept into Chicago in the 1960s, Mayor Daley's "civic notable" strategy of elite recruitment yielded disastrous unintended consequences. As the black community began applying pressure on the
machine's ward leaders, demanding substantive rather than nominal representation, Daley's civic notables, with their high community standing, experienced the greatest stress. They would be the
only black elites who eventually buckled and fell under the community pressure. Thus, Mayor Daley responded by abandoning his
civic notable elite strategy during the civil rights siege. He began
bringing in yet another type of black elite, minor functionaries from
the machine's patronage ranks who held no social stature to speak
of and who therefore would be invulnerable to community pressure.

In Perspective

A classic study of black politics by James Q. Wilson (1960) explained the Daley machine's firm hold over black voters from an economic perspective. Dire socioeconomic need compelled poor blacks to exchange their votes for the machine's favors and friendship. Wilson did not realize, however, that it was not until Mayor Daley's election in 1955 that black voters actually began providing the machine with substantial majorities. Nor did he recognize that the long overdue realignment had little to do with any desire to satisfy material or social needs.

The sociological and political perspectives get us closer to the actual basis for the realignment. When the U.S. Supreme Court's 1948 decision struck down the black belt, two class-distinctive black communities emerged. The middle class fled the black belt and began taking up residence beyond its boundaries. Without the countervailing middle class, the poor voters who remained were left only with the political choices provided by the machine. The situation was exacerbated by Mayor Kennelly's racist campaign against Daley and the machine in 1955, which delegitimized the anti-machine forces in the black wards. Thus, although black support of the machine appeared solid, it actually rested on a shaky foundation, in that the machine had done virtually nothing to earn it.

The sociological and political perspectives also are useful for understanding the organizational relationship between the black ward elites and the machine. Inasmuch as the black wards emerged as the Daley machine's electoral stronghold, this should have resulted, by the economic perspective's terms, in a substantial increase of benefits to the black ward organizations. However, as we saw, the black ward organizations reaped no more benefits than they had when they were only marginally productive.

The groundwork for the denial of benefits was laid by the social upheaval following World War II that radically altered the city's political landscape. The flight of affluent Protestants to the suburbs left the Republican party without any electoral foundation to speak of. By 1955 it even resorted to running a liberal Democratic alderman as its mayoral candidate. The decimation of the Republican party provided Daley with an unprecented advantage. With virtual impunity he could set aside the economic factor of productivity, which enabled him to reconstitute the machine on his own self-interested political terms.

This, as we saw, is exactly what he did in recruiting black ward elites. In place of elevating highly experienced politicians, Daley instituted the novel practice of recruiting "civic notables," men with high community standing, but virtually no political experience. The strategy achieved two goals. It provided the disaffected middle class with its first taste of representation from the machine. However, since the representatives lacked political experience and were deeply indebted to Daley for their good fortune, the representation was merely symbolic.

Accordingly, despite a population explosion, a significant increase in the number of wards under black leadership, and solid black support for the machine, the black community and the black ward organizations were no better off than before. Things would remain this way until yet another critical event, the civil rights movement, would once again radically alter black perceptions of the machine.

6

The Movement and the Machine:
The Cultural Limits
of Political Power

A distinction must be drawn between the first and second halves of the Daley mayoralty. The launching of the Daley mayoralty coincided with the black local Democratic realignment. Black support became so critical to the machine's success that from 1955 to 1963 the Daley machine was a black machine in electoral terms. In 1963, the black wards very likely saved Mayor Daley from defeat against the powerful challenge issued by the Polish renegade, Benjamin Adamowski.

Adamowski made heavy inroads into even the strongest of the Daley machine's white wards in 1963. Daley's majority in Finance Committee Chairman Thomas Keane's powerful Thirty-first Ward was cut to half of what it had been in 1959. In the crime syndicate's First Ward political headquarters, Daley's majority fell by 40 percent. Adamowski cut into Daley's majority in the mayor's own ward by 35 percent, and overall, the Polish renegade carried eighteen wards. This was an extraordinary showing, considering that Republican Timothy Sheehan had carried only a single ward, his own Forty-first Ward, in 1959. The black wards, however, came through for Daley in record numbers.[1]

Yet right on the heels of the black outpouring of support came a stunning reversal. Only six months after the mayoral election, a school boycott organized to protest overcrowding, underfunding, and racial segregation in the black schools was supported by 90 percent of the black students. A second, more controversial, boycott several months later kept over three-quarters of the black student population home (Anderson and Pickering 1986, 119–20, 133). The boycotts were backed up by marches, rallies, and picketing. The protracted civil rights protest generated so much heat that Daley finally felt compelled to withdraw his support from school superintendent Benjamin Willis in 1965, in the hope that Willis' ouster would placate the determined protesters.

Yet no sooner had Willis left than Martin Luther King came sweeping in, and the heat was back on, more intense than ever. Seeking to put his southern civil rights movement on a national footing, King went looking for the biggest northern challenge he could find. Against the advice of several of his aides, he selected Chicago, the most segregated big city in the nation and home of the last of the great political machines (Tillman 1986, 155–62). King soon discovered that the situation was even worse than he could have imagined. "The people of Mississippi ought to come to Chicago to learn how to hate," he concluded after a dangerous day of marching in the white ethnic neighborhoods (*Chicago Sun-Times,* January 19, 1986).

Daley refused to provide King with the political confrontation he needed to dramatize the conflict between the movement and the machine. "Your goals are our goals," the mayor assured King, luring him to the bargaining table. After two long hot summers, King and his movement wound up with only a handful of empty promises to show for their efforts. By all accounts, the movement had run up against a brick wall in Chicago (Anderson and Pickering, 1986). Yet, as we shall see, the electoral consequences of the seemingly unsuccessful confrontation were anything but inconsequential.

Several devastating developments followed in the wake of King's foray into the city. Large parts of the West Side were leveled by the massive rioting following Dr. King's assassination in 1968. The rampaging, looting, and destruction provoked an outraged Mayor Daley into issuing his infamous "shoot to kill" order to the police. "In my opinion," he declared at a press conference, "policemen should have had instructions to shoot arsonists and looters— arsonists to kill and looters to maim and detain" (Royko 1971, p. 169). Not long after the riot, a police raid led by State's Attorney Edward Hanrahan, widely held to be Daley's heir apparent, resulted in the deaths of two Black Panther leaders. After surveying the crime scene, a news reporter contradicted Hanrahan's version of the event—that the police had been met by a hail of gunfire—by concluding that all but one of the 80–100 shots had been fired by the police (ibid., 212). In a grand jury hearing, a machine-controlled judge threw up one stumbling block after another in an effort to prevent the state's attorney's indictment (Travis 1987, 446–55).

Still another police "riot," as the commission investigating the confrontation characterized it (Walker 1968), occurred at the 1968 Democratic Convention held in Chicago. The conflict between the young white protesters and the police signaled that the machine was in trouble along another front. The "lakefront liberal" political movement that would challenge Daley's machine was formed out of the violent struggle at the convention, in which the police used clubs and tear gas to put down the protesters (Rose, interview, 1984). Racial division and divergent agendas, however, prevented discontented blacks and white liberals from forming an effective coalition against the machine. In 1975 a lakefront liberal candidate, Alderman William Singer, gave Mayor Daley a good run in the middle-class black wards, even though Singer did little campaigning among black voters.

Thus, the novel political fault lines of race and liberal ideology emerged during the second half of the Daley mayoralty, displacing the class divide that has long pitted the poor inner-city wards against the more prosperous wards along the city's edges. The centrality of the new racial divide was revealed by the new electoral composition of Daley's machine in the 1970s. For the first time, white ethnic working-class and middle-class wards became the machine's most productive supporters, and the main stronghold of Daley's new white ethnic machine was located on the Southwest Side, the most racially embattled area of the city. For two decades, block by block, accompanied by white panic, violence, and flight, amply fueled by unscrupulous realtors, blacks had been moving slowly but steadily into the Southwest Side.

The classic anti-machine issues—honesty, efficiency, and lower taxes—paled into insignificance in the face of the volatile issue of racial containment. The city's political establishment, of course, always had come down on the side of racial containment, going back to the black belt era. In the 1960s, however, the race issue moved firmly to the forefront because the black population had reached a critical mass, and, as the population continued growing, blacks spread farther and farther across the city.

At the same time, inspired by the civil rights movement, blacks were making unprecedented demands on the city's resources. In addition to the "street heat" generated by numerous marches and demonstrations, several successful lawsuits were filed demonstrating racial discrimination in a wide range of areas: public housing, public schools, the park district, and employment in the police and fire departments. All in all, then, it became increasingly clear during the second half of Daley's mayoralty that the Democratic machine no longer could maintain even a pretense of being a New Deal "party of the little man." As the racial demands escalated, the machine increasingly took on the retrograde character of a southern white supremist Democratic party.

This, needless to say, left the Daley machine with a substantial problem on its hands in the black wards. Daley responded by abandoning his strategy of civic-notable elite recruitment, in favor of a policy that provided black voters with even less representation. In the face of the civil rights challenge, Daley chose not to accommodate it. Instead, he tightened the organizational screws even tighter on his black elite. In effect, he decided to wall off the machine against the rebellion taking place in the black wards. As the rebellion escalated and the estrangement spread, exacerbated by Daley's containment strategy, the mayor simply added more bricks to the wall, in the form of an ever more compliant black elite.

Reaching down into the lower and middle ranks of the machine's patronage army, Daley began recruiting a new type of ward committeeman in the 1960s, committeemen who would be at once intensely loyal to the machine—and, of course, to Daley in particular—and indifferent to the civil rights protesters' demands for representation and policy changes. These new "loyalist" elite, unlike their civic notable predecessors, lacked standing in the black community, their well-being was dependent on their patronage employment, and their Catholicism—unusual among blacks—served to insulate them from the essentially Protestant civil rights movement, while it bound them to the machine's Irish Catholic leadership.

At the same time, more good fortune fell on Daley's machine. Despite the black elite's long years of service in the machine and the rising number of black wards—increasing from five in 1955 to fourteen in 1975—the black ward organizations wound up nearly devoid of experienced leadership in the 1970s. Death claimed many of the established black elite—Dawson, Campbell, Holman, and Benjamin Lewis on the West Side. Their successors, as Daley sought to insulate the machine from the dangerous shocks of the civil rights movement, invariably were compliant men with limited skills and small ambitions.

The slow expansion of the black community into new areas also meant that many black committeemen would be new to the job in the 1970s. Thus, in 1976 only four of the fourteen black committeemen possessed more than a single term of leadership experience. Accordingly, when Daley died, few of the black elite were in a position to participate in the reconstituting of the machine. The long awaited "new pie" was carved without their help, they took what they were handed, and, as usual, that meant they wound up with the crumbs.

Electoral Disillusion and Revolt

Three distinct black political communities emerged during the course of the second half of Daley's mayoralty. The oldest political community consisted of the poor wards in and around the old black belt. The original two wards had been the Second and the Third; the Twentieth Ward was created in 1947; the Fourth Ward, to the east of the old black belt, was added in 1953; and the Sixteenth Ward, west of the old black belt and straddling the 63rd Street class divide, was added in 1971.

These were the wards (with the exception of the yet-to-be-formed Sixteenth Ward) that had constituted the machine's electoral stronghold during the early Daley years. During the second half of Daley's mayoralty, their productivity fell off sharply. Demoralization set in, as the civil rights movement challenged the machine's legitimacy, and as it became clear to poor black voters that they were receiving little for their solid support of the machine. It was no less evident, at the same time, that the civil rights movement was sweeping through the old black belt wards without having much effect on their fortunes. The sense of isolation and disillusion was particularly evident in the huge blocks of public housing developments, which made up a substantial proportion of the Second, Third, and Fourth wards. Accordingly, these wards did not turn against the machine so much as they turned away from politics.

To the south of the 63rd Street class divide, a sizable middle-class black political community began to emerge in the 1950s. By the 1970s, it made up about a third of the black population. The antipathy of the middle class toward the machine that had existed during the black belt era carried over into the new black areas. Despite the media's preoccupation with the emerging anti-machine posture of the white so-called lakefront liberal wards in the 1970s, the black middle-class wards actually displayed a stronger independent stance. All of them issued strong challenges to the machine, most of them elected an antimachine alderman, and they supplied the great bulk of black votes won by various white independent challengers to the machine. By 1971, there were five middle-class wards: Sixth, Eighth, Seventeenth, Twenty-first, and Thirty-fourth.

On the West Side, a third black political community emerged in the 1960s, and it was for all practical purposes a distant land apart. It was not simply a matter of physical separation from the South Side; the West Side was governed by a radically different political tradition. Here was where the machine's strongest white ward bosses—party chairmen Pat Nash and Jake Arvey; state chairman Jack Touhy; Al Horan—had held sway for for decades—and many of them were ruthless men with allegedly close ties to the crime syndicate.

A black West Side 1960s political activist explained to me, pointing to the murders of black Alderman Ben Lewis and black aldermanic candidate Octavius Granady, that "South Side blacks had it easy. Out here, these mob guys acted as though murder was just another political tactic. If they couldn't scare you off or buy you off, they weren't above knocking you off. And believe me, that put a real damper on our independent political movement. A lot of those black activists you see on the South Side wound up there because they had been run off the West Side" (Janney, interview, 1981). Even Mayor Daley in his prime felt compelled to maintain a hands-off policy toward West Side politics (O'Connor 1975, 174).

Thus, it is unsurprising that even after the West Side wards acquired majority black populations, they continued to be ruled by white ward bosses. For that reason, the black West Side wards came to be called the "plantation wards."[2] In most cases, white rule was indirect. A black ward committeeman, Benjamin Lewis, was installed in Arvey's Twenty-fourth Ward as early as 1961. However, when Lewis began displaying too much independence, threatening to replace some of the organization's white precinct captains, for example (*Chicago Defender*, July 10, 1963), and, more boldly yet, demanding a larger share of gambling proceeds, he was murdered in "classic gangland fashion," as the newspapers put it.

Needless to say, the murder had a chilling effect on any black elite flirting with notions about acquiring greater power within the machine. The other plantations acquired nominal black leadership in the late 1960s and 1970s. The exception to indirect rule was the Twenty-seventh Ward, whose white committeeman, Edward Quigley, described by Mayor Daley's press secretary, Earl Bush, as "one of the 'Irish Neanderthals' who influenced Daley" (Sullivan 1989, 33), retained office into the 1980s, when he was finally driven out by Mayor Harold Washington. In all, there were four plantation wards by the 1970s—the Twenty-fourth, Twenty-seventh, Twenty-eighth, and Twenty-ninth (see ward map).

If we look at the voting behavior of the three black political communities in aldermanic and mayoral elections, we can see that social class and political tradition shaped their orientation to the Daley machine. The middle-class wards on the Far South Side were by far the

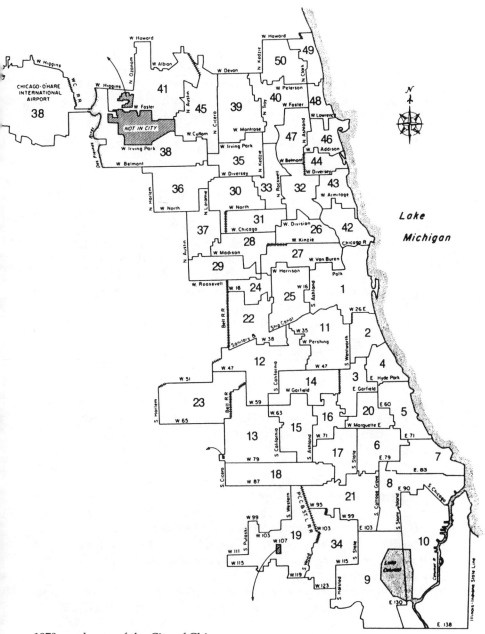

1970 ward map of the City of Chicago

most independent. The older and poorer black belt wards on the Near South Side generally displayed less independence, although middle-class pockets in some of them created problems for the machine. The plantation wards showed the least independence of all: They failed to elect an anti-machine alderman, and two of them were able to provide the Daley machine with substantial majorities even into the 1970s, after black support everywhere else had collapsed.

Aldermanic Elections

According to a leading student of black politics, one of the Daley machine's principal electoral advantages was the failure of the black middle class to flex its considerable muscle. Supposedly demoralized by a "you-can't-beat-city-hall" attitude, voter turnout in mayoral elections was actually lower in the middle class wards than in the poor black wards (Preston 1982, 94–100). Yet, when voting in aldermanic elections is taken into account, the outlook of the middle-class wards was anything but apathetic and defeatist. The machine was strongly challenged in all of the wards south of the 63rd Street class divide.

As we saw, Charles Chew scored the first anti-machine aldermanic victory at the close of the first half of Daley's mayoralty in 1963, in the middle-class Seventeenth Ward. Several other unsuccessful black anti-machine campaigns were launched in the same year (Matthewson 1974, 121–34). The breakthrough was extended in 1967, when two more aldermanic posts were secured by black independents. In a battle of the morticians in the Sixth Ward, A. A. "Sammy" Rayner defeated machine committeeman Robert Miller. However, as we shall see, Rayner received indirect and unsolicited assistance from the machine because of Mayor Daley's displeasure over a momentary spark of independence Miller displayed in the city council. In the Eighth Ward, a late Democratic convert, William Cousins, who finally abandoned the GOP in 1964 after it nominated the extremist Barry Goldwater as its presidential nominee, defeated a black machine candidate.

A third victory nearly was achieved in the Twenty-first Ward. Two strong independent challengers, James Montgomery and Augustus "Gus" Savage, divided the anti-machine vote in 1967, enabling the machine's candidate, Wilson Frost, to win. After the ward boundaries were redrawn in 1970, Frost moved over to the Thirty-fourth Ward, where he won another close election over Savage.

Thus, anti-machine challengers won in three of the five middle-class wards, and they mounted strong challenges in the other two wards.

The middle class revolt spilled over the class divide in the wake of its success in 1967. The once impregnable Second Ward fortress of "Boss" Dawson fell in 1969, in a special election. Fred Hubbard, a social worker who had unsuccessfully sought the Second Ward seat in 1967, defeated a badly divided Dawson organization in 1969. Dawson, gravely ill in Washington, D.C., had abandoned the organization to his aides years earlier, and they could not agree upon a successor. Several of Dawson's prominent aides even chose to side with Hubbard in an effort to discredit the organization's candidate (Love, interview, 1979). Hubbard also was aided by a strong vote from a sizable middle-class housing development that had been put up in the ward.

A feisty female attorney, Anna Langford, defeated the machine in 1971, in the racially changing Sixteenth Ward that straddled the 63rd Street class divide. The ward had been run for many years by the politically powerful Sheridan family, first father and then son, and Mayor Daley was unable or unwilling to get the younger Sheridan to see the new handwriting on the wall. Sheridan ran for alderman, and despite Langford's limited resources and modest capacity for political organizing, she was able to defeat what little was left of the Sixteenth Ward's machine.

The problem for the independent movement, however, was that in virtually every case the successful anti-machine alderman displayed no staying power. Some of them were coopted by the machine. Charlie Chew abandoned his aldermanic seat midway through his first term and won a state senate seat. After entering the senate, Chew made his peace with the machine he had twice defeated. As he explained it, he did not feel he could rely on independents to keep him in office over the long haul (Rose, interview, 1984). Fred Hubbard in the Second Ward also defected from the independent movement after defeating what was left of the Dawson machine, opting for security over the precarious existence of a political independent.

What both men understood was what Anna Langford and Sammy Rayner discovered when they prepared for reelection. The machine would throw everything it had at independent aldermen to prevent a second defeat. Since many of the black machine ward organizations were confronted by only nominal challenges or none at all, they could send over their best precinct captains to aid their beleaguered colleagues in the independent areas. Substantial financial resources also were allocated to machine ward organizations under siege. At the same time, after failing to establish much of a record in office, the independent aldermen were hard pressed to secure much help in their reelection bids. Thus, Rayner chose to not even stand for reelection, and Langford probably wished she had done the same, after getting soundly defeated.

The sole successful challenger over the long run was Bill Cousins. In several respects, Cousins was the mirror image of the other independents. They tended to be flamboyant, he was quiet. They relied heavily on rhetoric to carry their campaigns, Cousins was an energetic "nuts-and-bolts" organizer. They spent much of their time "in the media" and little in the ward. Cousins worked his ward year 'round, attending block club meetings, church affairs and neighborhood events, and meeting as best he could the residents' "housekeeping" demands. Thus, although the machine came after him time and again, Cousins won because he worked his ward in the same dedicated way that the machine worked its wards.

On the West Side, the independent challengers had no success at all. In the most middle class of the plantation wards, the Twenty-ninth Ward on the Far West Side, an independent challenger, Robert Biggs, came close in 1963. However, the ward's prudent machine committeeman, Bernard Neistein, promptly coopted Biggs, and ran him as the machine's candidate in 1967, badly demoralizing Biggs' independent followers (Janney, interview, 1981; Barnett, interview, 1983).

The electoral success of independent aldermanic challenges to the machine in the three black political communities can be seen in table 7.

Mayoral Elections

The shift in black voting at the mayoral level during the latter half of Daley's mayoralty was less dramatic and more drawn out. The lack of drama had to do with the lack of choice. In 1967 the Republicans ran another lackluster candidate, who wound up getting buried by Daley in all fifty of the city's wards. Still, even under these limiting circumstances, there were discernible signs of discontent in the black wards.

All but one black ward produced a smaller margin for Daley in 1967 than it had in 1963. More significantly, the bulk of the black wards no longer ranked among the machine's most productive units, as they had in 1963, when all but one of them was ranked

Table 7   **Successful Aldermanic Challenges in the Three Black Political
           Communities, 1963–75**

Black Belt Wards	Middle-Class Wards	Plantation Wards
2 Hubbard (1969)	6 Rayner (1967)	24
3	8 Cousins (1967)	27
4	17 Chew (1963)	28
16 Langford (1971)	21	29
20	34	

Source: Chicago Board of Election Commissioners. Wards were included when they acquired a black alderman.

among the top ten producers. In 1967 only the two West Side plantation wards and one of the poor black belt wards remained among the machine's top producers.

This was the first firm indication that race was replacing class as the city's main political divide. White ethnic voters saw Daley as finally coming around to their side (Madigan 1986, 114–15). Black voters saw Daley turning his back on them. The civil rights challenge forced Daley into taking a stand. Although with considerable skill he finessed King's foray into the city, refusing to confront him and luring him to the bargaining table, voters across the city came to understand where the mayor stood on the issue of racial expansion versus racial containment. As Daley's press secretary at the time, Earl Bush, explained years later, "What Daley did was smother King. What Daley couldn't smother was the civil rights movement" (*Chicago Sun-Times*, January 19, 1986)[3].

By the 1970s it became evident that Daley's black machine had been replaced by a white ethnic working- and middle-class machine. The Southwest Side, the area experiencing the greatest racial change, became the Daley machine's new electoral stronghold. At the same time, black voters expressed their growing disillusion with the machine by staying away from the polls. Only one black ward, Arvey's old Twenty-fourth Ward on the West Side, the premier plantation ward, produced a turnout that exceeded the citywide turnout in 1971. Only two plantation wards remained among the machine's top producers.

At the other end of the scale, three of the black middle-class wards provided the Republican's liberal mayoral candidate in 1971, Richard Friedman, with a sizable vote, despite his hopelessly doomed candidacy. Thus, just as we saw at the aldermanic level, the three black political communities were responding to the machine in distinct ways. The black belt wards were largely mired in disillusion, the middle-class wards were in revolt, and the plantation wards, controlled by their white overlords, proceeded along a path of indifference.

The 1975 Democratic mayoral primary produced the most dramatic development in the black wards. In it, Daley faced his first party challenge since his initial election in 1955, when he had to take on incumbent Mayor Kennelly. Daley's two primary challengers reflected the city's new political fault lines: Alderman William Singer represented the white lakefront liberal forces, and black State Senator Richard Newhouse (from the liberal, racially integrated Hyde Park community) stood for the black middle class. Poorly funded and no less poorly organized, Newhouse ran only a token campaign. Singer, running as a classic reform candidate, flailing away at the machine's corruption and wasteful spending, was the main alternative. He mounted an impressive citywide campaign; however he had only a small organization in the black wards. As a participant in the campaign, I found no black leadership at the top level and observed that Singer made few appearances in the black wards and no appeal was developed that specifically addressed black voters.

Mayor Daley won all fourteen black wards, and he did it with ease in all but two cases. Newhouse, in turn, trailed Singer by large margins in all the black wards. However, when the Singer and Newhouse numbers are combined into a composite anti-machine vote, it can be seen that Daley fared far less well among black voters than it appeared, as he failed to carry all the middle-class wards. He also lost the Second Ward and nearly lost the Fourth Ward, the two black belt wards with sizable numbers of middle-class voters. Only in the West Side plantation wards, that world apart, was Daley able to handily turn back the composite white liberal–black middle-class challenge.

Thus, at the close of his long mayoralty, Daley clearly was in trouble with the voters who had been instrumental in putting him into office in 1955 and who had kept him there when even the strongest white machine wards, including his own ward, had let him down in 1963 against Adamowski. When the performance of the black wards is viewed over the length of Daley's mayoralty, the considerable effect of the civil rights movement and ensuing racial and civil disorders is strikingly evident (see table 8).

By comparing the performance of the black wards in mayoral and presidential elections, it can be seen that the Democratic divergence that had characterized the black vote during the 1940s re-

Table 8   **The Rise and Fall of Daley's Black Machine: Citywide Ranking in Mayoral Elections, 1955–75**

Political Community	1955	1959	1963	1967	1971	1975
Black belt						
2	4	7	5	26	36	30
3	8	10	1	3	23	37
4	16	6	7	16	16	23
16					37	35
20	11	11	3	12	31	34
Middle class						
6	19	16	10	26	43	36
8				17	45	32
17			14	22	29	36
21				19	44	32
34					27	31
Plantation						
24		1	2	7	4	25
27					10	21
28					40	47
29				6	24	41
Proportion in top ten producers	40%	66%	86%	30%	14%	0%

Source: Chicago Board of Election Commissioners. Wards were included when they acquired a black alderman.

asserted itself in the late 1960s. Once again, many black voters began drawing a sharp distinction between what they perceived to be a supportive liberal Democratic national agenda and an increasingly conservative and racist Democratic machine agenda.

The greatest divergence appeared in the middle-class wards. They consistently ranked among the city's most productive wards in presidential elections; however, on only one occasion over the length of Daley's mayoralty did a middle-class ward rank among the top producers in mayoral elections. In the black belt wards (see table 9), the Democratic divergence reappeared in the late 1960s, and in the West Side plantation wards, it emerged in the 1970s.

When the performance of the original black belt wards is viewed in even broader perspective, the extent to which political values, as opposed to economic necessity, shaped the electoral behavior of even the poorest black wards is readily apparent. During the re-

Table 9   **Black Voting in Presidential Elections: Citywide Ranking,
           1956–76**

Political community	1956	1960	1964	1968	1972	1976
Black belt
2	3	6	10	11	9	9
3	5	9	3	4	11	14
4	6	3	6	8	8	10
16					12	8
20	10	8	1	5	7	6
Middle class
6	17	4	2	3	3	4
8				1	2	2
17			4	6	6	5
21				2	1	1
34					5	3
Plantation
24		1	11	10	10	13
27					15	17
28					14	15
29				7	13	16
Proportion in top ten producers	80%	100%	86%	90%	64%	64%

Source: Chicago Board of Election Commissioners. Wards were included when they
acquired a black alderman.

alignment period, when the middle class lived among the poor in
the black belt, the machine had a difficult time securing a bare majority in mayoral elections, and a Republican alderman represented
one of the wards. At the same time, the black belt wards were voting
overwhelmingly Democratic in presidential elections. During the
first half of Daley's mayoralty, the black belt wards finally and firmly
came into the local Democratic fold. However, as we saw, even this
shift had more to do with political values than material inducements. Mayor Kennelly's racist campaign tactics against Daley drove
black voters into the machine. Then as the civil rights movement
emerged in the 1960s, during the second half of Daley's mayoralty,
an increasing proportion of black voters once again began turning
against the machine.[4] (see fig. 5.)

The Organizational Response to the Electoral Revolt

We have argued that an economic explanation of decision making in the machine is misleading because it focuses only upon the organization's interest, to the exclusion of an elite interest in maintaining and enhancing their positions and power in the organization. The elite are not simply interested in maximizing the machine's electoral efficiency in order to acquire greater profit for the organization; they also seek to acquire benefits in a more direct way by increasing their control over the organization. By controlling the decision-making centers, the elite are better able to maintain and extend their own privileges and power.

Depending upon the goals pursued by the elite, and the means used to secure the goals, organizational dynamics and outcomes will be quite different. We saw at the outset of Daley's acquisition of the party chairmanship that he eschewed highly experienced and skilled black elite in favor of bringing men with limited political experience into the leadership ranks. At the same time, Daley's new

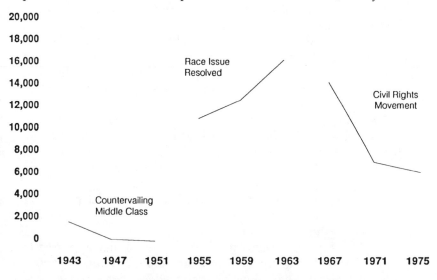

FIGURE 5.   Voting and values in the poor black belt wards: Mayoral elections, 1943–75. Source: Chicago Board of Election Commissioners. The Second, Third, and Twentieth wards (the original black belt wards) are included. The Twentieth Ward became a black ward after the 1947 mayoral election. The figures represent the average Democratic margin for the wards.

type of elite possessed high standing in the community. Thus, the civic-notable strategy of elite recruitment was designed to secure two distinct goals. The inexperience of the notables provided Daley with the control he sought. The prestige of the notables provided the middle class with a novel, albeit nominal, measure of representation.

With the rise of the civil rights movement, however, it became clear that Daley's civic-notable elite recruitment strategy was not working. Nominal representation failed to stem the rising anti-machine fervor of the middle class. Daley's black elite came to be castigated as the "silent six." The older black elites, the politicians (notably "Boss" Dawson and Kenneth Campbell), were not much troubled by the criticism. However, the civic notables, not purely creatures of the machine in the way Dawson, Campbell, and the West Side plantation elite were, were far more vulnerable to community pressure.

Thus, during the course of Daley's long mayoralty, he sacked only three black elite, and all three of them were civic notables who were unable to stand up to the intense pressure put on them by an aroused community. Accordingly, Daley altered his elite-recruitment strategy in the mid-1960s, as the civil rights movement transformed the black political relationship to the machine. In doing so, he also intervened much more forcefully in the decision making of the ward organizations, stripping them of the measure of autonomy many of them traditionally had possessed.

Daley had never granted the black ward organizations much autonomy. Virtually all of his black elite had come from outside or the periphery of the ward organizations they came to head. However, in the 1960s Daley had to force some of his new black elite down the throats of ward organizations that fought to retain the right of selecting their own leadership. The repressive measures reflected Daley's growing awareness that the civil rights movement constituted a grave threat to the machine in the black wards.

Indeed, as the civil rights revolt intensified, Daley appeared to become obsessed with the idea of maintaining absolute organizational control over the black ward organizations, particularly in the middle-class areas, where the prospects of revolt were greatest. The change was consistent with the general view of machine insiders who found that Daley became far more rigid, withdrawn, and autocratic during the latter half of his mayoralty. "In later years, he ignored the advice of many . . . The longer his career matured, the less he trusted anybody at all. It had to be just Daley and his family.

He would see you and listen to you for a little while. But you could always tell that he was suspicious" (Clark 1979, 346–54). Yet nowhere was the shift more evident than in his changing relationship to the black community. Any earlier notions of accommodation and cooptation were swept aside by Daley's growing preoccupation with containment.

Daley's New "Loyalist" Black Elite

One cannot say definitively when Daley's relationship with the black community began to change. But it well may have been in June 1963, less than two months after he had been reelected by a landslide margin in the black wards. He had accepted an invitation to address a rally organized by the local NAACP, a conservative black organization that had been infiltrated and taken over by the Daley machine years earlier (Wilson 1965, 63–65). The rally should have gone well, then, but it did not, for when the mayor attempted to speak, a loud chorus of protests drowned out what he had to say. Following failed efforts by the NAACP's leadership to quiet the crowd, Daley was forced to leave the stage, stunned and angered by the hostile reception he had received (Anderson and Pickering 1986, 112).

Two months later, Daley announced that two new black acting committeemen had been selected. William Shannon would head the Seventeenth Ward, where Charlie Chew had successfully defeated the machine, and Fred Coles would take over the racially changing Twenty-first Ward, where a white independent alderman had just turned back a black machine candidate. Both men were replacing white machine committeemen.

Neither man bore any resemblance to the civic-notable elite Daley had recruited earlier in his mayoralty. Both were patronage "hacks," holding minor jobs with the city, and they had little standing in the community. Thus, both men were tied to the machine by a cash nexus, they had limited ability to earn a living outside politics, and, because of their modest status in the community, they were unlikely to be unduly influenced by the anti-machine sentiment welling up in the community from the civil rights movement's activities.

Reflecting Daley's long organizational arm, increasing arrogance, and growing obsession with control, Shannon was imposed on the Seventeenth Ward organization without even the benefit of the traditional mock trappings of machine democracy: a vote by the precinct captains (*Chicago Defender,* July 31, 1963). Several months later the ward organization's president remained incensed enough to file a law suit seeking to prohibit Shannon from using the name of the Seventeenth Ward Regular Democratic Organization. However, within weeks, the precinct captains were assembled and they duly elected Shannon to the office, thereby nullifying the law suit (ibid., December 19, 31, 1963).

Daley also imposed his autocratic will on the Twenty-first Ward organization. The precinct captains there had unanimously elected Fred Coles, the organization's vice president, to the committeeman post (ibid., July 31, 1963). Daley, however, had another cadidate for them, preferring a protégé of his favorite black committeeman, Ralph Metcalfe, by the name of Joseph Robichaux, a popular athletic coach at Catholic St. Elizabeth High School.

The mayor's choice was not even a member of the Twenty-first Ward organization (ibid., July 19, 1963). However, as Daley had shown before, he did not regard this as a drawback. Indeed, from the mayor's viewpoint, strong ward ties constituted a deficit, inasmuch as he demanded undivided loyalty from his black elite. This in itself, then, made the outsider Robichaux more attractive than the insider Coles. Moreover, since Robichaux was sponsored by Metcalfe, a man who had demonstrated his loyalty by publicly denouncing Dr. King, the outsider merited the mayor's solid support.

Coles complained bitterly that his ward organization's job holders were being pressured into abandoning him in favor of Robichaux by the threat of losing their jobs (ibid., December 19, 1963). Even after he was dumped, Coles chose to challenge the outsider Daley was imposing on the organization. However, the conflict never came to a head. As often happened to the machine's opponents, Coles' nomination petitions were challenged, and the Board of Election Commissioners ruled him off the ballot, leaving Robichaux unopposed (ibid., April 13, 1964).

Thus, Mayor Daley had two more black elite aboard, and both of them owed their positions to the mayor's forceful intervention. Both could therefore be counted on to back Daley to the hilt. The fact that both men were Catholic added yet another bond between them and the machine's Irish Catholic leadership, while it estranged them from the community they were supposed to represent. Since the black political tradition, and the civil rights movement in particular, was rooted in the black Protestant church, both Shannon and Robichaux—as well as Metcalfe, another Catholic—were culturally marginal in their communities as well as racially marginal in the machine.

The third of Daley's new black committeeman, John Stroger, was also Catholic, and he reached office along the same imperial road in 1968. The peculiar thing here was that when Stroger was selected to head up the Eighth Ward, he was serving as a precinct captain in Metcalfe's Third Ward organization. Moreover, Stroger was elevated not simply without Metcalfe's support, but over his strenuous objections (Caldwell, Washington, interviews, 1982). Metcalfe's opposition was based on the fact that Stroger had slipped over to the Eighth Ward without Metcalfe's knowledge to work a precinct there, while he continued to work his Third Ward precinct. Thus, the appointment amounted to a sharp slap in Metcalfe's face.

In this way, Daley sent a message to Metcalfe, as well as to the other black committeemen: Daley was willing to grant Metcalfe preferred status—the best committee assignments, putting his man Robichaux into the Twenty-first Ward committeeman post, and so forth,—however, he would not give anyone too much power. The appointment drove a deep wedge between Metcalfe and Stroger, as Daley had undoubtedly intended, and, of course, the mayor's political "gift" provided him with Stroger's deep gratitude.

That same year, an incumbent black committeeman, the civic notable Robert Miller, was dumped by Daley—the first of three civic notables the mayor eventually would remove—and replaced by Eugene Sawyer, a protégé of Miller. Sawyer, just like his counterparts in the Eighth and Seventeenth wards, Stroger and Shannon, held a minor patronage job and had no standing independent of the machine in the community. Sawyer was a meter reader in the city's water department, Stroger examined financial records for a state agency, and Shannon helped organize parades and such for the city's office of special events.

Sawyer did possess two distinctive features. He was not a Catholic and he was the only one of Daley's new "loyalist" elite who had been recruited from within the organization he had been selected to head. This break in Daley's firmly established pattern of recruiting outsider black elites apparently had to do with an agreement the mayor reached with Miller when he dumped him. If Miller would go quietly, he would be given a say in selecting his successor (Caldwell interview, 1982).

Miller's choice of Sawyer provided Daley with the assurance that he need have no fear of divided organizational loyalty or community ties. In general, Daley's black elite, given the severe constraints he imposed on them, possessed an infamous reputation for docility and public silence. Yet even among them, Sawyer stood out as a virtual mute (*Chicago Tribune*, June 9, 1974). An aide to Mayor Washington who worked with the city council could not recall Alderman Sawyer's ever showing an interest in any issue or speaking in a meeting except briefly in response to a direct question.

Thus, with the exception of Metcalfe's protégé Robichaux, who was well regarded in the community for his coaching at St. Elizabeth High School and work with the Catholic Youth Organization, the loyalist elite recruited by Mayor Daley in the 1960s during the civil rights era differed in several significant ways from the civic notables, just as the civic notables had differed from the politicians recruited by Daley's predecessors.

The first black machine elite, the politicians, were long on political experience and demonstrated skill. However, they were widely regarded in the community as machine hacks with little interest in representing community interests. Conversely, the civic notables came up short on political experience, but they possessed high stature in the community, at least at the outset, before it became evident that Daley would permit no more than nominal representation.

The loyalists possessed neither virtue. They had little to offer the machine by way of skill, and little to offer the community by way of standing in it. What they did bring to the job was unswerving loyalty to the machine—and of course to Mayor Daley in particular—which was exactly what was required, from Daley's viewpoint, given the pressure being brought to bear on his black elite by the civil rights movement. Representation—offering the middle class some token recognition with the civic notables—had not worked. Perhaps the new loyalist strategy of containment would work. At any rate, Daley was determined that the cancer of revolt would not spread into his machine (see table 10).

Expansion and Turnover: More Yields Less

During the 1970s the black political landscape changed dramatically. The population continued to expand, to the point where blacks constituted nearly 40 percent of Chicago's population by 1976, the year of Mayor Daley's death. Between 1968 and 1976, the number of wards headed by black committeemen increased from nine to fourteen. Even on the West Side, blacks acquired ward leadership posi-

Table 10   **Politicians, Civic Notables, and Loyalists: Three Types of Black Machine-Ward Elite**

Committeeman	Political Experience	Community Prestige	Religion
Politicians (1940–48)			
Dawson	High (alderman)	Medium (political leader)	Protestant
Wimbish	High (state senator)	Medium (political leader)	Catholic
Campbell	High (alderman)	Medium (political leader)	Protestant
Civic Notables (1952–64)			
Metcalfe	Medium (board member)	High (olympic star)	Catholic
Holman	Medium (congr. aide)	High (prominent attorney)	Protestant
Miller	Medium (fundraiser)	High (prominent businessman)	Protestant
Robichaux	Medium (fundraiser)	Medium (athletic coach)	Catholic
Loyalists (1964–68)			
Shannon	Low (precinct captain)	Low (city employee)	Catholic
Stroger	Low (precinct captain)	Low (state employee)	Catholic
Sawyer	Low (precinct captain)	Low (city employee)	Protestant

Source: Newspaper files and interviews.
The table excludes committeemen recruited at the ward level without input from central party leadership. Thus, "Mike" Sneed from the Third Ward and Benjamin Lewis and George Collins from the Twenty-fourth Ward are not included. The three ward-based elite constitute a fourth type of black elite—overseers—subject to the informal dictates of the white ward leaders who put them in office and retained control over them.

tions in most of the plantation wards, although informal white leadership continued to exert much of its traditional influence.

The expansion was accompanied, however, by a high rate of leadership turnover. Several of the older black leaders died, thus almost entirely stripping the original black belt wards of their old-line leadership during the 1970s. Mayor Daley also sacked those black ward leaders, all of them civic notables, who displayed the temerity, however limited in scope, to take a community position in opposition to the machine.

The end result, then, was an expansion in the number of wards under black control, but a contraction in terms of experienced black leadership. Thus, when the party leadership changed hands in 1977 following Daley's death, only four of the fourteen black ward leaders possessed more than a single term of leadership experience. Moreover, three of the four seasoned black elite were loyalists, who could be relied upon to advance no forceful claims for a greater share of the long-awaited redistribution of power and privileges. The ulti-

mate contradiction, then, was that as black power expanded numer-
ically and in terms of protest and disillusion in the streets, black
power within the machine scarcely existed. The city's black population had to make do without any political representation to
speak of.

Mayor Daley's handling of the black elite provided further assurance that they would provide little representation of black interests
within the machine. The prime criterion for success in Daley's machine was not effectiveness but fidelity to Mayor Daley. None of the
black elite was removed for failing to perform in the electoral sphere
(although several of them, particularly the loyalist elite in the
middle-class areas were deficient in this respect). According to several observers inside the machine, Shannon, Stroger, and Sawyer
ran weak organizations, and the results they turned in—low turnouts, limited machine support, and organizational dissension—confirmed the negative evaluations. Yet the only black elite Daley removed were those who displayed divided loyalty, which was
understood to mean taking a community position in opposition to
the machine.

Mayor Daley's first sacking of a black elite had a chilling effect on
the other black ward leaders, largely because the harsh punishment
resulted from such a minor infraction. Bowing momentarily to intense community pressure from his middle-class constituents, Alderman Robert Miller, the civic notable from the Sixth Ward, voted
in a city council committee against the reappointment of a highly
conservative and therefore controversial black school board member, Mrs. Wendell Green. Since Green's reappointment was assured,
the vote merely amounted to a symbolic protest. Moreover, Miller
promptly recanted by supporting Green's reappointment when the
full council voted.

However, as far as Daley was concerned, Miller had gone too far
to be taken back into the organization. Thus, when Miller came up
for reelection in 1967, he was publicly endorsed by the machine, but
the machine's precinct captains were quietly ordered to withhold
support from him (Travis 1987, 252–53). Left on his own, Miller fell
to his independent challenger, A. A. "Sammy" Rayner. The following year Miller was dumped as committeeman and replaced by the
loyalist, Eugene Sawyer.

The next sacking came in the 1970s. It involved the least likely of
Daley's black elite, and the conflict was protracted and intense.
Ralph Metcalfe, the first of the black elite elevated by Daley, had
been given Dawson's congressional seat in 1970, another indication

The Movement and the Machine   137

that he was Daley's favorite among the black ward committeemen. The falling out between "the father and son," as one machine insider described the relationship between Daley and Metcalfe, was precipitated by the one issue that united the black community across the class spectrum: police brutality. The victim in this instance was one of the congressman's top aides, and the incident drove the usually cautious Metcalfe over the edge (Robinson, Washington, interviews, 1982).

Metcalfe began with a public call for disciplinary action against the officers involved in the incident. That produced no action. He escalated the confrontation by assembling a board of inquiry of his own to look into the issue of police brutality in the black community. That produced more heat, but again no results. Next he broke ranks with the machine over its reslating of State's Attorney Edward Hanrahan, who had ordered the raid resulting in the death of Black Panther leaders Fred Hampton and Mark Clark. After Hanrahan won the Democratic primary, Metcalfe took the extraordinary step of crossing party lines to endorse Hanrahan's Republican opponent, Bernard Carey, who wound up carrying all but one of the fourteen black wards.

By 1975 the fiercely determined machine renegade had emerged as a heroic figure in the black community in his David and Goliath struggle against the machine, and he was being urged by anti-machine activists to challenge Daley for mayor in the Democratic primary. After seriously exploring the prospect, but finding insufficient money for a strong challenge, Metcalfe backed away. However, he signaled his continuing dissatisfaction with the mayor by endorsing Daley's white liberal challenger, Alderman William Singer, in the Democratic primary.

The endorsement of Singer must have been the straw that snapped Daley's judgment. The following year, Daley dumped Metcalfe both as congressman and as committeeman. However, buoyed by a flood of volunteers that poured into his camp, Metcalfe decided to fight back. He easily retained his congressional seat, although he had no public support from any of the black committeemen, carrying all but a few dozen of the district's 400 precincts.

Even more remarkable, he narrowly retained his committeeman post. Drunk with pride and jubilation over the latter victory, the congressman reeled around his ward headquarters as the results rolled in, pressing money into the hands and pockets of the precinct captains who had remained faithful to him in the face of intense pressure by the machine to abandon him. Metcalfe's committeeman post, of course, no longer carried any power, since Daley had transferred all of the patronage to Metcalfe's opponent. But Metcalfe understood, just as his captains and volunteers understood, that Daley had thrown everything he had at Metcalfe in an effort to strip him of the coveted party post, and the mayor had failed where the machine always had been invulnerable.

The only real loser in Metcalfe's drawn-out confrontation with the mayor was his protégé in the Twenty-first Ward, Joseph Robichaux. One week after Robichaux was reelected committeeman in 1972, it was announced that he was stepping down, and that the ward's alderman, Bennett Stewart, would be taking his place. Robichaux, who had left his coaching job at St. Elizabeth when he became committeeman in 1964 to become an executive with a milk company and then to head the Baldwin Ice Cream company, went quietly. Lacking Metcalfe's prominence, political skill, and determination, Robichaux elected to settle for wealth in the private sector rather than jeopardizing it by getting into a battle with the mayor.

Significantly enough, the two men who had been under civic notable Robichaux's command emerged to become the leading black elite during the Daley machine's twilight years. However, Wilson Frost, who had been alderman of the Twenty-first Ward until he moved to head up the Thirty-fourth Ward in 1972, and Bennett Stewart, replacing Robichaux, took up the loyalist line more vigorously and faithfully than any of the other black ward leaders, and Daley rewarded them for it. Stewart was the only freshman alderman given a coveted committee chairmanship in the city council (*Chicago Tribune*, June 9, 1974). Frost emerged as the head of the black aldermanic bloc, and he was admitted into the exclusive inner circle of the Daley machine (Rakove 1975, 94).

Thus, although Daley could not defeat Metcalfe or stem the tide of the black revolt taking place in the streets, he could still contain the problem by using the compelling organization weapons at his disposal. He made it clear that any of the black elite who dared to side with the movement or Metcalfe's revolt would be destroyed, whereas those who stood by Daley in the struggle would be rewarded with prominent places within the machine. How long Daley's containment strategy could withstand the rising tide of black discontent was the critical issue he left his successors to contend with when he died in the winter of 1976.

In Perspective

A variety of exchange theories, rooted in the economic perspective, have been developed to explain the black-machine relationship. Edward Banfield and James Q. Wilson (1963) advanced the classic economic explanation of a face-to-face exchange of favors and friendship for votes. Steven Erie (1988) explained the relationship on the basis of resources made available to the machine through intergovernmental relations. When the intergovernmental faucet is turned on, machines thrive because they have the resources to secure black support; but when the faucet is turned down, the relationship dries up. Richard Keiser (1988) modified the exchange thesis in still another way by arguing that the machine-black relationship is conditioned by electoral competition and only when compelled by keen competition will machines enter into exchange relations with black voters in order to gain their support. Each of the economic exchange theories, then, maintains that a mechanical device of sorts regulates the black-machine relationship.

Yet time and again we have seen how critical events surface, to which the political perspective draws attention, which serve to radically alter black political values and black perceptions of the machine, thereby transforming the black-machine relationship. The New Deal's promise in its closing days to deal with the issue of racial discrimination altered black perceptions of the national Democratic party, which served to complete the black national Democratic realignment. Similarly, the U.S. Supreme Court's 1948 decision enabling the middle class to leave the black belt wards, coupled with Mayor Kenelly's racist campaign against the machine in 1955, served to drive poor black voters into the machine. Then in the 1960s, the civil rights movement, followed by a host of locally generated racial upheavals, once again profoundly rearranged the black-machine relationship.

By coupling the sociological perspective to the political perspective, it can be seen that the response to these critical events was not uniform across the black community. As we saw, three distinct black political communities had emerged by the 1970s, and each of them responded to the civil rights movement in a different way. Not surprising, the middle-class wards were the most responsive, turning sharply against the machine. At the other extreme, the West Side plantation wards under white control hardly responded at all, remaining firmly under the machine's control.

The machine was also compelled to modify its relationship to the black community by the force of the civil rights movement. Daley's initial civic-notable strategy of elite recruitment backfired because the notables' high standing in the community made them vulnerable to the movement's pressures. Daley responded by installing a new type of black elite, the loyalists, who were without community standing and therefore invulnerable to community pressure. In this way, Daley walled off the machine from the movement.

Yet, of course, Daley's containment strategy failed to address the rising tide of black discontent and disillusion with the machine. Thus, by the time of his death in 1976, he left his successors to cope with a black electorate that had been severely suppressed and denied representation and which was therefore ripe for revolt.

Part 4
Transformations

7

The Daley Legacy: From Machine
Politics to Racial Politics

We saw in the preceding chapter that prolonged racial strife during
the latter half of Daley's mayoralty transformed the relationship between the machine and black voters. The machine's electoral stronghold of the 1950s and early 1960s became the machine's nemesis during the 1970s and 1980s. Following Mayor Daley's death in 1976, the
machine experienced trouble along a wider range of fronts. Inside
the organization, elite rivalry and ethnic conflict, long suppressed
by Daley, resurfaced with a vengeance. Electorally, the machine was
rocked by discontent in nearly every quarter of the city. Only the
Southwest Side, which had replaced the poor black wards as the
machine's electoral stronghold during the racially turbulent 1960s,
remained steadfast.

Within hours of the mayor's death, the Daley inner circle was
confronted by a challenge from the so-called Young Turks. Headed
by aldermen Edward Vrdolyak and Edward Burke, the Young Turks
were a small group of young, talented, ambitious, and therefore
frustrated, ward committeemen. They were frustrated because
movement up the organizational ladder had been tightly controlled
and sharply limited by Daley. The challenge to the Daley bloc
yielded a radical redistribution of power atop the machine. The Daley bloc managed to hold on to the two top positions of mayor and
party chairman. However the men selected for the posts, Michael
Bilandic and George Dunne, respectively, were men with limited
leadership skills and ambition.[1] They were loyalists, cut along the
lines of the black committeemen Daley recruited, men who could be
counted upon to preside without the verve or ruthlessness of a
Mayor Daley.

The aggressive Young Turks acquired the top positions in the
city council, and the council steadily acquired more influence under
the less forceful and inexperienced Bilandic administration. The
Turks also acquired more say in the party's decision making under

its congenial and conciliatory leader, George Dunne. Thus, the post-Daley machine quickly and increasingly took on the characteristics of the pre-Daley machine. Multiple centers of power and patronage emerged, and the more energetic and ambitious ward committeemen acquired more influence in government and party affairs.

The reorganization of the machine by the Daley bloc and Young Turks did not, however, pacify the hunger of the city's two largest ethnic blocs, blacks and Poles. Leaders from both groups had hoped that the transition would yield them a greater measure of representation and power in the machine. Yet neither group wound up profiting from the reorganization. It did not appear that way on the surface. Yet ironically, the black committeeman, Wilson Frost, and the Pole, Walter Kozubowski, who were elevated during the reorganization testified to the weakness of blacks and Poles within the machine. Neither man actually represented a racial or an ethnic interest, but rather, each was representative of a stronger bloc in the machine, the Young Turks.

Frost owed his promotion to the chairmanship of the powerful Finance Committee in the city council to the two heads of the Young Turks, Vrdolyak and Burke. Working out of Burke's law office, they had helped Frost negotiate the deal with the Daley bloc. In turn, black activists who had been urging Frost to run for mayor perceived Frost's acceptance of the Finance chair as a setback rather than an advance. In their estimation, Frost had "sold out" black interests by collaborating with the Young Turks (Travis 1987, 510–15). In the same way, Kozubowski's acquisition of the newly created post of vice mayor resulted from his long years of faithful service in Burke's Fourteenth ward organization. As far as the Northwest Side Polish leadership was concerned, then, the elevation of Burke's Polish aide constituted a reduction of Polish representation.

Accordingly, because the reconstitution of the machine by the Daley bloc and the Young Turks failed to incorporate the city's principal racial and ethnic groups, the machine was hit by a second shock wave in the 1977 special mayoral election. Black and Polish insurgents from the periphery of the machine, black State Senator Harold Washington, and Polish Alderman Roman Pucinski from the Northwest Side, announced their entry into the special Democratic mayoral primary against Bilandic. This represented the first mayoral challenge from within the machine since party chairman Daley had taken on Mayor Martin Kennelly in 1955. Thus, the ethnic rivalry that Mayor Daley had managed to hold in check for over two decades was in full flower again.

Although Bilandic received only 49 percent of the vote, he handily turned back the insurgents. Pucinski's candidacy was largely confined to the Northwest Side, reflecting a regional "friends and neighbors" base of support. Poles and eastern Europeans elsewhere did not respond strongly to his candidacy. Washington's candidacy reflected a similar limitation. He carried several of the middle-class black wards; however, he ran poorly elsewhere, including the poor black wards. Given the city's deep racial division, neither Pucinski or Washington received any support from across the racial divide. Thus, in the land of the blind, the one-eyed machine remained in power.

When Bilandic filed for reelection in 1979, it appeared as though he had successfully bridged the machine's transition into the post-Daley era. The only source of turmoil was the black wards, where Mayor Bilandic experienced several problems. Only one challenger emerged, and this was a disgruntled former member of the Daley machine, Jane Byrne, who had been driven out of the party's leadership ranks by party chairman George Dunne and out of her government post by Mayor Bilandic. Bitter over her ouster, Byrne campaigned against what she called the "evil cabal," notably men from the Young Turks, whom she contended had taken over and subverted the party after Mayor Daley's death.

Virtually unknown, and lacking organizational support and financial resources, Byrne's hopeless candidacy was blessed by a devastating series of snowstorms that almost brought the city to a standstill. As the Bilandic administration coped ineptly with snow removal, Byrne was handed a dramatic issue that enabled her to gain large amounts of free media exposure. She was able to present dramatic evidence that the legendary "city that works" was no longer working well at all. The media exposure gave Byrne an opportunity to tap into the deeper wells of discontent with the machine which had been spreading across the city since the waning days of the Daley administration—in the black wards, along the liberal lakefront, and out on the ethnic Northwest Side. Thus, Byrne's deficits—her limited "biography" and lack of ties to any particular electoral base—were transformed into assets. She became a lightning rod through which discontented voters across the city could strike out at the machine.

Byrne's greatest support came out of the middle-class black wards. This was where the machine's strength had been diminishing since the mid-1960s. State senators Newhouse, in 1975, and Washington, in 1977, had issued mayoral challenges against the Daley and Bilandic machines. Mayor Bilandic also had taken several hostile actions against the black community. Byrne's next largest block of support came from the lakefront liberal wards. These were the wards Alderman Singer represented when he challenged the machine for mayor in 1975. Byrne ran strongly, as well, in the Northwest Side wards, the wards that had given Alderman Pucinski strong support in his 1977 mayoral bid against Bilandic.

Bilandic wound up carrying only two areas of the city. The bulk of his support came from the machine's electoral stronghold on the Southwest Side, and he also carried the poor white "river wards" on the West and Northwest sides, the machine's original electoral stronghold, during the Kelly-Nash era. Yet despite the unprecedented broad base of support for Byrne's candidacy, the race was only narrowly—a plurality of 16,775 votes out of 809,043 votes cast—decided in her favor. In the general election, the machine moved firmly behind Byrne, and she retained the reformer image she acquired in challenging the machine. Thus, she handily defeated the Republican party's "throwaway" mayoral candidate, Wallace Johnson.

When Byrne entered the mayor's office, she faced a critical trio of problems. To begin with, she lacked a base from which to govern. A large number of the votes that she had received in the primary were not as much votes for her as they were votes against Bilandic and the machine. Moreover, her diverse electoral coalition of the discontented—blacks, lakefront liberals, and Northwest Side ethnics—held sharply conflicting agendas. Forging policies that would satisfy the antagonistic members of her coalition would be no simple matter. Finally, the elected representatives of her coalition possessed little influence within the machine or the city council. That was exactly why the Daley bloc and the Young Turks had been able to readily reconstitute the machine on their own terms in 1977.

Thus, as mayor Byrne had to choose between forming a governing coalition out of the weak, antagonistic, and discontented groups that had elected her or forging a new alliance with those among the machine's ruling elite who were willing to cooperate with her. Byrne flirted briefly with the idea of an alliance of the discontented. She asked lakefront liberal Alderman Martin Oberman to devise a plan for reorganizing the city council's leadership (Granger and Granger 1980, 19), and she appointed Louis Masotti, a liberal academic from Northwestern University, to head her transition team. Then, however, she abandoned her electoral coalition in favor of a governing coalition of the strong. She boldly turned to the very "cabal of evil men" she had campaigned against, principally the Young Turks, and made them her managing partners. She explained her choice in pragmatic terms: "It takes 26 votes to get things passed in the City Council" (*Chicago Sun-Times*, no date).

Byrne's decision meant that the Young Turks would remain the prime beneficiaries of the machine's tumultuous passage through the post-Daley years. They had risen to power under Bilandic, when they emerged as influential junior partners in the machine, sharing power with the Daley bloc. Now the Young Turks were full fledged partners in the Byrne administration, because they were sharing power with a mayor who, first of all, lacked a base of her own in the machine, and who, no less important, was determined to drive the Daley bloc out of power.

Virtually from the outset of Byrne's mayoralty, the Daley bloc became her great nemesis. A "government in exile" formed by the Daley bloc emerged around the late Mayor Daley's eldest son, State Senator Richard M. Daley. Young Daley came to be widely viewed as Byrne's inevitable challenger in 1983. The media, relishing a big fight, regularly splashed fuel on the speculation. A Byrne press conference, regardless of its purpose, usually wound up as a commentary on the feud.

Accordingly, two grave problems plagued Byrne throughout her mayoralty. Every move she made had to be calculated with an eye to its effect on the fortunes of the government in exile, which grew increasingly bolder in its opposition to her. At the same time, Byrne had to contend with a bureaucracy over which she had only limited control. It was the product of twenty-one years of Daley's firm control, which meant that it was filled with loyalists to the Daley bloc's treacherous government in exile. The mayor was thus beset from without and within throughout the course of her administration.

Byrne's other grave problem had to do with her relationship to the electoral coalition she had abandoned in favor of the powerful Young Turks. Black voters were particularly incensed by what they perceived as her betrayal. They had provided her with the great bulk of her support in her narrow victory against Bilandic, and they accordingly anticipated playing a large role in Byrne's administration. Moreover, black anti-machine sentiment had been growing increasingly since the waning Daley years, and so Byrne's alliance with the Young Turks, the machine's new ruling elite, was perceived as a further betrayal of black interests. Despite their growing numbers and the electoral muscle they had flexed, blacks were no better off under Byrne than they had been under Daley or Bilandic.

As it turned out, the black political condition actually worsened under Byrne, and so, in turn, did her relationship with the black community. She chose to solve one of her two principal problems, contending with the Daley bloc's government in exile, in a way that exacerbated her other principal problem—her relationship with black voters. In her struggle against the Daley bloc, black political interests frequently were used as a pawn. Byrne would lure ethnic support away from young Daley by dramatically favoring ethnic interests over black interests. Accordingly, during the Byrne mayoralty the city's politics swirled more openly and tumultuously around racial antagonism and conflict than ever before. The old class-based machine—poor inner-city wards against affluent outlying wards—was giving way increasingly to a racially based machine—white against black.

In this regard, Byrne, as well as Bilandic, patterned their behavior toward the black community on the model established by Mayor Daley in his waning years rather than on the model when he was in his prime. Early in his mayoralty, Daley had employed finesse and guile in undercutting black interests. In this way, he continued to enjoy strong black electoral support while he eliminated black influence within the machine. His handling of "Boss" Dawson is a prime case in point. Daley never publicly challenged Dawson, however, he effectively checked his empire-building designs by bringing in new and inexperienced black committeemen who owed their success to him rather than to Dawson. Dawson was allowed to retain his congressional seat, and he even continued to serve as the ceremonial leader of the black elite. Dawson thus was accorded prestige, while Daley acquired virtually all of the power.

In sharp contrast, Daley's handling of black political interests in his waning years revealed a growing arrogance and declining skill. Consequently, during the mayor's protracted feud with Congressman Metcalfe, for example, the congressman was transformed from a machine hack into a folk hero in the eyes of the black community. Then when Daley unsuccessfully tried to defeat Metcalfe in 1976, the black community received a rare taste of the machine's blood, which emboldened blacks to seek more. Thus, the seeds of the machine's collapse in the black community were planted in the waning Daley years and bore more bitter fruit during the Bilandic and Byrne years.

Both mayors Bilandic and Byrne appeared to go out of their way on numerous occasions to publicly antagonize blacks. Thus, there

was a terrible continuity, stretching back into the closing of the Daley
era, of racial humiliation, exploitation, and conflict that undergirded
the city's new post-Daley politics of discontinuity. As the machine
deteriorated organizationally, wracked by elite rivalry, it also was
falling apart electorally in the black community. Accordingly, when
the mayoral primary election rolled around in 1983, Chicago's political forces were divided into three bitterly divided camps: Byrne
seeking survival and the Daley bloc and the black community bent
on revenge.

The Bilandic Mayoralty

The political legacy Bilandic inherited from Daley placed him at a
substantial disadvantage in the black wards right from the outset.
Moreover, the obscure Bilandic's introduction to the black community was disastrous. The day after Mayor Daley died, Alderman Wilson Frost, the black president pro tem. of the city council claimed
that by law he was entitled to hold the position of acting mayor until
the council convened to elect a permanent acting mayor. However,
the Daley inner circle, which occupied the mayor's office, immediately rejected Frost's claim, and they backed up the rejection by post-
ing police at the doors of the mayor's office in order to prevent Frost
from physically entering the office.

Then while the succession battle was being waged in the media,
the Daley inner circle and the Young Turks entered into secret negotiations to settle it among themselves. Frost's candidacy for a higher
post was promoted by Vrdolyak and Burke, the heads of the Young
Turks. Meanwhile, unaware of the secret negotiations, a remarkable
mix of machine and anti-machine blacks was promoting Frost's mayoral candidacy. Frost concealed his secret negotiations from his black
backers while he encouraged speculation that he was considering a
run for the mayor's office. When word began drifting out that a deal
was under way which would give the mayor's office to the Daley
bloc, with the finance committee chairmanship going to Frost as a
concession, Frost vehemently denied that he was a party to any such
settlement (Travis 1987, 511).

As the election neared in the city council, a headcount indicated
that the vast majority of black aldermen would be backing Frost. Bilandic, alderman of the late Mayor Daley's Eleventh Ward and chairman of the finance committee, emerged as the Daley bloc's candidate. Vrdolyak, head of the Young Turks, surfaced as a possible

third candidate. This, of course, posed the threat of a split in the white vote, which undoubtedly enhanced Vrdolyak's bargaining leverage with the Daley bloc.

However, a settlement sending Bilandic to the mayor's office and Frost to head the finance committee was announced before the election. Vrdolyak acquired the pro tem. post, and Burke received the chairmanship of the police and fire committee. A new position of vice mayor, designated to go to a Pole, was created in order to resolve the acting mayor issue in the future. However, the Pole designated for the position, Walter Kozubowski, came from Burke's ward organization rather than from one of the Polish organizations. Thus, everything of substance had been divided between the Daley bloc and the Young Turks, and everyone else remained out in the cold, where they had always been.

Frost's decision to forgo a mayoral campaign infuriated his black activist backers, and his response to their anger and frustration did not help. He lacked the votes to win, he explained; therefore if he had run, he "would not have come out with any benefit other than knowing that I gave some people a good feeling. . . . Why should I be the one to take the suicidal leap?" Frost asked (Travis 1987, 514). The aborted Frost for Mayor committee immediately evolved into a candidate search committee for the upcoming special mayoral election. After a number of starts and stops, State Senator Harold Washington emerged as the committee's choice.

Washington was a machine maverick and an enigma even to his friends (McClory, 1984; Grimshaw, 1987). He had spent years in the machine, entering it the year his father died, 1954, and taking over his father's precinct and job in the corporation counsel's office. By the early 1970s Washington had become convinced that the black community would have to challenge the Daley machine if it were ever to gain a fair share of benefits from it. Thus, he had been among those urging Metcalfe to launch a mayoral campaign in 1975. When the cautious Metcalfe finally decided to back away from the challenge and endorse the lakefront liberal challenger, Bill Singer, the long and often tenuous relationship between Washington and Metcalfe (his committeeman) was breached beyond repair. Even years later, Washington remained bitter about Metcalfe's unwillingness to challenge Daley, criticizing him as being paralyzed by excessive caution: "a man who plotted every step of the way before he decided to cross a street" (Grimshaw 1987, 200).

For his part, Washington appeared to enjoy living on the edge. Shortly after beginning his career in the state legislature in the 1960s, he infuriated Mayor Daley by steering a bill out of committee which would have created a civilian review board for Chicago's police department. Only adroit maneuvering saved Washington's neck from a furious Daley's chopping block (ibid., 198). Later, Washington created a black caucus of state legislators, violating Daley's firm principle about not permitting any "other organizations within the Organization" (Weisman and Whitehead 1974). When he moved up to the state senate in the 1970s, Washington worked with a band of black and independent white senators against the machine's candidate for senate president, Thomas Hynes. After a record stalemate, involving nearly 200 votes over a five-week period, the machine's leadership finally compromised; several leadership posts were granted to Washington's faction in exchange for the presidency (Travis 1987, 498–99). Thus, Washington's mayoral campaign amounted to one more daring tilt at the windmill by the black machine maverick.

Formed late and with little organization or financial backing, Washington's campaign barely got off the ground before election day arrived. None of the black committeemen supported his candidacy. They had all gone over to Bilandic after Frost withdrew his mayoral candidacy. The machine's long, strong arm also kept black financial contributors away from Washington's campaign. Washington did receive the endorsement of the city's leading reform organization, the predominantly white Independent Voters of Illinois. However, by the 1970s the IVI's influence was limited mainly to the South Side precincts of the Hyde Park–University of Chicago area in the Fifth Ward. Thus, the endorsement generated few votes in the northern lakefront liberal wards. By and large, Washington ran a campaign geared to black interests. A broader reform message had been crafted; however without money or troops to transmit it, it was barely heard.

Despite the numerous deficits, Washington managed to carry five wards containing substantial middle-class black populations, and he narrowly missed winning a sixth middle-class ward. This represented a significant gain over State Senator Richard Newhouse's 1975 campaign—Newhouse having run a distant third behind Daley and Singer in all the black wards. Outside the black middle-class wards, Washington's modest support also surpassed Newhouse's vote (see table 11).

During the 1977 general election, the machine continued to exhibit the declining electoral strength that had surfaced in Daley's final election in 1975. During the course of Daley's mayoralty, it had

Table 11   **Support for Black Mayoral Candidates in the Three Black Communities: 1975, 1977**

	Newhouse (1975)		Washington (1977)	
	Votes	%	Votes	%
Black belt wards				
2	2,206	17	2,931	28
3	1,343	13	2,121	26
4	1,854	14	3,101	30
16	1,750	14	2,770	29
20	2,133	17	2,909	31
Total	9,286	15	13,832	29
Middle-class wards				
6	3,325	23	4,557	41*
8	3,746	22	6,514	45*
17	2,174	19	3,395	41
21	4,009	23	5,960	45*
34	3,209	22	4,342	37
Total	16,463	22	24,768	42
Plantation wards				
24	1,480	15	2,414	28
27	1,452	14	1,538	15
28	1,446	18	2,001	27
29	1,430	15	2,200	31
Total	5,808	15	8,153	24
All	31,557	14	46,753	33

Source: Adapted from Lodato (1989).
*Wards won by Washington. He also carried the Fifth and Ninth Wards, wards with large black middle-class populations that were headed by white aldermen.

been standard practice for all 50 of the city's wards to deliver a minimum of 10,000 votes for Daley. Even when the Polish renegade Benjamin Adamowski had challenged Daley in 1963, and did so well, only a handful of wards failed to produce the standard 10,000 Daley votes. However, in 1975 over half the wards failed to meet the standard, and in 1977 the number increased to nearly two-thirds (see table 12).

It is important to recognize, though, that the machine's declining productivity in the mid-1970s did not occur across the boards. The productivity problem essentially was confined to the black wards and the lakefront liberal wards. All fourteen of the black wards failed to produce the standard 10,000 Democratic votes in 1975, and all but one of them failed again in 1977. None of the five lakefront liberal wards produced 10,000 Democratic votes in either election. Most of the other wards that failed to meet the standard in 1975 contained sizable black populations. In 1977, however, some Hispanic and white working class wards also fell below the 10,000 Democratic votes standard.

Mayor Bilandic exacerbated his problem in the black wards by attempting to punish Washington for challenging him in 1977. When Washington came up for election to the state senate in 1978, he was reslated by a majority of the five committeemen in the senate district. However, Bilandic took the rare step of allowing the two dissenting committeemen to openly oppose Washington by running a candidate against him. Washington, backed by an independent band of volunteers as well as two of the machine committeemen, managed to win the election, but by only a few hundred votes.

Bilandic's extraordinary decision to override the district slating process and openly challenge him convinced Washington that he had to get out of the machine. Thus, just as Daley had driven Metcalfe out of the machine and transformed him into a heroic figure in the black community, Bilandic's treachery did the same thing for Washington. As soon as he broke with the machine, Washington began supplanting the cautious Metcalfe as the reigning spokesman for the rising number of independent forces spreading across the three black communities.

Bilandic launched a second major assault on black political sensibilities later in 1978. Congressman Metcalfe died shortly before the November congressional election, and, in a highly controversial move, the folk hero was replaced by a notorious machine hack, Al-

Table 12   **The Machine's Declining Productivity in Mayoral Elections, 1955–77**

Year	Democrat	Republican	Wards with Less than 10,000 Democratic Votes
1955	708,222	581,555	2
1959	778,612	311,940	0
1963	679,497	540,705	5
1967	792,283	272,542	0
1971	740,137	315,969	3
1975	542,817	139,335	26
1977	490,688	135,282	31

Source: Grimshaw 1982.

derman Bennett Stewart. Both the decision and the manner in
which it was made infuriated a large segment of the congressional
district's voters, as well as several black committeemen. The committeemen's resentment stemmed from Stewart's limited tenure. He
had been a committeeman only since 1972, and several other committeemen believed they held a prior claim on the congressional seat
because of their longer tenure.

The selection of Stewart in tandem with the earlier elevation of
Frost (who also had been elected committeeman in 1972) to the finance committee chair constituted a changing of the guard among
the black machine elite, and it did not sit well with the committeemen who held longer tenure and equivalent loyalty. Thus, when
Metcalfe died, two of the senior black ward committeemen, John
Stroger and Eugene Sawyer, announced their interest in succeeding
to the coveted congressional seat, the highest office to which blacks
in the machine could reasonably aspire.

The way in which Stewart was selected also did not sit well with
the community or the committeemen. All of the black committeemen in the district except Stroger were ordered down to the mayor's
office by Bilandic's patronage chief, Thomas Donovan, who informed them that Stewart would be taking the seat. Donovan then
sent the committeemen over to party chairman Dunne's office.
Dunne personally supported his fellow county board member John
Stroger for the position; however he declined to challenge Donovan's action. Unable to win Dunne's backing, Stroger quietly returned to the fold to await another opportunity to move up the
ladder.

Unfortunately for the black committeemen, the imperious manner in which Stewart had been imposed on them by the mayor's patronage aide was leaked to a news reporter (*Chicago Sun-Times*, October 13, 1978). When the formal slating session was held in the
district, an angry crowd of 2,000 turned out and castigated the committeemen. By then, however, all the black committeemen were
firmly back in the fold, and they presented a united front for Stewart's candidacy. In the election that followed, the Republican candidate, A. A. "Sammy" Rayner, running without money or organization, received over 40 percent of the vote, indicating the
overwhelmingly Democratic district's dissatisfaction with the machine's candidate. Two years later, Stewart would be challenged and
soundly defeated by the black community's new anti-machine
champion, Harold Washington.

The most fateful of the Bilandic administration's miscalculations in the black community came during his reelection campaign in 1979. At the outset, Bilandic had an unimpeded track to reelection. No black, lakefront liberal nor any Polish challenger emerged to oppose his candidacy. The machine's sole obstacle was a disgruntled former machiner, Jane Byrne. She had become a favorite of Mayor Daley during the latter half of his mayoralty, when he made her his commissioner of consumer affairs in 1968, and then co-chairman of the party in 1975—needless to say, a ceremonial post, but still a coveted place in the sun. Under Bilandic and Dunne, she lost both posts. Dunne dumped her immediately as party co-chairman, and Bilandic fired her after she publicly accused him of corruption in regard to a taxi cab fare increase. Byrne's campaign centered on the corruption issue; however, among jaded Chicagoans, such an issue generated scant attention. Short of staff and funds, the Byrne campaign was going nowhere.

Then came the snowstorms and sub-zero temperatures that nearly paralyzed the city. Bilandic's response to the natural disaster provided Byrne with a new issue that guaranteed her a regular and prominent place in the news. Bilandic appeared variously as inept, dishonest, indifferent, and racist, and each time he stumbled, Byrne attacked, often featured for the cameras huddled out on a cold street, voicing the collective anger and frustration more and more Chicagoans were coming to feel.

On its own, the media had a field day with Bilandic. This was the kind of David and Goliath story the media cannot resist, and Bilandic's numerous missteps further whetted their appetites. Reporters learned at the height of one bad snowstorm that the Bilandic administration had issued a lucrative contract to a machine insider for a worthless snow-removal plan—it essentially duplicated a previous study. Then the mayor went on television to announce that numerous public school parking lots had been cleared of snow, enabling cars to move there and allow snow cleaning equipment to get down blocked side streets. However, television cameras revealed that many of the school lots Bilandic claimed had been cleared remained covered with snow. Reporters also found Bilandic vacationing in Florida during one of the snow storms. With one week to go in what once had been a walk-away campaign, Byrne was running neck and neck with the beleaguered Bilandic.

The crowning blow in the black community came when the Bilandic administration implemented a bizarre plan to improve the flow of snowbound rapid transit trains into the central business district: Traffic from outlying areas was speeded up by closing several stations in black communities on the south and west sides of the city. The black community exploded in anger, needless to say, over what was widely interpreted as a blatant racist assault. After the furor erupted, Bilandic ordered the plan rescinded, but that failed to undo the damage.

Despite Bilandic's numerous missteps, an extraordinary effort by the machine nearly saved him from defeat. Three-quarters of the city's fifty wards actually managed to produce a larger vote for Bilandic in 1979 than they had in 1977. With their patronage and perquisites on the line, most of the machine's ward organizations demonstrated that they could still produce. However, a huge outpouring of votes for Byrne provided her with a narrow margin of 16,775 votes. The anti-machine vote in both 1975 and 1977 had amounted to a nearly identical 337,000 votes. Byrne's 413,000 votes thus represented an increase of over 22 percent. The snowstorm had generated an extraordinary response by both sides.

The media attributed Byrne's victory to Bilandic's failure to cope with the snowstorm, and the snowstorm undeniably played a critical role in generating support for Byrne's initially floundering campaign. Yet when the voting returns are put into a broader perspective, it can be seen that Byrne actually won by tapping into the deeper discontent with the machine that had first surfaced during the late Daley years. Byrne's principal support came from those three areas of the city that had sent up mayoral challengers against the machine in 1975 and 1977: the black wards, the lakefront liberal wards, and the ethnic Northwest Side wards. Byrne won, then, because all the mounting discontent with the machine finally was marshalled behind a single candidate. Bilandic's main support came from the machine's electoral stronghold on the Southwest Side and from the poor white river wards. In the West Side plantation wards, the race was fought to a virtual draw (see table 13).

The Byrne Mayoralty

The sense of liberation and empowerment that swept through many parts of Chicago following Byrne's remarkable upset victory was something to behold. In the mother ward of reform, the Fifth Ward, even strangers greeted one another the next day with jubilant smiles and delighted cries of, "We did it." But within a stunningly short time the jubilation dissolved into dismay and nervous laughter, as the new mayor careened from one pitfall into the next, trying to get a handle on the complex enterprise that kept eluding her grasp. By

Table 13   **The Sources of the Byrne and Bilandic Electoral Coalitions**

Byrne's Coalition Unit Wards	Margin	Bilandic's Coalition Unit Wards	Margin
Middle class black	5,127	Southwest Side	4,910
Lakefront liberal	3,822	White river	2,203
Northwest Side	1,461	Plantation	462
Black belt	1,110		

The figures represent the average winning margin for the wards in each category. Thus, Byrne carried the seven black middle-class wards by 35,890 votes, amounting to a per-ward average of 5,127 votes.

the end of her first year in office, anger and frustration had replaced the wonder and the laughter. The alliance she struck with the "evil cabal" she had campaigned against, three back-to-back labor strikes, a "revolving doors" administration, black voters taken on an emotional roller coaster ride, and Byrne's wild tilts with the Daley bloc stunned and transfixed Chicagoans. Nothing like it had been seen since the Roaring Twenties, when that clown prince of Chicago mayors, William Hale Thompson, had presided.

Looking back, the basic course for Byrne's extraordinary mayoralty was fixed six months after she entered office. With President Jimmy Carter in town to address a gala Democratic fund raiser, Mayor Byrne appeared by all accounts to endorse him for reelection. Two weeks later, however, she switched directions by formally endorsing Ted Kennedy. After ramming her remarkable endorsement through the machine, she took young Daley and his bloc to task for failing to go along with the party's choice. Presidents, of course, never ranked high in the machine's highly material hierarchy of interests. Yet this was the first time that a Chicago politician had attempted to dispose of a sitting Democratic president in order to gain an organizational advantage.[2]

Daley responded to Byrne's bold gambit with one of his own, by announcing his candidacy for Cook County State's Attorney. The mayor, in turn, prevented Daley from securing the machine's endorsement, and put up Alderman Edward Burke, one of the ambitious twin heads of the Young Turks, to oppose him. (The Young Turks were a bloc of talented and ambitious younger ward leaders whom Mayor Daley had suppressed.) With the mayor playing an active public role in the race, the campaign turned mainly into a referendum on Byrne. A hapless Burke—pleading with voters at the end to recognize that he, not Byrne, was the candidate—wound up getting trounced. In the general election, Byrne veered along several courses: she was for Daley, then she was neutral, and finally she came out more or less openly for the Republican incumbent, Bernard Carey. This, of course, was the last thing Carey wanted or needed. With the referendum-on-Byrne factor figuring strongly once again, Daley won. The victory transformed the lowly regarded Daley—a poll sponsored by the liberal *Chicago* (November 1977) magazine had ranked Daley among "the ten worst legislators" in the state, and, alluding to his father's influence, said, "If he were named Richie M. Schwartz, he wouldn't even be in the legislature"—into a formidable force, and it set the stage for a direct confrontation with Byrne in the 1983 mayoralty.

While Mayor Byrne was tilting wildly with the Daley bloc, she also was taking on the city's public unions in several bitter public jousting matches. This battle was no less extraordinary than the open conflict that had broken out within the machine. One of the cornerstones of peace and prosperity in the "city that works" had always been a close collaborative relationship between the machine and the unions, particularly between Mayor Daley and the union heads, several of whom were old and close personal friends. Mayor Byrne was rewriting the rules in some fundamental ways.

The private unions had benefited far more than the public unions from the machine's arrangement—receiving, for example, a generous "prevailing wage," the right to draw up the city's complex and costly building code, and seats on several public boards and commissions. Mayor Daley had always drawn the line at conferring collective bargaining rights on the public unions; they, after all, were public employees, and, as such, their allegiance had to be to him and the machine. He conferred generous wages and good working conditions with his informal "handshake" agreements. Thus, the public unions were "birds in a gilded cage," who, despite their lack of freedom, chirped happily most of the time (Grimshaw 1979, 1982). However, under Byrne, the time-honored understanding between the unions and the machine was cast to the winds.

The public transit workers union, a union the late Mayor Daley had inherited, was the first to trade blows with Byrne. It enjoyed a highly beneficial cost-of-living adjustment provision in its contract, and when the mayor attempted to cut back on the costly provision, the transit workers went on strike in order to preserve it. Then about one month after the transit strike was settled, the teachers' union went on strike, again after Byrne had attempted to cut back on some costly contract provisions. This strike ran two weeks, and the public exchanges between the mayor and the teacher union leadership were as acrimonious as the verbal blows Byrne had traded with the transit union.

The longest and most bitter strike came from the firefighters, in February 1980. Byrne had promised them a collective bargaining contract during the mayoral campaign as a means of gaining their support. After winning, however, she had second thoughts. After the stalling had dragged on for a year, the firefighters finally went out on a strike that lasted over three weeks. Determined not to give in, Byrne hired new firefighters to replace the strikers, thereby earning Byrne the unprecedented reputation for a machine mayor of being a "union buster." In the end a contract was negotiated. However, to the dismay of the striking firefighters, the settlement allowed many of the replacement "scab" firefighters to retain their jobs. This generated acrimony between the returning and the new firefighters which raged in the fire stations for years after the settlement was reached. Thus, despite granting the firefighters their long-sought contract, Byrne wound up reaping their enmity—a Pyrrhic victory indeed.

In addition to splitting the machine into armed camps through her war with the Daley bloc and taking on the city's sacrosanct labor union establishment, Byrne also ripped into the black community during her first year in office. This seemed a most bizarre choice of opponents, inasmuch as strong support from the black middle-class wards had provided Byrne with her narrow margin of victory against Bilandic. She had even carried the poor black belt wards, once the machine's electoral stronghold. Even more impressive, she had fought Bilandic virtually to a draw in the West Wide plantation wards. Thus, the black community constituted Byrne's largest and strongest ally in her struggle with the Daley bloc.

Things between Byrne and the black community started out as expected in view of the election returns, when she named Samuel Nolan, a veteran black police official, as her acting police superintendent. In light of the late Mayor Daley's long and bitter battle with Congressman Metcalfe over police brutality in the black community, the Nolan appointment represented a powerful symbolic gesture by the mayor of "a new day." However, by the end of the year Nolan was out. After announcing that a national search would be conducted to find a permanent superintendent, Byrne wound up replacing Nolan with a white ethnic from within the department, Richard Brzeczek.

The replacement of Nolan by Brzeczek came on the heels of the

promotion of Angeline Caruso, another white ethnic, to school superintendent over Manford Byrd, a black candidate who stood
higher in the school bureaucracy and who had the vocal support of
Reverend Jesse Jackson's Operation PUSH and several other prominent black organizations. Inasmuch as the public school clientele
was overwhelmingly black, the feeling was widespread in the black
community that a black deserved the superintendency, and that
Byrd had been passed over by a less qualified candidate.

A short time later, in April 1980, Byrne further exacerbated her
schools problem in the black community by threatening to disband
a newly appointed school board after it selected a black member,
Reverend Kenneth Smith, as its president, over a prominent white
businessman favored by the mayor. Thus, by the end of her first year
in office, Byrne had sent several compelling messages to the black
community that were sharply at odds with the electoral support it
had given to her. Given the city's deeply embedded "to the victor
belong the spoils" tradition, many blacks felt betrayed by the mayor
they had put in office.

Yet from Byrne's vantage point, there actually was method behind her apparent madness. To begin with, she understood that in
the nation's most racially segregated city many voters kept racial
"scorecards," putting a racial spin on the "friends and enemies" political game the machine played. Thus, the best means of drawing
white ethnic support away from her rival, Daley, was to demonstrate
her preference for white ethnics over blacks, which she did repeatedly.

At the same time, she could rest assured that the black committeemen would remain behind her, regardless of her assaults on the
black community. Their loyalty to the machine, after all, had been
tested time and again over the years, often under the most trying
circumstances, and they had always remained faithful. Finally, by
assaulting the black community she was almost certain to lure a
black mayoral candidate into the race, who in turn would serve the
purpose of preventing dissatisfied black voters from rallying behind
Daley. Thus, blacks became pawns in Byrne's contest with the Daley
bloc, and the city's politics became all the more openly divided along
racial lines.

The open assault by Byrne on black interests surfaced in three
critical arenas: in the city council, where the boundary lines of a new
ward map eliminated black majorities in three wards (and Hispanic
majorities in four wards), and in the public schools and public housing, two majority-black institutions, where black leadership was re-

duced by Byrne. In each instance, the reduction of black representation produced a large outcry from a rapidly growing black independent leadership, and the media provided prominent coverage of each conflict. Thus, in accordance with her apparent electoral strategy, Byrne came to be widely perceived as favoring white ethnic over black interests.

The ward remap issue played out over the full course of Byrne's mayoralty because the map became embroiled in a lengthy challenge in court. Late in 1982, the federal court decided in favor of the black and Hispanic plaintiffs, creating three additional black-majority and four Hispanic-majority wards. However, the ruling was challenged, and the issue spilled over into the post-Byrne period before it was finally settled. Despite the lack of resolution, the issue was instrumental in galvanizing a new coalition among black, Hispanic, and lakefront liberal—represented in the form of counsel for the plaintiffs—forces.

The replacement of two black school board members by white ethnics in the spring of 1981 generated another furious outcry from the black community on two counts. Not only was black representation reduced by Byrne's action, but both the white replacements had been leaders of the anti-desegregation school movement on the Northwest and Southwest sides as well. The black reaction to the appointments was so intense that several of the machine's usually faithful black aldermen even felt compelled to vote against the appointments in the city council. The racial antagonism Byrne was furiously stirring in the electoral arena was spilling over into the machine's normally indifferent organizational confines.

A year later, in the summer of 1982, a similar scene was played out in the public housing arena. Under intense pressure from the federal housing authority to remove the scandal-ridden white chairman of the Chicago Housing Authority, Charles Swibel, Byrne finally capitulated by naming an inexperienced white campaign aide, Andrew Mooney, to replace him. Byrne also used the occasion to replace two black board members with whites, giving the overwhelmingly black agency a predominantly white leadership. Black protest was no less intense than it had been over the school board controversy. Once again the conflict spilled over into the city council, as several black machine aldermen turned against the machine to vote against the white appointments.

Several indications began to surface in the summer and fall of 1982, with the mayoral primary looming in February 1983, that Byrne's racially rooted electoral strategy was critically flawed. A newspaper poll and private polls indicated that young Daley had acquired a commanding lead over Byrne in terms of voter esteem (Day, Andreasen, and Becker 1984, 86–88). The mayor was in trouble with a substantial number of white voters as well as black voters. With Daley clearly poised to challenge her, Byrne's strategy of relying upon the certain loyalty of her black committeemen began to take on profound significance.

Yet her black-loyalist strategy appeared all the more flawed when several black anti-Byrne actions bore fruit in 1982. One critical development emerged when the mayor tried but failed to dump one of the machine aldermen who had voted against her white replacements on the school board. In a special election in June, Byrne threw the machine's full arsenal of weapons at Allen Streeter, Seventeenth Ward alderman, and came up short.

During the election, several black committeemen from neighboring wards sent over precinct captains to aid the machine's candidate—a standard tactic when the machine is under siege—and independent activists from across the black community rallied to Streeter's cause. Streeter, for years a machine loyalist who felt compelled to convert to independence under the intense community pressure generated by Byrne's actions, wound up winning what came to be hailed as a major independent victory over the machine. Streeter's victory reflected the magnitude of the rising black antagonism toward Byrne and the machine since Streeter possessed none of the stature, skill, or eloquence of a Metcalfe or a Washington. The independents had not rallied to Streeter so much as they had used him as a vehicle to express their burgeoning opposition to Mayor Byrne.

In a similar way, the black community rallied in opposition to a gala summer event, ChicagoFest, sponsored by the mayor. In a galaxy of special events favored by Mayor Byrne, ChicagoFest was the crown jewel. Black opposition to the festival initially was launched by the Reverend Jesse Jackson, but soon a broad array of black organizations joined in, which included several new and reinvigorated groups with political orientations that were springing up like mushrooms in response to Byrne's racial assaults. The opposition to ChicagoFest took the form of a black boycott, which proved so successful that the popular festival's revenues were driven down into the loss column.

The most spectacular of the several black protests came, however, in a massive voter registration drive. An earlier attempt at voter registration the previous summer had failed, as usual, to accomplish much. But the drive in the fall of 1982 wound up exceeding everyone's wildest expectations. A combination of several unusual ingredients created the unprecedented success.

First of all, a remarkably broad based collectivity was put together under the rubric of POWER (People Organized for Welfare and Employment Rights), which drew leadership and support from the West Side and South Side black communities as well as from Hispanic and white independent organizations. The drive also acquired an unprecedented amount of financial support, principally from the black president of Soft Sheen Products, Edward Gardner. The money provided radio commercials, eye-catching posters, and bumper stickers that spread the registration message—"Come Alive October 5"—across the black community.

The organizers also managed to convince state officials to allow them to conduct voter registration sessions at state welfare agencies. This provided unprecedented access to the low-income population, the most difficult group to reach in voter registration drives. Finally, the drive was aided by black antagonism to President Ronald Reagan's welfare program cutbacks and Mayor Byrne's openly hostile actions toward the black community. Although the registrars were supposed to be nonpartisan, some of them used anti-Reagan and anti-Byrne appeals to lure welfare recipients to the registration tables.

The voter registration drive wound up producing an additional 125,000 black voters. This convinced Congressman Harold Washington that what he had been hearing in his reelection campaign was not merely idle rhetoric. Everywhere he had campaigned, voters were urging him to forget about Congress and run instead for mayor (Washington interview, 1985).

The results of the November elections further convinced Washington that a black mayoral campaign stood a chance of success. The key outcome was a near Democratic victory in the gubernatorial race. According to numerous polls, the Democratic candidate, Adlai Stevenson III, was given no chance of defeating the incumbent Republican governor, James Thompson, yet Stevenson wound up losing by merely a few thousand votes. The media initially attributed Stevenson's remarkable showing to the renewed vigor of the Chicago machine, now under the leadership of Edward Vrdolyak. (With Mayor Byrne's backing, Vrdolyak had replaced George Dunne as party chairman.) However, when the vote was examined more

closely, it became evident that a huge outpouring of black voters actually had been responsible for nearly putting Stevenson into the
governor's office (Kleppner 1985, 150).

Thus, as the 1983 Democratic mayoral primary rolled around,
Mayor Byrne found herself challenged not only by young Richard
Daley but by Congressman Washington as well. As State's Attorney
since 1980, Daley had confounded expectations by appointing a
number of highly qualified aides, not machine hacks. His brief tenure was conducted without scandal. Thus, with his newly acquired
reform image, his favorable family name in many quarters, and the
support of several committeemen, who would be openly or discreetly aiding his candidacy, Daley represented a formidable opponent.

Nobody, of course, gave Washington's candidacy any chance of
success. The great success of the voter registration drive and the
huge outpouring of black voters in the November elections were
heavily discounted by historical considerations. The media, going
along with Mayor Byrne's electoral strategy, took it for granted that
the machine firmly controlled a certain proportion of the black electorate. As one of the city's leading political activists, Don Rose, once
observed: "The Organization owns a lock on a solid 20 percent of
the black vote. This is the vote the Machine would deliver for a
George Wallace against Martin Luther King" (Whitehead and Weisman, 1974, 80). Finally, the last two black mayoral candidates certainly had not fared well. Thus, when the machine's slatemakers
came together, only one of the fifty committeemen supported Washington, and that was the white committeeman of the Fifth Ward,
Alan Dobry. All but one of the black committeemen went with
Byrne. Thus, the only question about Washington's quixotic candidacy was which of the white candidates would be hurt the most
by it.

In Perspective

Long held in check by Daley, the centrifugal forces within the machine, to which the sociological perspective draws attention, exploded following his death. Holding far fewer resources (stemming
largely from the Shakman decree's prohibitions on political hiring
and firing) and less authority (the offices of mayor and party chairman
were separated), Daley's successor's were compelled to devote much
of their attention to coalition-building. Yet as elite rivalry flowered

again inside the machine, they also had to attend to the task of power-building in order to protect themselves.

As the political perspective would lead us to expect, both Mayor Bilandic and Mayor Byrne wound up devoting more attention to power-building than coalition-building. Both mayors attempted to achieve both goals simultaneously, reconstituting the machine and shoring up their own positions by striking an alliance with the Young Turks. Under Bilandic, backed by the Daley bloc, the Young Turks acquired "junior partner" standing, and under Byrne, beset by the Daley bloc, they moved up and became "senior partners."

The new ruling elites emulated Daley's elite recruitment strategy of providing only nominal representation to other factions within the machine. Thus, the two largest electoral blocs, blacks and Poles, acquired little from the reconstitution of the machine. Their representatives in the new order, Wilson Frost and Walter Kozubowski, merely appeared to represent black and Polish interests, whereas both were actually associates of the ruling Young Turk faction.

Accordingly, the ruling elites' narrowly conceived coalition-building strategy yielded disastrous electoral consequences. Bilandic was strongly challenged by insurgent black and Polish candidates in 1977, and in 1979 he was defeated by a coalition of the discontented who rallied in Byrne's side against the machine. In turn, in 1983 Byrne, who had returned to the machine after having defeated it, was defeated by a coalition that she had empowered and then disempowered.

All three theoretical perspectives contribute to an understanding of the machine's decline and fall. The economic perspective points to the machine's critical loss of resources under the Shakman decree's constraints. With far fewer field agents to engage voters in face-to-face exchanges, the machine's productivity declined sharply. Half of the city's fifty ward organizations failed to deliver what had been a minimum standard of 10,000 votes for Daley in 1975, and two-thirds of the ward organizations failed to do so for Bilandic in 1977 (as seen in table 12). Yet when the productivity problem is viewed more closely, it can be seen that it was confined primarily to the black and lakefront liberal wards. Thus, the machine was hampered by more than a problem of socioeconomic exchange.

The sociological and political perspectives' respective concerns for representation and empowerment are useful, then, in completing our understanding of the machine's difficulties. While the fateful snowstorm undeniably was important in aiding Byrne against Bilandic in 1979, Byrne in fact secured the bulk of her support from exactly those groups that had been denied representation by the machine: blacks, lakefront liberals, and Northwest Side ethnics. (Both the Daley bloc and the Young Turks were primarily based on the Southwest Side.)

Byrne's defeat, in turn, by Washington had much to do with the compelling sense of disempowerment she engendered among blacks. As her principal backers, blacks acquired high expectations and a powerful sense of themselves. Accordingly, when she turned on them, in an effort to draw ethnic support away from rival Daley, black voters retaliated by turning on her.

8

Harold Washington:
Reform Mayor, Black Messiah

Harold Washington had several things going for him in the 1983 Democratic mayoral primary. The advantages were not evident, however, from news coverage of the campaign. The media dismissed him as "the black candidate," a designation that implied he was not a serious contender. After all, the media had been awaiting the showdown between the city's two Irish titans, Byrne and Daley, for nearly four years. A third candidate, much less a black candidate, was not going to be allowed to spoil the spectacle.

Nevertheless, Washington brought a substantial base of black middle-class supporters into the campaign. In his 1977 mayoral campaign, despite severe financial and organizational deficits, he had carried most of the wards in which these voters lived, and there was every indication that he would do even better in "the base," as he called it, in 1983. The media, however, chose to dwell on Daley's base of support on the Southwest Side, even though Washington's middle-class base was of comparable size.[1]

Moreover, black antagonism toward the machine had been steadily mounting, particularly since 1979. Byrne's breakthrough victory over Bilandic had been achieved primarily in the middle-class black wards, yet her most extraordinary achievement came in the poor black wards. Although she carried them by only a small margin, no independent mayoral candidate had ever come close to carrying them before, including Washington in 1977. Byrne's unprecedented showing accordingly provided black voters with a new sense of themselves, and the machine lost its aura of invincibility. If black voters could elect a female mayor, why not a black mayor?

Then, of course, when Byrne shifted direction after winning she exacerbated the burgeoning problem between black voters and the machine. By collaborating with the machine she had defeated and then turning on the black voters who had put her into office, she heaped fuel on the very bonfire she had fanned to new heights in the black wards. Black voters perceived Byrne's perverse actions as a betrayal.

Byrne's actions against the black community did appear to undermine her apparent electoral strategy of relying on a core black vote. Historically, the machine had been able to take a certain level of black support for granted. Even Don Rose, a savvy campaign strategist who had helped turn black voters against the machine on several occasions, most recently as Byrne's campaign manager in 1979, acknowledged the apparent soundness of the assumption. "The Organization owns a lock on a solid 20 percent of the black vote. This is the vote the machine would deliver for a George Wallace against Martin Luther King" (Whitehead and Weisman 1974, 80).

Yet no mayor had ever accentuated the machine's racist character as openly and consistently as Byrne was doing. Thus, for a rapidly growing number of blacks, Byrne redefined the machine in highly negative terms. In the process, she was undermining both the conventional electoral assumption along with her own prospects for reelection.

The 1980s ushered in another critical advantage for Washington in the form of yet another enemy, this one the White House. President Ronald Reagan's dismantling of the welfare state and introduction of "Reaganomics" had a devastating impact on the black community, an impact that was felt across the boards. Poor blacks were, of course, hit hard; yet so was the black middle class, which derived a disproportionate share of its income from government employment. In several middle class black wards, the proportion of government employment exceeded 30 percent, while in white middle class wards the proportion ranged between 10 to 15 percent (City of Chicago, Department of Planning, 1980 Ward Profiles, 1984).

The rising black dissatisfaction with Byrne and Reagan was revealed in the unprecedented success of the fall 1982 voter registration drive. Although the drive was supposed to be conducted on a non-partisan basis, many registrars found it easy to lure prospects to the registration tables with appeals to "send Reagan a message" and "get Jane Byrne." This was particularly true for registrars working at public aid and unemployment offices. The registration drive added about 125,000 black voters to the rolls, expanding the size of the black electorate by nearly 30 percent.[2]

The deep dissatisfaction generated by Byrne and Reagan thus provided Washington with a pair of unprecedented assets. The black electorate was substantially larger than ever before: the seventeen black wards held 552,993 voters. Moreover, black voters were as angry as they ever had been, and therefore the turnout for Washington would be large.

Finally, not only had the political landscape dramatically changed during the 1980s, but so had Harold Washington. When he had challenged Mayor Bilandic in 1977, Washington had represented a small and generally poor state senatorial district. Since 1980, however, he had been representing a much larger and more diverse black electorate as the congressman of the First District. As one of three predominantly black congressional districts in the city, the First District covered most of the black South Side, including several of the politically potent middle class wards.

His performance during his first term was such that the machine's leadership chose not to oppose him for reelection in 1982. In anticipation of a challenge by the machine, Washington had returned home from Washington on most weekends in order to make the rounds of his district. He assembled a network of churches and community organizations across the district, and he also established a strong independent political organization. The scope and depth of his backing convinced the machine's leadership that opposing him would be futile and counterproductive.

Washington had what amounted to a two-dimensional organizational base. He established a broad base in the black church, the black community's historic institution of protest. The church's longstanding political role stretched back into slavery, when it had constituted the only institution to which blacks could turn. After blacks migrated north to the big cities, the church's political role became all the more pronounced (Frazier 1964). During the 1960s, the church was at the vanguard of the civil rights movement. Thus, when Washington appeared at church social gatherings on Saturdays and addressed congregations from the pulpit on Sundays, he was there in an integral, historical capacity, interweaving the political with the moral dimensions of the black church.

Washington also put together his own political organization. On most Saturday mornings, his organization held meetings at the "Packing House," a meatpackers union hall on the Near South Side. The meetings addressed a range of public policy issues. By creating several task forces, issue leaders and interest groups from across the district became involved in the process of creating a "Washington Agenda."

Workshops on electoral politics were also conducted at the Saturday morning meetings. All the nuts and bolts of running an effective local political campaign were covered: fundraising, recruiting volunteers, developing issues, devising electoral strategies, and working a precinct. These sessions drew established and aspiring independent political leaders from across the city. Several participants wound up putting their workshop skills into practice in aldermanic campaigns in 1983, which were run in tandem with Washington's mayoral campaign.

Thus, when Washington entered the 1983 mayoral campaign, he possessed a firm moral base in the black church, and a solid political organization in the black wards. He also had developed positions on a range of issues, which he could draw upon in the campaign. Reflecting the peculiar moral-political base of his campaign, when Washington announced his candidacy he was flanked by several pastors as well as by political leaders. Startling the case-hardened political reporters, the press conference was launched with a prayer from one of the pastors: "Lord, we thank you, for the man, the moment, and the movement have come together" (*Chicago Sun-Times*, November 11, 1982). It was going to be a crusade as well as a campaign.

The great disadvantage Washington faced was the widely held view, shared by most blacks as well as virtually all whites, that he was unelectable. As long as this perception persisted, two things almost certainly would occur: Turnout among his supporters would be low, and many voters who preferred Washington would not vote for him, for fear they would be "wasting" their votes. Accordingly, Washington faced two great hurdles: He first had to convince voters that he was qualified to govern, and then he had to convince them that he could actually win.

In related fashion, Washington had almost no support among the black ward committeemen. This reinforced the perception that he stood no chance of winning. Three black committeemen—Timothy Evans, Eugene Sawyer, and Niles Sherman—endorsed Washington, as did the white liberal committeeman, Alan Dobry, of the racially integrated Fifth Ward. The black defections were a small, but unprecedented break with tradition, reflecting the extraordinary new dynamics sweeping across the black wards. Yet all but one of the other black committeemen openly cast their lot with Byrne, despite the deep discontent she had engendered among black voters.

As the campaign progressed, however, and Washington developed a commanding lead in the black wards, several black ward bosses publicly broke with the machine and endorsed Washington. This extraordinary defection gave Washington's campaign a dramatic boost. Yet, of course, given their histories and their chains, few of the black committeemen could be expected to actually honor their public pledges of support. Most were only donning disguises in order to protect themselves from the voters' wrath. If Washington were going to win, he would have to do it on his own.

The 1983 Mayoral Campaigns

Washington's campaign proved to be unique in the city's history. It was, as he liked to say, *sui generis*. It was unquestionably the largest independent political organization ever assembled against the machine. In the four lower income black wards that I supervised for Washington during the final days of the primary election, we were training over 500 election-day volunteers in each ward. Ordinarily, a campaign is fortunate to find 100 volunteers in these hard-to-organize poor wards. The level of enthusiasm was unprecedented and proved to be a blessing. Campaigning was a new experience for many of the volunteers, and their dedication to the cause compensated for their limited political skills.

Although I had participated in several forays against the machine, I never experienced anything remotely like Washington's campaign. Phone calls came in on election day inquiring about the amount of Chicago's poll tax. We ran an extensive free "taxi" service, delivering scores of elderly and impaired voters to the polls. Several bus loads of students, from as far away as Southern Illinois University, arrived on election day. After fifteen-minute orientation sessions, the students were sent out in crude waves to sweep across low-turnout precincts. By early afternoon, we were getting calls from persons who had already voted, urging us to please stop knocking on their doors. The student-waves tactic did not win high marks for efficiency, but it certainly worked.

The campaign was different in other ways as well. It was actually three campaigns rolled, more or less, into one, thus presenting campaign manager, Al Raby, and the central office staff with a formidable task of coordination. In turn, extraordinary claims were made on Washington's time and attention. Candidate, manager, and central staff had to devote much of their effort to keeping all three components of the campaign reasonably content and moving. Fortunately, both Washington and Raby appeared to thrive amidst what Raby, a veteran of Chicago's hectic "freedom movement," called the campaign's "creative chaos."

First, there was the formal campaign organization, which was structured and conducted along conventional campaign lines. Full field operations were mounted in over half of the city's fifty wards, including all the black, Hispanic, and white lakefront liberal wards. Partial operations existed in another dozen wards which contained sizable black, Hispanic, and white liberal populations. In all, three-fourths of the city's wards were being worked by the formal Washington campaign organization.

The campaign also contained an elaborate network of interest groups that worked largely outside of the formal structure. Some of the interest groups were activated at the instigation of the formal campaign, but many others simply emerged on their own. The range of the groups was extraordinary; from Artists for Washington to Women for Washington, and just about everything else in between: labor, education, business, and, of course, students, but there were dozens more as well.

A healthy, if sometimes combative, competition existed between the formal campaign and the interest groups. The groups preferred "doing their own thing" to ringing doorbells for the formal campaign. Several of them developed their own literature, and all of them, of course, fashioned campaign appeals geared to their particular constituencies. In this regard, it was a campaign of a 100 mirrors, each one flashing a particularly appealing feature of the candidate or his platform. Washington, seasoned by years of debating in the legislative arena, proved up to the task. He rarely used a stock stump speech. To his speechwriters' dismay—for wordsmiths love their own words—the candidate wanted only a few basic themes to work with.

The campaign's third principal component was what the formal campaign organizers sometimes called the "Sound and Light Show." The derisive term conveyed the tension existing between the two groups. Here there were fundamental differences over goals as well as tactics. The nucleus of the Sound and Light operation was a group of black nationalists, whose idealistic, "separatist" goals clashed with the more practical and "integrationist" goals of the formal campaign.

The general character of the conflict had a history. It traced back to the waning days of the civil rights movement, when young northern black power advocates, such as Stokely Carmichael and Malcolm X, emerged to challenge Martin Luther King's leadership and the movement's ties to white liberal allies. In the nationalist's estimation, white liberals exercised excessive influence on King and the movement, which set sharp limits on what could be accomplished.

During the Washington campaign, black nationalists—such as

radio commentator Lu Palmer, academics Conrad Worrill and Robert Starks, and the Reverend Al Sampson—voiced varying degrees of public and private opposition to the formal campaign's racially integrated leadership and its racially inclusive goals of "fairness" and "equity." The nationalists wanted the campaign to be run by blacks for the purpose of black empowerment; but as long as white liberals exercised their influence, such goals could not be achieved.[3]

The nationalists constituted only a small element in the black community, however, they were intensely committed to their cause, and passionate and often eloquent in expressing their views. Most blacks understood and were not unduly troubled by the nationalists, but this was not the case, though, with the vast majority of whites. They were appalled and frightened by the black nationalists' often fierce demeanor and the fire and fury of their rhetoric.

The fact that campaign manager Al Raby and field operations director Jacky Grimshaw were avowed black "integrationists" with strong ties to the white liberal political community poured fuel on the conflict. Washington's several white advisers, some closely tied to him, further strained relations between the two camps. Even Washington himself was not above suspicion. In the darkest corridors of the campaign, anti-Semitism reared its ugly head, where sick whispers about a "Hyde Park Jewish conspiracy" and the like could be heard.

The formal campaign and the black nationalists also did not see eye to eye on tactics. However, the disagreement over tactics yielded a more comprehensive means of getting out the vote. The nationalists disdained the conventional campaign practice of sending out workers door-to-door to identify supporters and win over undecided voters. This conventional "precinct captain" practice was dismissed as a "white" tactic appropriate for "bureaucratic" machines but not for black movements. The nationalists' preferred form of communication was the spectacular event: big rallies and large parades that drummed up a powerful emotional response. Black voters were emotional, the nationalists contended; they had to be "turned on" before they could be "turned out" to vote.

I attended one such parade, that worked its way down South State Street, where much of the city's public housing is located, and it was, indeed, a spectacular event. Sound trucks preceded the parade, with their speakers set at maximum level, as volunteers fanned through the buildings along the way, urging residents to come out and meet "Harold." What started as a small parade quickly turned into a huge, jubilant rally. Music, mixed with cries of exhortation, blared out of the sound trucks; hundreds of the famous blue Washington campaign buttons and countless pieces of campaign literature were dispensed; and everybody was screaming "Harold, Harold, Harold," as they pressed in closer and closer around him.

These extraordinary street rallies presaged the huge and joyous culminating rally the formal campaign staged at the University of Illinois Pavilion, which drew over 12,000 wildly enthusiastic supporters. It was emotional events such as these that undeniably helped transform the campaign into a movement. Washington thus campaigned as a reform candidate for mayor as well as a messiah for the black community. Without the capacity to encompass both roles, he could not have won.

Three critical events fueled Washington's campaign, driving it forward in a series of explosions. In the first event Washington successfully addressed the critical issue of his capacity to govern. In a rare move for an incumbent, Mayor Byrne insisted on a series of televised debates. She intended to expose Daley's limited debating skills, letting him strangle himself with his own tongue, as it were. The strategy paid off with white voters. Polls taken after the first debate, the most widely watched of the four debates, gave the mayor a substantial boost and Daley plummeted. Among black voters, however, the mayor's strategy backfired as Washington's financially strapped campaign received an even larger boost from the first debate: he moved past Daley into second place, and Byrne's stock began to fall (Day, Andreasen, and Becker 1984, 89–90).

Washington's campaign strategy, and for the debates in particular, was provided by Patrick Caddell's polls, which showed Daley without support among black voters, and without prospect of getting any. This knowledge enabled Washington to ignore Daley and focus all his attention on Byrne. Thus, instead of a three-candidate race, there were actually two discrete two-candidate races; Washington versus Byrne in the black community, and Daley versus Byrne in the white community (*Chicago Sun-Times*, January 19, 1983; *Chicago Tribune*, February 2, 24, 1983).

The existence of discrete campaigns can be seen from the distinctive reactions voters had to the first debate. Although it was widely acknowledged that Washington had scored a stunning victory then, it did not alter his standing among white voters. They were measuring Byrne against Daley. Thus, Byrne gained six points, Daley lost nine, and Washington gained one. (This is according to a Gallup poll. It and several other polls are summarized in Kleppner 1985, 171.)

Black voters, however, watched a different debate: They were sizing up Washington against Byrne. This version of the debate cost Byrne six points, Washington gained eight, and Daley lost two (ibid.). In broader terms, the debates profoundly altered Washington's status among black voters. The political editor of the *Chicago Tribune*, Steve Neal, agreed with Washington in an interview that the debates had turned the tide; "they convinced blacks his candidacy was not just symbolic, but a serious bid to gain control of City Hall" (*Chicago Tribune*, February 24, 1983). Washington's campaign literature, playing on the media's insistent characterization of him as the "black" mayoral candidate, proclaimed him the "qualified" candidate.

The second stage of the campaign came near the end, and it involved the campaign's biggest gamble, but an essential one. The debates had given Washington a substantial boost; however, he still lagged well behind the front running Byrne. A sizable number of black voters remained convinced that Washington stood no chance of winning. Mayor Byrne retained a firm grip on about 20 percent of the black vote, according to Washington's own polls as well as published polls. Thus, a decision was made to hold one final rally at the University of Illinois' huge, 12,000-seat pavilion. Washington had jumped successfully over the "qualifications" hurdle. He still had to get over the "electability" hurdle.

The bold decision to hold the rally at the University of Illinois Pavilion wildly violated the cardinal rule of the political advance man. Events must always be held, goes the rule, in small places; in that way the appearance of a large crowd is created, regardless of its actual size. Washington's campaign turned the rule on its head. By the best estimates of those skilled in organizing rallies, a crowd of 6,000 would constitute a huge success. Yet at the colossal pavilion, the huge success would appear to be a dismal failure. The outrageous plan did not sit well at all with the field organizers. They would have to divert their attention from the precincts for several weeks in order to organize for the rally.

By the day of the rally, the Washington campaign's organizers estimated that they could fill about half of the 12,000 seats. Anybody else who showed up would be coming on his own. As it turned out, the rally drew a standing room only crowd of well over 12,000. It was at this point that a good many individuals, inside and outside the campaign, became convinced that Washington actually had a shot at it.

Being inside the Pavilion that Sunday afternoon was like being inside a living thing. It rocked and pulsated in a way that touched all the senses. A corps of black elected officials from across the country addressed the crowd. Responding to that rousing, inimitable black style that blends the role of politician and Baptist minister, the huge crowd was brought to its feet time and again. Black, Hispanic, and white entertainers kept the show moving with their music, all of which, good and bad, was wildly approved. This was a starry-eyed celebration of universal brotherhood. So while the crowd was overwhelmingly black, it rocked along to whatever it was offered: mariachi bands, folk guitarists, soul singers, and gospel choirs.

Washington did not enter the huge hall until the end, after three hours of non-stop excitement. The only question was whether he could rise to the occasion, topping the best political orators black America had to offer. He did, and that was what the crowd had been waiting for: "Harold, Harold, Harold." It seemed as though it would never end, and nobody wanted it to end. It was a fitting climax to a long, exhausting, and joyous campaign.

The aftereffect of the huge rally was electrifying. An exhilarating air of impending victory swept across the black community. The impossible suddenly seemed within reach. Washington declared that he had the election locked up. News reporters confirmed that he was campaigning in the final days with a new aura of confidence. His only worry now, Washington told supporters and the press, was that the machine would try somehow to steal the election from him.

The confident air, however, was merely designed to get him all the way over the high hurdle of "electability." The rally had closed the gap, and each day the race became a little tighter. Momentum was on Washington's side, but Byrne remained the front runner. Washington's field organizers reported that the recalcitrant West Side plantation wards remained a problem. Washington's pollster identified another problem: a sizable number of older black women still were holding out for Byrne.

Both campaign workers and new literature that hammered away at Mayor Byrne's numerous assaults on the black community were poured into the West Side plantation wards during the final stage of the campaign. Washington's campaign schedule was modified, giving him more time before women's groups. He made headway among both holdout groups, but time was running out.

At the very end, Washington's final surge was unintentionally supplied by the machine. Recognizing that Washington was closing in, Byrne's campaign took its own wild gamble at the end. It rolled out the volatile racial dice. Given the onus of racism that Byrne carried into the campaign, this was a high-risk strategy that could easily backfire. She needed to shake her backers out of complacency and to draw voters away from Daley; but she risked driving her remaining black supporters away, and alienating her lakefront liberal supporters.

Byrne's campaign initially managed the risk brilliantly by scheduling a tour for Byrne through the black public housing developments. As anticipated, Byrne was met by scores of Washington supporters, who loudly denounced her with open scorn and sang out with cries of enthusiasm for Washington. Byrne, however, was not playing to them, but to the television cameras accompanying her. Here, she was saying in effect to white voters, take a look at what I am up against: a wildly charged black electorate that is solidly behind Washington. Thus, the racial issue was raised; yet in a way that made Byrne appear to be its victim rather than its instigator.

In the precincts, though, away from the media's eye, the racial assault was made much more directly. The Byrne-Vrdolyak machine responded to Washington's candidacy by defining it in openly racist terms. For some time, in fact, Byrne's campaign had been putting a racial spin on the election by characterizing Daley as a "spoiler" (*Chicago Tribune*, January 30, 1983). Since Daley stood no chance of winning, Byrne's campaign argued, a vote for Daley only helped Washington. It was a difficult notion to sell, however. Few white Chicagoans found the prospect of a black mayor even remotely credible, and Byrne appeared to be well ahead in the race.

Three days before the election, however, Byrne's campaign slipped up, inadvertently exposing its racist argument to the entire city, and the election went out of control. A few news reporters, without party chairman Vrdolyak's knowledge, were mingled among the precinct captains at a Northwest Side campaign rally, and they heard Vrdolyak spell out the Byrne campaign's racist message in no uncertain terms: "A vote for Daley is a vote for Washington. . . . It's a racial thing. Don't kid yourself. I am calling on you to save your city, to save your precinct. We are fighting to keep the city the way it is" (Travis 1987, 593).

When Vrdolyak's racist appeal was splashed across the front page of Sunday's papers and newscast leads, it washed away Byrne's remaining black support. Many of Byrne's lakefront liberal supporters also abandoned her in favor of Daley, boosting Daley's campaign out of the doldrums where it had been languishing. Her lakefront supporters may have been liberal, but they were not liberal enough to shift their support to Washington. The combination of shifts gave

Washington just enough of a boost to cross the finish line ahead of Byrne by 36,145 votes. The racial fires Byrne could not resist feeding wound up consuming her in the end.

The General Election

The difference between the primary and general elections was as stark as day and night. The race issue, stoppered until the final days of the primary campaign, exploded on the general election scene and turned the city into a racial battleground. The carnival atmosphere that had marked the black community's participation in the primary evaporated. Hunkered down, bitter, and resolute, black voters conducted a forced march to the finish line in the general election.

The race issue did not emerge at the outset, although the first several weeks of the campaign were anything but typical. Twenty years earlier, when Washington was managing the campaign of the first black presidential candidate for Chicago's Young Democrats (a subsidiary of the machine), he had angrily denounced its white members for failing to honor their obligations: "You don't play the game by the rules. When we get in the game, you change the rules" (Travis 1987, 228). Washington's candidate, William Harris, was supposed to have succeeded by tradition to the presidency since he was vice president. But faced with the prospect of a black president, the Young Democrats' white members had turned tradition aside and elected a white candidate in his place.

Twenty years later, nothing had changed. Racial considerations still dictated the rules. After winning the primary, Washington found only a handful of white committeemen who were willing to support him, mainly those heading wards with sizable black or Hispanic populations. Of the lot, Washington's field organizers determined that only two were making a genuine effort on his behalf: former party chairman George Dunne, whose "Gold Coast and Slum" Forty-second Ward encompassed the huge Cabrini-Green public housing development, and Alan Dobry, head of the liberal Hyde Park-University of Chicago Fifth Ward with its majority black population.

Party chairman Edward Vrdolyak conveyed word to Washington that the machine was willing to support him, but only on a conditional basis. If Washington agreed to abandon his reform platform and work in concert with Vrdolyak to maintain the status quo, then the machine's support would be forthcoming. Otherwise he was on his own, and the machine might well oppose him (Raby interview, 1983; Washington interview, 1985).

Washington rejected Vrdolyak's proposal and attempted to win over several white committeemen on a direct basis. However, this path was firmly blocked; nearly all the white ward leaders were committed to following Vrdolyak's lead. This confirmed Washington's surmise that in a partnership with Vrdolyak, he would be expected to serve as the junior member. Infuriated by the rejection, Washington resorted to threatening political retaliation. Unless the machine's full support was forthcoming, Washington would withhold his support from the machine's county ticket in 1984 (*Chicago Tribune*, March 14, 1983).

The threat produced no more support than did Washington's calls to individual committeemen. Some committeemen believed that Washington could not win without their support. Others assumed that Washington was bluffing about taking on the machine as mayor. Some simply wanted nothing to do with a black mayoral candidate. Thus, the battle lines were drawn, with the racial issue being clearly present. Yet the cutting organizational issue was political: reform versus machine. As one of the machine's most outspoken ward leaders, Vito Marzullo, put it: "I like Epton [the Republican mayoral candidate] better than the other guy. The other guy don't want no machine, don't want no committeemen, and don't want no Democratic party" (*Chicago Tribune*, March 16, 1983).

Then all hell broke loose in mid-March. Race reared its ugly head when Jane Byrne announced that she was entering the general election as a write-in candidate. Presaging the racial code words Bernard Epton would adopt in his campaign, "Epton—Before It's Too Late," Byrne said she felt compelled to run as a "unity" candidate in order to save a "fragile" city that she said was "slipping" (*Chicago Tribune*, March 18, 20, 1983). For the next two weeks the city was plunged into a cataclysm of racism.

A few days after Byrne's stunning announcement, Epton tore into Washington during the campaign's only televised debate. He aggressively turned the spotlight on a series of tax and legal issues that focused attention on Washington's personal integrity. Washington appeared stunned and dumbfounded by the assault. The next day Epton escalated the attack by launching his media campaign. The television ads were a double-barreled shotgun. The main message, "Epton—Before It's Too Late," activated racial fears, and the particular messages, focusing on Washington's past legal and tax problems, raised doubts and fears about Washington's character.

White voters began pouring into the Epton camp. Byrne, for lack of support and in response to the heavy white shift to Epton, abandoned her write-in candidacy.

A few days after Byrne's withdrawal, the devastating effects of the twin racial assaults by Byrne and Epton became all too apparent. When Washington, accompanied by former vice president Walter Mondale, attended a Sunday service at St. Pascal Catholic Church on the far Northwest Side, a crowd that appeared nearly out of control disrupted the visit. "Nigger die" was spray-painted on a wall. "Crook," "tax cheat" and worse the crowd screamed at Washington (Rose 1984, 199–20).

The crowd's frenzied anger marked a critical turning point in the mayoral campaign. Prior to the St. Pascal's explosion, Washington had campaigned across the Northwest and Southwest sides without encountering any problems. He had marched at the head of the St. Patrick's Day parade without incident. But after Washington's mayoral opponents unleashed the tiger of racism, it ran wildly through the white wards, and ripped the city apart.

During the two weeks between Byrne's write-in announcement and the St. Pascal's explosion, the mayoral campaign was recast almost entirely in racial terms. Uncertain about how to counter the racial assault, the campaign continued to rely on the classic partisan appeal, Democrat versus Republican, in an effort to expand its base of support. To a lesser extent, the reform versus machine theme also was advanced. Both messages, however, were overwhelmed by Epton's more focused, resonant, and dramatic racial assault.

The Epton campaign maintained the offensive by issuing a steady flow of exaggerated charges calling Washington's character into question. After setting Washington up as a "tax cheat" (he had paid taxes but had failed to file tax returns for several years), a "disbarred" lawyer (his license had been briefly suspended for failure to provide service), and a "convicted felon" (he had served a jail sentence for the misdemeanor of not filing tax returns), the stage was set for reinforcing the negative image with a steady stream of lesser charges. A utility bill from an earlier campaign had not been paid. Washington co-owned a building with code violations, and so forth. The individual charges were minor, several were spurious or overstated, and none of them challenged Washington's public credentials; yet the cumulative effect was devastating. Most Chicagoans were left wondering: what next, and where does it end?

With a week to go, the election was up for grabs. Most white voters were voting white. Virtually all black voters were voting black. The only significant bloc of undecided voters was the white lakefront liberals. They certainly had not been immune to Epton's message—pollster Patrick Caddell graphically described the lakefront liberal wards as "hemorrhaging." Yet many lakefront liberals remained torn. So during the final week, Washington focused nearly all his attention on what Washington's strategists came to think of as "the thin white sliver of hope."

As it turned out, Washington once again was unintentionally aided by his nemesis, Vrdolyak, when Vrdolyak once more overplayed his hand. Looking to land the decisive blow, Vrdolyak's aides tried peddling a rumor to the media that Washington once had been arrested for child molestation, and that the arrest was being covered up by the police and the *Chicago Tribune*, which had the evidence but refused to print it. Unable to uncover any evidence to support Vrdolyak's story, the media rejected it. Nevertheless, the rumor flourished in the precincts, spread by pamphlets an enterprising reporter traced to an organization run by one of Vrdolyak's top aides (Rose 1984, 118).

Washington, as angry as anyone had ever seen him, finally took his stand on the spurious morals charge. Campaigning along the lakefront, he linked Epton to Vrdolyak, and the morals charge to the broader race issue. Holding up Vrdolyak's pamphlet, he told a stunned audience: "This particular piece of literature happens to describe me as a child molester. Here I am running a campaign in which little children all over my community are ecstatic . . . telling their mothers to vote for me. . . . Why am I the victim of this scurrilous, incessant low life kind of attack? Well, I've had enough" (*Chicago Sun-Times*, April 8, 1983). Turning the tables by shifting the focus to Epton's character, Washington went on: "I say to you, Mr. Epton: Do you want this job so badly. . . . Are you so singularly minded that you would try to destroy character? . . . If these are the kinds of dogs of racism and scurrilousness you are going to unleash, I say to you, Mr. Epton, I will fight you day and night" (*Chicago Tribune*, April 8, 1983).

At the same time, Washington returned to the reform versus machine theme that had been buried under Epton's racial assault. Referring to the machine as the "greed merchants," he denounced them "for injecting race into the campaign to cover up their fear of his proposed reforms" (*Chicago Sun-Times*, April 10, 1983). He dismissed Epton as a creature of Vrdolyak and the machine. As one of Washington's lakefront supporters put it, "I think people should realize that this isn't really a battle between Washington and Epton.

It's a battle between Washington and Eddie Vrdolyak. Epton would be just a figurehead if he were elected" (*Chicago Tribune*, April 3, 1983).

By invoking the reform versus machine theme and confronting the race issue head on, a critical number of lakefront liberals were drawn back into the Washington camp during the final weekend of the campaign. In Patrick Caddell's words, Washington had "snatched victory from the jaws of defeat." What Caddell knew from his polls was that if the election had been held only five days earlier, Washington would have lost. In the end, however, the hemorrhaging in the lakefront wards was staunched. "In many ways, this was a miracle," Caddell told reporters (*Chicago Sun-Times*, April 14, 1983).

Washington had won the primary election by 36,145 votes. He won the general election by 48,250 votes. In both elections, well over one million votes were cast. Chicago had its first black mayor; but it had not been easy. In the "last of the great machine cities," Washington had been compelled to run through a hurricane of racism to reach the mayor's office.

The Limits of the Reform Revolution
In the City Council

Accounts of the Washington revolution give little attention to the broader dimensions of it. An unprecedented number of new and reform-minded black and Hispanic ward leaders were swept into office, clinging to Washington's long coattails. By 1987, over 80 percent of the black aldermen in the council had been elected during the Washington era, and nearly all of them had built their political careers outside the machine. A comparable change occurred among the black ward committeemen. Only one-third of the eighteen black committeemen elected in 1988 had been put in office before Washington's election. All three of the black communities, as well as the two Hispanic communities, were transformed by the Washington revolution.

Four of the five old black belt wards on the Near South Side—the Daley machine's original electoral stronghold—came to be headed by new aldermen, none of whom had come up through the machine's ranks. The sole holdover was Timothy Evans, elected in the early 1970s, and he promptly shifted course to become one of Washington's leading spokesmen. The "mother ward" of black politics, the legendary "Boss" Dawson's Second Ward, came to be headed by a former Black Panther, Bobby Rush. The Third Ward was taken over by Dorothy Tillman, a former aide to Martin Luther King, who had veered over to the black nationalists in the 1980s. The old black machine stronghold was now the headquarters of the black empowerment movement.

The transformation of the West Side plantation wards, the last black bastion of machine strength, was no less remarkable. After a fifth black West Side ward was created by federal court order in 1986, four of the five plantation wards were headed by new reform-minded aldermen, all of whom had made their way up the political ladder without the machine's help. The only survivor was William Henry, the most dyed-in-the-wool of the old guard machine loyalists. A crude and blustery but cunning man, Henry struggled, if without conviction, to master the new rules and rhetoric of reform. Indeed, most of the old guard, and more than a few of the new guard, publicly praised Washington while they privately yearned for the old machine ways, when the victors reaped the spoils (*Chicago Tribune*, July 30, 1983; Sept. 7, 1986).[4]

Ironically, it was in the great engine wards of the Washington revolution, the middle class wards, where the least amount of change occurred. Fewer new elites emerged, and the commitment to reform was remarkably modest. The old guard, Eugene Sawyer, John Stroger, and Wilson Frost—loyalists recruited during the civil rights crisis—seemed to set the tone. They learned the new language of reform, and they lavished praise on Washington; but they also kept one leg discreetly planted in Vrdolyak's tent, waiting patiently for the storm of revolution to pass.

One of the newer committeemen from the middle class area, Niles Sherman, elected in 1980, voiced the frustration many of the black committeemen felt over the new rules of the game: "Those individuals who put the mayor where he is deserve something more than a pat on the back" (*Chicago Tribune*, July 30, 1983). Alderman Marian Humes, from loyalist Stroger's Eighth Ward organization, tried without success to convince a black radio talk show audience that she had a "right of conscience, just like the mayor did," and thus there would be times when she would have to oppose Washington in the council. A third alderman, Perry Hutchinson, whose Ninth Ward bordered Vrdolyak's ward, was widely rumored to be in league with the party chairman. On crucial votes in the council, both Humes and Hutchinson turned up missing (ibid., June 3, 1986).

All three of the openly wavering alderman were replaced in the 1987 elections, victims of greed and the revolution. Humes and Hutchinson were brought under indictment for accepting bribes and did not stand for reelection; Sherman ran and was defeated. Washington's reform movement, contested at every critical turn by the "Vrdolyak 29" bloc (denoting the number of aldermen siding with the machine against the "Washington 21" bloc), had come to be perceived by blacks as a "holy war." Accordingly, any expression of opposition to the mayor was regarded as heresy, and retribution was exacted from the "sinners."

Yet at the same time, Washington himself showed little interest in ousting the recalcitrant black ward leaders. There was no question about who they were. Political aides and advisors repeatedly urged the mayor to purge the worst of the lot, the old Daley loyalists, notably Sawyer, Henry, and Frost. But Washington turned a deaf ear to the appeals. In his estimation, matters were well in hand: "There's nothing those snakes in the grass can do to me."

However, in refusing to purge the machine loyalists, Washington was doing more than exercising caution. He was advancing his own political self-interest at the expense of institutionalizing his reform movement. The old loyalists came to understand that as long as they were willing—however reluctantly—to go along with the mayor's reforms, they would be allowed to survive. In this way, then, none of the fault lines opened into fissures. Washington kept his monolithic black base intact, but at what would prove to be a terribly high price.

Consequently, support for reform actually was far less well established among the black aldermen than it appeared to be. The mayor had a small, but mainly inexperienced, bloc of genuine reformers on his side. Then there was a bloc of aldermen who had come in on Washington's coattails; but their commitment to reform was mixed with a desire for spoils in the machine tradition. Finally, there was the loyalist machine bloc, biding its time while it waited for the revolution to spend itself. Thus, when an advisor challenged the mayor's selection of Timothy Evans as his council floor leader, recounting Evans' numerous deficiencies, Washington merely shrugged and replied: "Sure, but who else is there?"

Backed in this limited fashion, Washington was forced to run through the same deluge of racism in the council that he had endured during the mayoral campaign. Party chairman Vrdolyak organized a majority of the aldermen into a solid band of twenty-nine members, all white, that opposed the mayor at every critical turn. The black aldermen sided with Washington, as did the reform-minded white aldermen from the lakefront liberal wards. After the special aldermanic elections in 1986, three of the four new Hispanic aldermen also sided with the mayor. Thus, the conflict revolved around both race and reform.

Chicago, the textbooks say, has a weak mayor—strong council form of government. Yet government never was actually practiced that way until Chicago elected its first black mayor. When Mayor Daley was elected in 1955, he stripped the council of its budgetary authority, and virtually every other form of authority, and ruled in dictatorial fashion. His council floor leader, Alderman Thomas Keane, regularly disposed of huge blocks of legislation in only a few minutes time. He plowed ahead after consulting with the mayor, of course, but without saying a word to his council colleagues.

Under Washington, the council acquired a mind of its own with a vengeance. The first big fight broke out only a month after Washington's election, coming over the allocation of federal Community Development Block Grant funds. The guidelines earmarked the money for lower income communities; however, the Vrdolyak 29 insisted on allocating a share to middle-income white wards (*Chicago Tribune*, May 9, 27, 1983). This initial "us versus them" fight set the tone for the bitter race war that would persist for the next three years.

In the reorganization of the council following the mayoral election, all of the committee chairmanships went to backers of the Vrdolyak 29. When the mayor attempted to reduce the deficit he had inherited from Mayor Byrne by firing several hundred city employees, Alderman Burke, the co-leader of the 29 faction, went to court seeking an injunction. Mayor Washington's efforts to win a tax hike also were blocked, leaving him, just as the 29 intended, in serious fiscal straits, unable to substantially cut the sizable deficit he was saddled with. Several "Shakman suits" (resulting from the federal court ruling prohibiting hiring and firing on political grounds) were filed against Washington, and few of Washington's appointments to boards and commissions were approved by the council. At year's end, the Vrdolyak 29 rejected the mayor's budget in favor of its own budget.

In other American cities, such give and take between executive and legislature—with less rancor and racism, of course—is the norm. Moreover, the council wars almost always were resolved through negotiation and compromise. Yet this was Chicago, where things customarily were accomplished by mayoral fiat, and by the end of Washington's first year in office, the *Chicago Tribune* had had enough. In three furious back-to-back editorials, it decried the "paralysis" gripping city government and urged the warring factions to work out their differences (April 8–10, 1984). The *Wall Street Journal* weighed in with its devastating characterization of Chicago as "Beirut on the Lake." Virtually everyone in the media seemed ready to abandon reform in favor of peace and order. The development infuriated Washington, who took to bitterly calling those who were pleading for an accommodation with the machine the "new cynics" (*Chicago Tribune,* August 26, 1984).

The confrontations were played out annually throughout the first three years of Washington's administration. So firmly were the battle lines drawn from the outset that within only four months of Washington's election, a local comedian, Aaron Freeman, was able to stage an elaborate nightclub comedy routine called "Council Wars." Patterned after the popular movie *Star Wars,* the skits featured Darth Vrdolyak as the villain and Harold Skytalker as the hero. Less amusing was the decision by the bond-rating agencies to lower the city's credit rating because of the council wars (ibid., August 5, 1983; March 14, 1984). The nadir was reached in May 1984 when Alderman Burke sought Washington's impeachment in the courts for failing to submit a financial disclosure statement on schedule.

In the Executive Branch

Washington's central conception of political reform was rooted in the black political experience and had little to do with classical reform. Classical reform is rooted in a white managerial culture, which conceptualizes good government in essentially economic terms. Government, the classical reformers argued, ought to be conducted as a business: honestly, without partisan considerations, and, above all, with businesslike efficiency (Banfield and Wilson, 1963, 138–50; Welch and Bledsoe, 1988). In practical terms, the rallying cry of reform in the big cities was bare bones economy: low levels of service that required low levels of taxation. Thus, the aldermanic reformers who fought the Chicago machine in the 1940s and early 1950s were aptly called "the economy bloc" by the newspapers of the day.

Washington's conception of reform was rooted in the black church, and it was accordingly cast in moral, rather than economic, terms. The principal goal was "fairness," and given the city's prevailing white middle class bias, this required redistributing government benefits so that the "have-nots" began receiving "fair shares." Washington's novel fairness reform, then, essentially amounted to eliminating the long-standing, well-fortified barriers of race, gender, and class.

Few white ethnic Chicagoans, however, perceived Washington's agenda in such terms. They had been "schooled" in a far more political institution, the machine. The machine's "political" school taught that government revolved around "rewarding friends and punishing enemies." The white middle class attended an "economic" school of politics, where government was regarded as a corporation dedicated to sound management practices and businesslike efficiency. The black church's "moral" school of politics understood government's principal mission in terms of achieving fairness and equity (Grimshaw 1984).

Accordingly, what Washington regarded as a moral basis for redistributing benefits to a range of "have nots," his opponents took to be political punishment. Given the city's long and deep immersion in the machine's political culture, the reaction was altogether understandable, and both sides could find evidence that supported their opposing interpretations. Racial considerations further skewed the picture. A cornerstone of the mayor's fairness reform was affirmative action, and since blacks, by sheer number, were the prime beneficiaries of the reform, it was a simple matter to conclude that the new reform politics amounted to the same thing as the machine's old "reward and punish" politics.

That, of course, is exactly what Washington's opponents charged. Republican Governor James Thompson contended that the conflict between Washington and the machine was not over reform but "power, politics, contracts and patronage" (*Chicago Tribune*, March 2, 1985). Alderman Burke, co-leader of the 29 bloc with Vrdolyak, offered a pithy definition of how Washington's reforms looked from his perspective: "Your guys are out, our guys are in" (ibid., September 7, 1986).

Some members of Chicago's cynical press corps, however, who initially were highly skeptical of the mayor's reform agenda, wound up siding with him in the end. Thus, *Chicago Tribune* columnist Clarence Page dismissed the opposition's "phony reformer" charge as a tactical political shift, after an earlier tactic had failed: "his opponents, unable to prove him inept as the next election campaign heats up, are sure to claim he is getting too powerful" (ibid., September 7, 1986).

Even some scholars questioned Washington's commitment to reform. The editors of a book on the 1983 mayoral campaign, historians Melvin Holli and Paul Green, expressed their skepticism by asking in the book's introduction if "the 'ethic of fairness' is simply a fancy name for a black version of old-fashioned patronage" (Holli and Green 1984, p. xvi). These historians subsequently (1989, 158) conducted a study in which they characterized Washington's reforms in just such terms, describing them as "affirmative action patronage," amounting to no more than a "new wrinkle" on the "spoils system" practiced by Chicago's machine mayors.

Yet it is difficult to sustain the "black patronage" thesis inasmuch as a much wider range of "have-nots" wound up benefiting from the fairness reforms. Several new commissions were established, enabling women, Hispanics, gays and lesbians, Asian-Americans, and others to create their own agendas, and a wide array of groups was given unprecedented access to city government. The mayor's "set aside" programs, affirmative action, and open bidding on contracts, for example, benefited all these groups, not simply blacks. Similarly, the top ranks of Washington's administration reflected the same fundamental difference between his fairness reform and machine governance. Washington's "rainbow coalition" administration stood in stark contrast to Daley's administration, which had been composed almost entirely of white males.

Other groups not customarily encompassed by the term "have-nots" also benefited: City employees, the machine's forced labor pool for political work, were prime beneficiaries of the new reform agenda. Washington provided 20,000 city employees with collective bargaining rights, and he installed a professional bargaining process in place of the machine's "handshake deals." He issued an executive order prohibiting the solicitation of city employees for campaign work and financial contributions. He signed the Shakman decree prohibiting hiring and firing on political grounds. All these steps transformed tenuously held patronage jobs into permanent government careers.

By executive order, Washington created a Freedom of Information Order, lifting the shroud of secrecy that had long hidden Chicago government from scrutiny by the media and civic groups. Public hearings on the city's budget, one of the machine's principal secrets, were established in neighborhoods across the city. A panel of neighborhood organizations was formed to determine the distribution of federal Community Development Block Grant funds. All fifty of the city's wards benefited equally from a $169 million bond issue for infrastructure repairs and improvements.

Yet, oddly enough, when I asked the mayor at the end of his first

term to evaluate his achievements, he responded as a classic managerial reformer by citing his fiscal accomplishments. Laughing at my
look of amazement, he said: "Being fair is easy. That's what it's all
about, sure. But getting hold of the financial mess we inherited from
Jane Byrne was something else. She ran this place like a Ma and Pa
candy store, and we had to spend a lot of time straightening it out."
He then launched into a lengthy "nuts and bolts" description of the
various management reforms that had been initiated. When he finally paused, I teasingly remarked that his obvious relish for and
mastery of detail made him sound like a "sepia Daley," and he
seemed pleased by the comparison. In my time with him, the harsh-
est criticism he leveled was reserved for those "who did not do their
homework."

Shortly after Washington entered the mayor's office, the fiscal
burden he had inherited was compounded. The credit agencies, first
Standard and Poor and then Moody, responded to what came to be
called "council wars" by reducing the city's bond rating. The mayor's
efforts to reduce the deficit, either by workforce reductions or tax
increases, were largely stymied by the Vrdolyak 29 bloc. Not until
Washington finally acquired control over the city council in 1986 was
he able to eliminate the deficit, at which point the credit agencies
restored the city's bond rating to the "A" level.

Expanding the Reform Revolution

The critical turning point in Washington's capacity to govern was
reached in the spring of 1986. The federal court finally ordered, after
several challenges by the machine, that special aldermanic elections
would be held on March 16, 1986, in four Hispanic wards and three
black wards. The court confirmed that the seven wards had been
racially gerrymandered during the Byrne administration. With control of the city council riding on the outcome, Vrdolyak and Washington threw everything at their disposal into the elections.

After a final and decisive run-off election in the predominantly
Hispanic Twenty-sixth Ward, in which all three of the white factions—Vrdolyak, Byrne, and Daley—united behind the machine
candidate, Washington emerged victorious. The 29–21 division in
the council that had thwarted Washington for three years was reconfigured into a 25–25 draw, and Mayor Washington held the tie-
breaking vote.

Washington took full advantage of his new edge. The council
was reorganized, and the lion's share of committee chairmanships

went to the mayor's supporters. The mayor's appointees to boards and commissions, many of whom had been held hostage for years by the Vrdolyak 29, finally were approved. The mayor's budget, always a subject of fierce contention and final hour compromise, sailed through the council a full two months before deadline. Cracks in what had been a monolithic opposition bloc began appearing on more and more votes.

As momentum was shifting to the mayor in the council, the opposition leadership was falling into deeper disarray. Vrdolyak had assembled a solid white ethnic bloc of opposition in the council; however, no agreement could be reached over who Washington's challenger would be in the 1987 mayoral primary. Three factional leaders were fighting and maneuvering for the opportunity: Byrne, Vrdolyak, and Daley.

Byrne made the first move, stunning her rivals when she announced her candidacy nearly two years in advance of the 1987 Democratic mayoral primary. Her preemptive strike assigned the dreaded role of "spoiler" to any other white challenger who had the temerity to enter the primary. Byrne's bold move virtually assured her of a one-on-one match against Washington. Her only problem was that Washington played a cat-and-mouse game, refusing to say whether he would run in the Democratic primary or as a third-party candidate in the general election.

Vrdolyak, who had been Byrne's principal ally while she was mayor, was now sharply at odds with her. He vacillated between challenging Byrne in the primary, running as a third party candidate in the general election, and urging prominent Republicans (notably former Republican Governor Richard Ogilvie) to enter the race. The latter tactic raised some eyebrows inasmuch as Vrdolyak still chaired the Democratic party. Yet "Fast Eddie," as he was called, had built his career on bold and opportunistic moves, and was not fazed by the criticism. He had, after all, been caught earlier by reporters for making overtures to President Reagan's top political aides shortly after Washington was elected (*Chicago Tribune*, November 21, 1983).

Daley, lacking the audacity and dash of his two flamboyant rivals, relied upon stealth and guile to advance his candidacy. When Byrne began hinting that she would challenge Washington, Daley announced that he would not be a candidate in 1987. However, two weeks after she announced her candidacy, members of Daley's faction, but not Daley himself, proposed an extraordinary change in the mayoral election rules: They wanted to eliminate party primaries and replace them with a non-partisan election (*Chicago Tribune*, April 30, 1985).

The rules change would enable Daley to enter the election as a Democrat without bearing the terrible "spoiler" stigma, a festering wound he had acquired for his role in splitting the white vote in the 1983 primary election. The success of the proposed change, from Daley's viewpoint, hinged on the assumption that Washington could not get a majority vote in the non-partisan election, and thus he would be forced into a one-on-one runoff election against a white candidate. Further assuming that Daley were the white runoff candidate, he then would secure the one-on-one advantage Byrne had acquired with her bold preemptive strike. Byrne accordingly joined Washington in denouncing the Daley faction's efforts to change the rules of the game. Key Democratic leaders in the legislature, determined to avoid a devisive "council wars" in Springfield, also opposed the Daley bloc's effort to change the rules (Madigan 1986).

After an elaborate and often imaginative series of moves and counter-moves, Washington wound up facing Byrne in the Democratic primary. In the general election, he would be opposed by two candidates. Vrdolyak relinquished his chairmanship of the machine in order to run as a third party candidate in the general election. Daley dropped out of contention after his non-partisan election ploy failed. However, the Daley faction did come up with a candidate, Cook County Assessor Thomas Hynes, who ran in the general election as a second third party candidate. However, after failing to force Vrdolyak out of the race, Hynes folded his candidacy a few days before the election.

The Republicans entered the race with a political activist academic, Donald Haider, a professor of public management at Northwestern University, as their candidate. Haider had worked for a short time in Mayor Byrne's administration, until she fired him. After that he had served as an issues advisor to Daley in the 1983 Democratic primary. Then, after a stint back at Northwestern, Haider emerged as a Republican. But the new guise did not work well either. Mired at rock bottom in the polls, the general election effectively amounted to a one-on-one contest between Washington and Vrdolyak.

In both campaigns, Washington took the position that the election boiled down to a choice between reform and machine politics. His principal opponents, Byrne and Vrdolyak, sometimes with finesse and at other times boldly, tried to cast the choice in racial terms. After dancing fitfully around the racial issue for a time, Byrne finally struck with an explosive television ad. It featured a scowling Mayor Washington, followed by a bolt of lightning cracking Washington's angry visage in half, and closed with the message: "Jane Byrne: A Mayor For All Chicago." The media howled in outrage over the ad's racist implications, and Byrne bowed to the reaction by promptly pulling it off the air. Vrdolyak, on the other hand, whom the polls gave no chance of winning, apparently concluded that he would go down swinging the racial club. His bold use of racial themes throughout his campaign repeated Epton's wildly divisive campaign in 1983.

In the Democratic primary, Washington defeated Byrne by 78,158 votes, amounting to 54 percent. His margin in the general election against Vrdolyak was 131,797. The mayor's share of the vote once again came to 54 percent, with Vrdolyak winning 42 percent, and Haider picking up the remaining 4 percent. Comparing the 1983 and 1987 elections reveals an interesting pattern of both continuity and change (see table 14).

The table indicates that Washington solidified his hold on the mayor's office and advanced his reform agenda by achieving three goals. First, his level of support in the black wards remained remarkably solid and strong. This was particularly true in the middle class wards, where his support remained nearly as robust in 1987 as it had been in the breakthrough 1983 election. In ten of the city's seventeen black wards, he received 99 percent of the vote. In the other seven

Table 14 **Sources of Mayoral Support: 1983, 1987**

Wards	1983	1987	Change
	The Washington Coalitions		
Middle class black	28,700	26,700	− 7%
Poor black	22,600	19,500	− 14%
Hispanic	600	3,000	+ 400%
Wards	The Epton-Vrdolyak Coalitions		Change
White bungalow	30,600	25,400	− 17%
White renter	16,300	11,000	− 33%
Lakefront liberal	4,300	800	− 81%

The figures represent the average winning margin for each voting bloc. For the sake of clarifying central tendencies, ten wards with racially heterogeneous populations were excluded from the calculation; eight (1, 7, 10, 15, 18, 19, 37, 42) contained black-white electorates and two (32, 33) had white-Hispanic electorates.

black wards, which contained small pockets of white voters, his level of support ranged from 89 to 98 percent. This extraordinary level of support in "the base" meant that Washington only required a modest level of additional support to win.

Second, Washington significantly improved his standing among Hispanic and lakefront liberal voters. In 1983 he had carried three of the four Hispanic wards, but only by small margins. In 1987 he won all four of them, and in the two predominantly Puerto Rican wards, his level of support reached the 60 percent range. The shift in the five lakefront liberal wards was even more dramatic, as Washington had not carried any of them in 1983 and in 1987 he carried three of them. Thus, in the city's small but critical number of swing wards, Washington's definition of the situation prevailed. The cutting issues were "fair and open government," as the mayor styled his redistributive reform agenda, not black "patronage and bossism," as his opponents had charged.

Finally, fear and hostility toward Washington subsided in the white ethnic wards, particularly in the "renter" wards, where the "stakes" were lower. The widespread expectation that he would create a black machine that would exact retribution from his white "enemies" did not materialize. There was no mass firing of whites at city hall, ward services were not rolled back, and scatter-site public housing was not spread throughout the ethnic wards—all of the dire things that the machine's precinct captains had said were certain to occur. Washington did not increase his share of white ethnic votes in 1987; however, the level of opposition to him diminished significantly.

The distinction between "bungalow" wards, where the homeownership rate exceeds 60 percent, and "renter" wards, with ownership rates of from 29 to 51 percent, has received little attention in analyses of the elections (City of Chicago, Department of Planning, 1980 Ward Profiles, 1984). The conventional analysis relies on the categories popularized by polling: income and education levels, occupation, religion, ethnicity, and gender (Kleppner 1985, 217–19). These traits undoubtedly help explain voting behavior. However, they do not get at the critical differences in ethnic voting behavior encompassed by the concept of "community attachment" developed by urban sociologists (Janowitz 1952; Suttles 1972; Guterbock 1980).

The white "bungalow" wards, located on the far Northwest and Southwest sides, were far more opposed to Washington than the white "renter" wards were in both 1983 and 1987. The homeowners tended to hold a deeper level of community attachment, in both material ("sunk costs") and psychic ("sunk roots") terms. Thus, the homeowners perceived that far more was at stake in the election, and they voted accordingly: overwhelmingly against Washington. The renters, with generally lower levels of community attachment and thus less at stake, experienced far less anxiety, and so they opposed Washington in substantially smaller numbers.

The "community attachment" interpretation of ethnic voting behavior is supported by two other observations. Opposition to Washington in 1987 subsided much less in the bungalow wards, by only 17 percent, than in the renter wards, where it fell by 33 percent. Moreover, when a closer look is taken at the renter wards, it can be seen that those with more at stake remained far more opposed to Washington. Opposition to the mayor in the "high stakes" renter wards (the Southwest Side wards located next to black wards and undergoing racial transition) declined by only 15 percent—the same rate as the bungalow wards. In marked contrast, opposition to Washington fell by 36 percent in the North Central renter wards and by 42 percent in the renter wards on the Northeast Side wards.

Accordingly, with support holding firm in the black wards and rising in the Hispanic and lakefront liberal wards, and opposition declining in the white ethnic wards, Mayor Washington could confidently boast, to the delight of friends and dismay of foes, that he would be "mayor of Chicago for twenty years." He was a messiah to his black supporters, their liberator from long years of bondage as second-class citizens under the machine. To a growing number of voters, he was a reform mayor, genuinely bent on providing fair and open government. The "last of the great machine cities" was now at the vanguard of the nation's progressive reform movement.

In Perspective

The sociological perspective's concern for organizational coalition-building and electoral representation direct attention to several critical aspects of Washington's election. Among blacks, Washington created a monolithic electoral bloc by bridging the historic differences that separated the three black political communities: black belt, middle class, and plantation wards. Inside the campaign, he checked the influence, but retained the support of the black nationalist bloc, which was bent on transforming the campaign into a narrowly conceived black empowerment movement. Citywide, Washington formed the most comprehensive reform coalition in the city's

history, adding substantial numbers of lakefront liberals and Hispanics to his monolithic black base of support.

Using "fair and open" government as a campaign theme, Washington drew a compelling distinction between his reform goals and
the machine's "friends and enemies" style of governance. Unprecedented access and representation were promised to a wide array of
dispossessed groups. After Byrne and Daley were eliminated in the
primary election, Washington picked up solid support from lakefront liberals and Hispanics. The success of his coalition-building efforts in office became apparent in the 1987 mayoral election. His
black base remained firm, he made significant gains among Hispanic and lakefront liberal voters, and white ethnic opposition declined, particularly in the Northside "renter" wards.

The political perspective's interest in the relationship between
events and empowerment as an electoral goal identifies two such
critical elements. Washington's pollster, Patrick Caddell, called his
election a "miracle," and in terms of the good fortune that fell his
way, Washington's election was miraculous. The twin "monsters,"
President Ronald Reagan and Mayor Byrne, provided an extraordinary context for Washington's campaign. Reagan's rolling back of the
welfare state and Byrne's numerous open assaults on black interests
enabled Washington to capitalize on a profoundly bitter sense of loss
and disempowerment running through the black community. The
registration of 125,000 new voters prior to the election testifies to the
depth of the discontent.

At the same time, the political perspective's concern with elite
self-interest points to the basis for the inability of the Washington
coalition to survive his death. Washington's inclination was to "win
over" opponents rather than to exclude and punish them in the machine tradition. Yet it also was in his political self-interest to treat
some opponents in this fashion. Thus, as we saw, during the campaign, the divisive black nationalists were tolerated and won over.
As mayor, Washington did the same thing with the divisive black
machine loyalists. In so doing, Washington served his own political
interest by creating no fissures in his monolithic black political base.

However, the support ultimately was secured at an extraordinary cost. Washington's reforms were not institutionalized as much
as they were personalized. His political skill and standing in the
black community compelled compliance from the recalcitrant black
nationalists and machine loyalists. When he died, therefore, the reforms were put in jeopardy and promptly undermined by the very

elements he had tolerated and left in place. The black machine loyalists collaborated with the white machine bloc and put one of their
own into the mayor's office. The black nationalists, in turn, took over
Evans' campaign, and killed whatever slim chance Evans might
have had of forming a reform coalition and winning.

9
Machine Politics, Reform Style

Harold Washington's sudden death in November 1987 exposed the weak foundation of his reforms. They had been "personalized" rather than institutionalized. Accordingly, without his charismatic leadership, power abruptly shifted from the mayor's office to the city council chambers, where the succession struggle would be settled. A coup, a turning back, clearly was in the offing. It was simply a question of who among the opposition's leaders would emerge on top.

Hats from many factions were tossed into the mayoral ring. Two black claims were advanced, one from the machine side and the other from the reform side. Alderman Eugene Sawyer, by virtue of seniority, temperament, and ties, emerged as the candidate of the black machine faction. Sawyer was one of the old guard who had publicly supported Washington's reforms, while yearning privately for the old machine way of doing business (*Chicago Tribune*, November 26, 1987). Alderman Timothy Evans, who had served as Washington's floor leader in the council, was the logical candidate of the black reform faction. He had been one of the few machine ward leaders whose conversion to reform was regarded as genuine by Washington administration insiders. Thus, Evans provided the prospect of a continuation of Washington's reform agenda.

On the white side, several claimants surfaced. Alderman Edward Burke, one of the fiery co-leaders, alongside Vrdolyak, of the anti-Washington bloc, wanted it. However, he had been so badly burned by the raging fires he had ignited during council wars that he was deemed unelectable. As one of the white machine leaders put it, the acting mayor had to be "a moderate, somebody who wasn't in the fray." Alderman Terry Gabinski, Congressman Daniel Rostenkowski's man, surfaced briefly as a possibility. But his lackluster and parochial style worked against him, and long years of divide-

and-conquer rule by the Irish had left the Polish leadership sharply divided.

This left Alderman Richard Mell, a mercurial opportunist from the Northwest Side, as the "great white hope." Mell apparently came within a single vote of pulling it off. Wild and desperate at the end, he allegedly offered a small fortune to Lawrence Bloom, the liberal alderman from the Hyde Park–University of Chicago area, who held the deciding twenty-sixth vote. Bloom, however, turned down Mell's deal, and then he presented himself as a candidate. The quirky reformer argued that since he had no ties to or support from any of the contending factions, this made him the ideal compromise candidate. The white side wound up stalemated.

The white machine leaders reluctantly conceded that they would have to settle for yet another black mayor. They would, however, have a say this time as to who it would be, and that, of course, meant that it would not be anyone remotely like Washington. A majority of Chicago's electorate had shown itself ready for reform. But most of the aldermen remained convinced that "Paddy" Bauler's wisdom still rang true, when he had declared on the eve of Mayor Richard J. Daley's election in 1955 that "Chicago ain't ready for reform."

Sawyer proved to be the ideal compromise candidate from the machine's point of view. He was, in the words of a white machine supporter, "flexible," which meant that he could be counted upon to cooperate with the white machine bloc. Indeed, Sawyer was one of the "loyalist" ward leaders Daley had recruited during the raging civil rights crisis in order to make certain that any black empowerment ended at the machine's door.

Sawyer had demonstrated his loyalty then, and even after the machine fell on hard times, his commitment did not waver until the bitter end. He backed Bilandic for mayor in 1977, and Washington carried his ward. He backed Bilandic again in 1979, and Byrne swept his ward. Only in the face of certain defeat in 1983, and under the threat of losing his own aldermanic seat, did Sawyer capitulate by endorsing Washington. Not surprisingly, however, Washington's field workers found that little help actually was forthcoming from Sawyer's organization.

Sawyer also was "well liked" by white and black machine leaders alike. He was regarded as someone who could be counted on to go along and who demanded little in return for his loyalty. He had no enemies because he had done nothing that would have created them. He had been virtually a mute during his many years in the council. He was the one black alderman that had profited from Vrdolyak's reorganization of the council under Washington. Vainly hoping to crack the mayor's monolithic black support, Sawyer was given the position of city counsel *pro tem*. Even in council caucuses, a mayoral aide was unable to recall ever hearing Sawyer speak: "He would just sit, all the time, puffing away on those thin brown More cigarettes, as though he wasn't even in the room."

Sawyer's critical virtue, though, from the machine's viewpoint, was that his election would drive a deep wedge into the monolithic black electorate that Washington had constructed. Sawyer was decidedly not the choice of the vast majority of black voters; Evans occupied that position, by virtue of his ties to Washington. Accordingly, if the council elected Sawyer, it was a virtual certainty that Evans would challenge him in the next election, producing a divided black vote. That would replicate the fateful white split between Byrne and Daley in 1983, which had enabled Washington to win. Sawyer, then, would fulfill in spades the divisive "loyalist" role that Mayor Daley originally had carved out for him during the turbulent 1960s.

Black Politics at the Crossroads

Within five days of Washington's death, the machine bloc backing Sawyer claimed to have thirty-one written commitments to his candidacy. Nineteen of the twenty-three white machine aldermen had signed on. Four of the five lakefront liberals held out, as did four Southwest Siders aligned with young Daley, and Vrdolyak, who after being defeated by Washington had become something of a party unto himself. (Vrdolyak was represented by his brother, Victor, who took his aldermanic seat when he ran for mayor.) Twelve of the eighteen black aldermen also pledged themselves to Sawyer. The four Hispanic aldermen formed a united bloc and withheld their support from Sawyer.

Two critical shifts developed, however, by the time the election was held in the wee hours of December 2, and only six of the black aldermen wound up voting for Sawyer. However, all but one of the white machine aldermen went for Sawyer (the holdout being Daley's alderman, Patrick Huels, who abstained). White liberal Lawrence Bloom, who despised Evans, cast the twenty-ninth vote for Sawyer. Yet although Sawyer won the council battle, he surely lost the impending regular election war. As the candidate of the white machine faction that had opposed Washington so fiercely, Sawyer became unelectable in the black community. That, needless to say, was exactly what the white machine leadership was banking on.

If any doubts remained about black sentiments, the raucous crowd of 4,000 demonstrators in and around City Hall on the night of the council election dispelled them. Furious cries of "traitor," "no deals," "Uncle Tom," and far worse filled the air. Five of the black aldermen who were pledged to Sawyer withered under the pressure and abandoned him; a sixth pledged black alderman was hospitalized and failed to vote. Some of the opposition was organized by the Evans bloc. However, most of the protestors made it to City Hall on their own, driven there by their outrage over the extraordinary turn of events.

Sawyer himself nearly buckled under the pressure. Not up to playing a leadership role under the best of circumstances, this was far more than Sawyer was prepared to endure. The council session had convened at 5:30 P.M., but the election was not held until 4:00 A.M. As one of Sawyer's white machine backers put it: "I think Gene lost his nerve. We had 27 votes at 5:30" (*Chicago Tribune*, December 2, 1987). Sawyer asked that the election be put off; but the white machine aldermen were unwilling to let him reconsider his decision. A television camera caught Burke angrily jabbing a finger in Sawyer's face. An alderman described the atmosphere in the room where Sawyer was sequestered as "like a football team at half time. We were jumping up and down and shouting 'Sawyer, Sawyer' and we had him all pumped up" (ibid., December 3, 1987). Sawyer himself described soul-searching sessions with his pastor.

When Sawyer finally agreed to go ahead with the election and entered the council chambers, an exuberant Alderman Mell, who had helped put together the white machine vote for Sawyer, leaped to the top of his desk and screamed, "We did it, we did it." Sawyer's knees buckled and he appeared ready to faint. Not in his worst nightmare could the loyalist have imagined anything more bizarre happening to him: an obscure hack for twenty years, miraculously lifted to the city's highest office, but compelled to get there by submitting himself to utter degradation.

After the smoke cleared, calm was restored, but things did not improve much for the acting mayor. He faced a number of compelling problems. To begin with, he lacked an electoral base from which to govern. When Sawyer delivered his "state of the city" address to the League of Women Voters in April, he wrapped himself in Washington's mantle of reform: "My agenda for our great city was

Harold Washington's agenda. My goals were his goals" (*Chicago Tribune*, April 17, 1988). He continued Washington's neighborhood-oriented reform programs, such as school reform and affordable housing. Much to the dismay of his machine backers, he also retained most of Washington's reform-minded cabinet.

Yet no amount of activity could overcome the terrible stigma of his election by—and his long ties and apparent obligations to—the machine. A few days after the election, an investigative reporter revealed a dubious "finder's fee" of $30,000 that Sawyer had received years ago from a real estate transaction in his ward. Another news report recalled that Sawyer's brother Charles had been fired by Mayor Washington "for accepting illegal contributions from an FBI undercover agent." Most of his family was found on the city payroll. None of this was unusual by machine standards; but measured by the reform standards he was espousing, Sawyer fell far short of the mark. A poll taken a few days after the council election indicated that only 10 percent of the black community favored Sawyer for acting mayor; two-thirds preferred Sawyer's black reform-minded rival, Evans (*Chicago Tribune*, December 13, 1987).

Sawyer also lacked the will to govern. His painfully diffident demeanor was such that reporters took to calling him "Mayor Mumbles." He attempted to distance himself from the most notorious members of the white machine bloc, notably Burke. However, the machine bloc, black and white, found Sawyer's efforts to bridge the machine-reform divide more than they were willing to tolerate. He was caught between an obligation to his backers and a desire to emulate Washington's reforms. By his backers' machine standards, government was supposed to be conducted on a "friends and enemies" basis, and yet Sawyer was going out of his way to punish the very friends who had elected him and reward the enemies who had opposed him. Sawyer, of course, realized that to do otherwise would doom his prospects, however slim, of reelection.

Finally in July, Sawyer's machine backers in the council had had enough. They tore into the Evans faction's members, stripping them of the committee chairmanships that Sawyer had allowed them to retain despite their outspoken opposition to him. Sawyer attempted to distance himself from the furious purge by claiming that he lacked control over the council. However, his press secretary exacerbated the mayor's problem by indicating that it was not so much a lack of control on his part, but a lack of will. "These guys have been chomping at the bit since December. Once the mayor indicated he could go with the reorganization, he unleashed the monster in these guys" (*Chicago Tribune*, July 15, 1988). Thus, much of Sawyer's hard work up on the highwire was dashed in a day.[1]

Caving into the reorganization reinforced the terrible image for indecisiveness Sawyer had acquired a few months earlier. News reporters learned that one Steve Cokely, a black nationalist employed in the mayor's office who was described by Sawyer's press secretary as "a wild-eyed, hare-brained, anti-Semitic bigot," had at one time issued a series of audio-tapes containing virulent anti-Semitic views. When the cry went up for the aide's firing, Sawyer vacillated for several days. Only after his archrival Evans called for the aide's termination did Sawyer finally bite the bullet and let Cokely go (Anderson 1991; Rose and Andrews, 1991).

Both of these problems and others were largely the result of a third compelling problem. Sawyer not only lacked a base from which to govern and a will to govern, but he lacked a governing strategy as well. He could not turn for help to any of the experienced white machine leaders; they were plotting his demise. His black machine backers were unhelpful; they lacked experience. Neither Mayor Daley and his successors nor Mayor Washington had ever allowed any of them to get near any of the important decision-making centers. Sawyer also could not trust many of the Washington holdovers in his administration because they did not trust him. Sawyer himself had never been in a situation where anything more than a simple ward reelection strategy was required.

Thus Sawyer had to construct a mayoral inner circle of strategists largely out of thin air, and the credentials of the group he assembled were, indeed, thin. The most able of the lot was Erwin France, a black consultant with years of government experience going back to the Daley era, when he had been hailed as one of the mayor's "whiz kids." He served as Sawyer's chief policy advisor. Unfortunately for Sawyer, over the years France had acquired a terrible reputation as a "contracts hustler." For this reason, Washington had denied France a position in his administration because, as a Washington advisor put it, France "engaged in conflicts of interest . . . [and] was too close to big developers and had used government positions to reward friends" (*Chicago Tribune*, February 11, 1988). When Sawyer signed a $200,000 consulting contract with France, even the mayor's supporters howled about the impropriety of a private consultant's serving as his chief policy advisor (ibid.).

For political advice, Sawyer turned to his brother Charles, who had helped him run the ward organization, and Marshall Korshak,

a white, elderly former ward committeeman who had not been politically active for several years. The rest of the acting mayor's inner
circle was even more limited, consisting of three businessmen who
had served as fund raisers for Washington, Sawyer's two pastors,
and an Hispanic former school board member. As the 1989 election
drew near, Sawyer hired a political consultant from New Orleans to
manage his campaign.[2]

For all that, Sawyer's gravest problem was Tim Evans. Evans
performed the same role young Daley had played during Byrne's
mayoralty. He was the "prince in exile," challenging the legitimacy
of Sawyer's right to govern. In his concession speech on the night
Sawyer was elected, Evans virtually announced his mayoral candidacy. He thus became a "shadow" mayor throughout Sawyer's term,
voicing the aspirations of the black and reform communities, while
discrediting Sawyer because of his ties to the machine.

Three and a half months after Sawyer's election, Evans' campaign was launched with a resounding boom. In what was viewed
as a "showdown" election for ward committeemen, three of the six
black committeemen who had voted for Sawyer were defeated. A
fourth committeeman, who had not voted for Sawyer but was
closely identified with him, was also defeated. Yet another Sawyer
backer declined to seek reelection. The fifth Sawyer backer ran his
brother in his place; he managed to win by a few hundred votes,
running against a Black Muslim with an Arabic name. Thus, the
only Sawyer backer to escape the harsh wrath unharmed was Sawyer himself, who ran unopposed.

Sawyer acknowledged the implications of the setback. "It shows
I've got a lot of work to do. I recognize the fact that I have a lot of
work to do, but just watch my smoke." A jubilant Evans described it
as "a mini-referendum on Sawyer," and one of the successful aldermen backed by Evans hailed his victory as "a continuation of the
Washington legacy." The vanquished Sawyer backers saw it the same
way. One cried: "Down, down, down, we're all done. Butler's
down, Henry's down, I'm down." Another explained why: "This is
a retaliation for my December 2 vote. I'm part of the Sawyer bloc,
and it's retaliation for his election" (*Chicago Tribune*, March 16, 1988).

Yet after the explosive launching, the Evans' campaign fell into a
long tailspin from which it never recovered. Evans wound up effectively discrediting Sawyer, but he never managed to credit himself.
By doing little more than draping himself in the mantle of the Washington legacy, he never emerged as a candidate in his own right and
failed to put together an effective political organization. In the end,

the black nationalist and white radical wings of the old Washington coalition took over his campaign. They transformed what had been a broad-based reform coalition under Washington into a reactionary racial movement, not unlike the old Daley machine they railed so passionately against.

Without Washington's strong and charismatic leadership, the reform center could not hold. Evans, by all accounts, was genuinely committed to reform, yet in a more fundamental way, he was cut from the same cloth as Sawyer, for both men were "loyalists" who had been elevated to leadership by Mayor Daley, and, given Daley's objectives, neither man had been chosen because of the leadership skills he possessed. They were functionaries in Daley's patronage government, with limited standing in their communities, men who could be counted upon to follow his leadership. Neither ever overcame the deficiencies Daley had found in them both.

Evans had not been highly regarded even within his own ward organization. When his predecessor, Claude Holman, had died in 1973, the precinct captains elected Evans to take his place as alderman; however, in recognition of Evans' limited leadership skill, they chose another member of the organization to take Holman's more critical committeeman spot, but Daley intervened and gave both positions to Evans.

Evans also was not well regarded by the reform activists in his ward. When the Independent Voters of Illinois overwhelmingly endorsed Washington for mayor in 1983, they rejected Evans for alderman in favor of a lackluster candidate with little standing in the ward. Even Mayor Washington had reservations about Evans. When he was preparing to name Evans to head his political organization, a political advisor objected that Evans had never demonstrated any leadership capabilities. The mayor acknowledged the problem by acknowledging his own problem: "Sure, but who else is there?"

Things grew worse for Evans without Washington to guide him. Until the end of June, he took virtually no steps to advance his mayoral candidacy other than publicly urging Sawyer to step down. At that point he held a long-awaited press conference, but only to announce the formation of an "exploratory committee," which would determine if he should enter the mayoral race. Meanwhile, by the end of August Sawyer had raised $2.5 million, which made it a virtual certainty that he would not be pulling out of the race, as Evans had vainly hoped. Evans, by contrast, had yet to hold his first fundraiser, and had only $100,000 in his campaign fund.

Evans also had not put together a campaign organization. A few volunteers worked out of a campaign office, but with little contact or direction from the candidate. Thus, when a group of black community activists announced that they would hold a "plebiscite" in September to rally the community around a single mayoral candidate, Evans was caught without an organization to seek the endorsement. Although he was widely regarded as the black community's leading candidate, Evans wound up running second to another reform-minded alderman from the West Side, Danny Davis. By then, the leadership vacuum was becoming apparent, and support began building for Jesse Jackson, who had shown no interest in running. Evans' status as the front-runner was disintegrating.

Evans finally announced his candidacy at the end of October. Yet he still had not made any serious effort to raise funds for his campaign, nor had he assembled a campaign organization. By this time, he had also lost the services of Jacky Grimshaw, Washington's highly regarded campaign manager and chief political organizer, who in bitter frustration departed for Pittsburgh to manage a mayoral campaign. Evans also lost David Axelrod, the city's premier media consultant, who had managed Washington's media in 1987. Axelrod wound up working for Daley against Evans. Many of Washington's political organizers, notably in the lakefront liberal wards, also pulled back from Evans' campaign, some because of his limited reform credentials and others because his campaign was floundering so badly.

By December it was apparent that Evans' campaign was in serious jeopardy. The *Chicago Tribune* published a poll indicating that Evans was slipping in the black community, and Sawyer was the beneficiary of the slippage. The poll also indicated that the two men held similar "esteem" ratings among blacks. Given Evans' earlier commanding stature as the front-runner, this amounted to a stunning reversal (*Chicago Tribune*, December 11, 1988).

Evans also was in serious difficulty in the lakefront liberal wards, the only place where a black candidate could reasonably expect to secure substantial white support. The poll indicated that Evans' negative rating among lakefront voters even exceeded those of Sawyer and Jesse Jackson. The interpretation of the poll attributed Evans' problem to a perception that the radical wing of the old Washington coalition was dominating Evans' campaign (ibid., December 14, 1988). With the stench of the Steve Cokeley affair obviously still fouling the lakefront air, this was bad news for Evans.

Lacking the money to mount an advertising campaign, Evans was unable to counter the negative image being projected in news accounts. Thus, at year's end Evans wound up announcing that he was withdrawing from the Democratic party primary. He would run instead in the general election as the candidate of a new party he had formed, the Harold Washington Party.[3] He went on to say that he would not be endorsing Sawyer over Daley.

Evans' decision to withhold support from Sawyer effectively doomed Sawyer's already long-shot candidacy. Even after several of Evans' prominent backers endorsed Sawyer—and urged Evans to do so as well—he refused to give in: "I will not tailor my principles to the passions of the moment" (*Chicago Tribune*, February 17, 1989). Daley wound up trouncing Sawyer. Then when Sawyer retaliated against Evans by refusing to endorse him in the general election, Daley trounced Evans.

Yet even if the black community had united behind either one of them, neither Sawyer nor Evans could have won, for neither candidate had generated any support to speak of outside the black community. Sawyer was tainted by his ties to the machine, and in Evans' case, the broad-based reform coalition Washington had constructed disintegrated into a narrowly conceived black empowerment movement (see fig. 6).

Machine Politics Reform Style

In kaleidoscopic fashion—a conventional machine mayor, then the city's first female mayor, followed by the first black mayor, and now a political androgyne: part machine/part reform—Chicago elected its fifth mayor, Richard M. Daley, in only a dozen years. His father had ruled the city for over two decades, and in dictatorial fashion as the last of the legendary machine bosses. It is difficult to say how long the son can survive in these more perilous and turbulent times. It is no less difficult to determine just what young Daley's agenda is. Tensions, contradictions, and complexities abound more than ever in both the political environment and between what the mayor professes and what he practices.

Daley appears to have put himself at odds with the machine that backed his candidacy. "Son of Boss," as reporters dubbed him in the 1983 mayoral campaign, has deep and intensely personal roots in the machine. Yet he insists that he has no interest in following in his father's footsteps as a machine style mayor, and his public persona is carefully crafted to deny any appearance of "bossism." Accordingly, Daley holds no political office, having relinquished his ward committeeman post when he was elected State's Attorney. He has

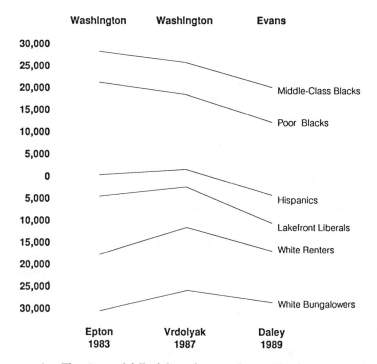

Washington   Washington   Evans

30,000

25,000

20,000   Middle-Class Blacks

15,000

10,000   Poor Blacks

5,000

0

5,000   Hispanics

10,000   Lakefront Liberals

15,000   White Renters

20,000

25,000

30,000   White Bungalowers

Epton   Vrdolyak   Daley
1983   1987   1989

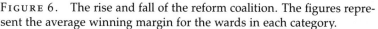

FIGURE 6. The rise and fall of the reform coalition. The figures represent the average winning margin for the wards in each category.

even declined to make political endorsements; although with his commanding lead going into the 1991 mayoral election, he descended from this lofty perch to endorse several aldermanic candidates. However, as we shall see, there is more here than meets the casual eye.

Daley also appears to have put himself at odds with the machine in the policy arena. He has pledged himself to a classical economizing reform course, making government more efficient and businesslike by vowing to trim the workforce, "privatizing" a number of government services, calling for greater productivity, and the like. Daley even has committed himself to maintaining Washington's moral reform agenda of "fair and open government." This, of course, would appear to set him up for the same clash Washington had with the machine, in that moral reform amounts to the antithesis of machine rule's commitment to a "closed, friends and enemies" style of government. Yet, as we shall see, tensions and contradictions again exist between what Daley says and what he does.

Given Daley's extraordinary pledges, it may well be asked what his purpose is in abandoning his machine backers and siding with the reformers. The source of the tension and contradiction is the new political environment of high expectations created by Washington's moral reforms. "Son of Boss" may well be bent on reinstating a centralized and closed style of machine government; however, he is entangled in the web of reform spun by Washington. Blacks, women, lakefront liberals, Hispanics, and other dispossessed groups who had been empowered by Washington's reforms are disinclined to give up their gains. They want to maintain the access, decision-making influence, and material and symbolic benefits they acquired under reform government.

These lofty expectations create an electoral contradiction for Daley that parallels his organizational conflict within the machine. Daley's problem is that it is far more difficult for him to maintain a reform position because Washington's electoral coalition was consonant with reform, and Daley's is not. The elements of Washington's coalition had two features in common: all were liberal and all had been consigned to second-class citizenship by the machine. Daley's coalition, however, is a volatile mix of liberal reform-minded and conservative machine-minded elements.

With their markedly different political values and policy preferences, Daley's electoral coalition is not unlike the contradictory coalition Jane Byrne assembled to defeat the machine. As we saw, Byrne felt compelled after her election to abandon her dissonant electoral coalition in favor of a conservative machine coalition. So far Daley has elected to remain up on the high wire, balancing the contradictory elements in his coalition. The critical difference, of course, between the two mayors' situations is that Daley is not confronted by a challenge, whereas Byrne had to contend with young Daley's "government in exile."

During his first two and one-half years in office, Daley has been remarkably successful. Large numbers of black voters remain skeptical, yet they are the odd men out. In every other quarter of the city, Daley's unusual strategy of machine politics reform style enjoys strong support. Along the way, the mayor has been helped immensely by the ineptitude of his opposition. The broadly based reform coalition Washington crafted has devolved into a narrowly conceived black empowerment movement, which holds some support among black voters, but none to speak of anywhere else. White reformers and Hispanics who would be willing to oppose Daley are unwilling to cast their lot with a movement that consigns them to a secondary status and which stands little prospect of success.

The descent from coalitional reform politics to black empowerment politics began, as we saw, in Timothy Evans' mayoral campaign. Washington had been able to hold the white radical and black nationalist elements in check; Evans could not, and, as a result, the extremists drove the moderates out of Evans' campaign. The Harold Washington party created by Evans was expanded into a county-wide organization for the 1990 county elections. In keeping with its black empowerment aims, an all-black slate of candidates was fielded, which won no offices. Yet in defeat it found victory for it could take credit for defeating some of the Democratic candidates it had identified as "enemies of the black community."

Daley also has had a free ride in the city council. A team of University of Illinois researchers found that only thirteen of the fifty aldermen opposed the mayor more than half the time during his first year in office (Simpson et al. 1990). Even that overstates the extent of opposition to Daley because the dissenting aldermen do not constitute an organized bloc. Evans is the nominal leader of the opposition, but he has proven to be no more effective in this role than he was as a mayoral candidate. Few meetings are held, strategy is not crafted, and coordination is absent. Thus, Daley's city council has reverted to a "rubber stamp" style of decision making.

Daley also has encountered little opposition in the media. Inasmuch as Evans generally has made himself unavailable to the press, the vacuum has been filled by aldermen of little stature and with dubious reform credentials. Thus Alderman Robert Shaw, who had been one of Acting Mayor Sawyer's principal backers, is often found in the role of spokesman for the opposition. Defeated as alderman in 1983 because he backed Byrne against Washington, Shaw jumped loudly on the Washington bandwagon in 1987 and won his aldermanic seat back. He then publicly vowed that he would "never be 'outblacked' again," and that he would "never again support a white mayor." If Daley were able to handpick an opposition spokesman (there is much suspicion that he actually has), he could not do much better than Alderman Shaw.

Yet the more intriguing questions involve Daley himself. In what direction is his hybrid government of machine politics, reform style headed? We have only a short mayoral record to examine. However, we can augment that by looking into the mayor's background before we take up his mayoral performance.

Daley's Background: From "Dead-End Kid" to Liberal Reformer?

Daley's emergence as a reform mayor in the Washington style was not his first remarkable transformation. He launched his political career early, at the age of 30, and at the top, in the state senate, and he clearly was not ready for the generous gift his father had bestowed on him. None of his colleagues was willing to speak to reporters for attribution, for fear of incurring the father's wrath, but they held little regard for young Daley's talents. "He isn't the most brilliant of people. . . . They don't give him too many things to do. . . . He has earned a reputation for sitting in his seat most of the time, with his mouth shut" (*Chicago Tribune,* May 6, 1973). One reporter, after observing Daley anxiously and fumblingly going about the simple task of collecting signatures for a senate resolution, sarcastically dubbed him "Richard the Lion-Hearted" (ibid.).

Midway through his first term, however, after his father bestowed the coveted chairmanship of the judiciary committee on him, the timid and uncertain young Daley suddenly emerged as "Richard the Terrible," and heads began to roll. His colleagues estimation of him changed accordingly. Now they spoke of his "drill sergeant demeanor" in running his committee, and looked askance at his "quick dispatch of bills, rough treatment of their sponsors, and often a civics lesson thrown in." He came to be regarded as "arrogant, ruthless, vindictive, and downright mean" (ibid., June 22, 1974).

Daley was particularly harsh on his liberal Democratic colleagues, earning a reputation as "the ringleader of the 'Dead End Kids,' the Chicago Democratic regulars who scuttled most reform bills at the behest of Mayor Daley" (*Chicago Sun-Times,* March 9, 1980). His favorite victim was Dawn Clark Netsch, who represented a Chicago lakefront liberal district: "Daley routinely scuttled her bills with the glee of a child pulling the wings off flies" (ibid., November 9, 1980). An enterprising reporter overheard Daley expounding on his contempt for liberals over dinner in a Springfield restaurant. "That—Katz [liberal senator from Glencoe] is just another phoney liberal. We're going to cut him up the next time he shows up in judiciary. We'll take him apart. He'll be defenseless." To which Katz could only reply, "God, I didn't even know I was on the enemies' list" (*Chicago Tribune,* June 22, 1975).

Daley did not, however, confine his wrath to the liberals, for even the Democratic leadership did not escape his reign of terror. Bills sponsored by senate president Cecil Partee and his deputy, Phil

Rock, were treated with the same low regard other bills received (*Chicago Tribune*, May 2, 1974). Reports began to surface that Daley's divisive behavior was threatening the Democrats' narrow hold over the senate. Partee, a Chicago machine man, was being assailed on all fronts: by the Republicans, of course; but also by maverick Democratic Governor Dan Walker; by the Senate liberals, who often allied themselves with Walker; and by young Daley, who was showing none of the regard for party discipline and loyalty that his father demanded from everyone else (ibid., June 22, 1974).

Daley then underwent a second transformation following his father's death in 1976. If the first transformation can readily be understood in psychological terms, the second one is better explained in political terms. The loss deprived him of the powerful political sponsorship he had relied upon to make his way up the machine ladder, and the cruel and arrogant use he made of his father's power left him with more enemies than allies inside and outside the machine. Liberals in particular despised him for the abuse he had heaped upon them.

Making Daley's path all the more difficult and precarious was the fact that times were changing. The machine was slipping, and the liberals were showing signs of a new-found ability to win. Daley himself took a powerful blow from the senate liberals. Pushing aside deputy president Phil Rock, who had shown the temerity to publicly criticize him for his roughshod tactics (*Chicago Tribune*, May 2, 1974), young Daley engineered the slating of his Springfield roommate, Thomas Hynes, for the senate presidency. However, Hynes' candidacy was blocked by a small band of independent senators, led by Dawn Clark Netsch and Harold Washington, for five weeks, during which time a record 185 ballots were cast. The independents wanted a share of leadership positions, and they would not back down, finally forcing Daley to capitulate in order to get Hynes elected.

Out of this cauldron emerged a very different Daley. He suddenly began sponsoring a range of liberal legislation: a revision of the state's mental health code, a nursing home reform bill, and an override of the governor's veto of a bill to repeal a sales tax on food and medicine (ibid., March 2, 1980). The flurry of liberal legislation was topped off by a dramatic appearance at the annual softball game sponsored by the Forty-third Ward, the base of liberal reform on the North lakefront. Daley was the guest of none other than the former principal victim of his wrath, Dawn Clark Netsch.

Yet Daley still was not ready to abandon the machine. He had to be kicked out of it. After completing two terms in the senate, Daley announced that he would seek the machine's endorsement for Cook County State's Attorney. However, Mayor Byrne would have nothing to do with giving her chief rival a leg up the ladder, and the machine wound up endorsing Edward Burke, one of the mayor's allies from the Young Turk faction. Daley was able to muster support from only nine of the city's fifty committeemen before withdrawing his name from consideration.

Cast out of the machine, Daley began to denounce it and Mayor Byrne in particular. He declared that he was now an independent Democrat, and he vented his outrage at Byrne's "bossism," while he scorned the machine's committeemen for "hiding at City Hall, just doing what the mayor tells them" (*Chicago Sun-Times,* January 10, 1980). The city's primary reform organization, IVI–IPO (Independent Voters of Illinois–Independent Precinct Organization), declined to endorse Daley, finding little difference between the new born-again liberal and his machine opponent. However, Daley wound up getting liberal reform backing from Senator Netsch.

Netsch led off with a tepid endorsement, expressing reservations about Byrne, rather than enthusiasm for Daley: "It is a question of whether the party will come under one person's domination" (ibid. February 14, 1980). A few days later, however, she came on a little stronger, saying Daley's "legislative priorities have shifted in a constructive direction," as she led a band of lakefront liberals into Daley's camp. One of the independents at the press conference explained the basis for the unusual alliance more candidly: "We need some allies. We can't expect people to be ideologically identical to us in order to be our friends." For his part, Daley pledged to honor the Shakman decree prohibiting political hiring and firing, and he promised to vigorously prosecute vote fraud (ibid., February 20, 1980).

The endorsement of Daley by his new liberal allies fell on deaf ears among skeptical lakefront liberal voters. However, a strong showing in his home base on the conservative Southwest Side and in the suburbs, where he campaigned hard against Byrne and the machine, put him over the top in both the primary and general elections. Thus, the machine's "Dead End Kid" was now Cook County's liberal state's attorney, as well as a virtual certainty to challenge Mayor Byrne in 1983.

Daley proved to be a curious mixture of conservative and liberal tendencies as state's attorney. On the administrative side, he received high marks for his liberalism. He signed the Shakman decree; made several high-quality appointments, even retaining some Republicans; and he did not load up the lower levels of the office with Democratic precinct captains. An early assessment of his administration found it to be: "serious-minded, hardworking, and apparently competent," and it was praised for having "avoided confrontation with Mayor Byrne" (*Chicago Sun-Times*, July 28, 1981).

On the policy side, however, Daley revealed the depths of his conservative roots and ties to the machine. He did nothing about prosecuting vote fraud, which undoubtedly pleased his friends in the machine. To the dismay of many of his liberal backers, he even disbanded the vote fraud unit after a time (*Reader*, February 10, 1989). His principal attention was devoted to cracking down on juvenile gangs, and here he attempted to take some decidedly illiberal measures: He lobbied, albeit unsuccessfully, in the state legislature for a bill lowering the adult age to fifteen, in order to prosecute juveniles as adults for serious and violent crimes, and he sought, but failed to win support for, legislation that would have opened juvenile court to the press and the public (*Chicago Sun-Times*, July 28, 1981).

Daley's politics also remained conservative. He voiced no objection to Mayor Byrne's racially gerrymandered ward map, which reduced black and Hispanic representation in the city council. In the same way, Daley sat quietly by during the volatile "council wars" period, although he was hardly neutral, inasmuch as his alderman, Patrick Huels, marched in lockstep with the Vrdolyak 29. When Mayor Washington urged Daley to get involved, Daley replied that the heavy press of his state's attorney activities prevented him from doing so (*Reader*, February 10, 1989).

Building on his solid administrative record in that office, he could present himself as a classic managerial reformer when he ran for mayor in 1983. He criticized Byrne's administration for its mismanagement and numerous inefficiencies, and he pledged to put government back on the businesslike basis he had established at the state's attorney's office. Further, his administration would be more honest, efficient, and nonpartisan than Byrne's. For the most part, he carefully avoided being drawn into the policy proposal arena. His awkward personal style and lackluster campaign strategy earned him third place in the three-way race. Such was the mixed character and direction Daley finally brought to the mayor's office in 1989. Just who he was and where he would be taking the city remained to be seen.

Daley's Mayoralty

By taking Daley at his word, evaluating his administration on the basis of its commitment to maintaining Washington's reform goals of "fair and open" government, we acquire a comparative standard while gaining more insight into the contrary course he is pursuing. Assembling evidence for the evaluation is complicated, however, by Daley's limited accessibility.

News reporters have complained of this, but to no avail. He is willing to speak candidly; even to express strong views, but only "on background." For the record, Daley has little to say (*Chicago Sun-Times*, February 17, 1991). His press conferences are carefully scripted with little give and take. Freedom of Information (an executive order initiated by Washington that requires prompt response to public inquiries) requests to city agencies are regularly shunted to the mayor's office, where they are often held or only partially answered (*Chicago*, August 1990, 14–15). In Daley's reform style machine, then, press agentry performs much of the work formerly done by precinct captains.

Open Government

Within days of his election, the new mayor made dramatic headlines by introducing a "rainbow" cabinet; fully half of the twenty-four appointees were minorities—black, Hispanic, and Asian. Moreover, Daley maintained that he would be giving his commissioners a free hand in shaping their agendas. As Timothy Degnan, a member of the mayor's inner circle, explained, Daley's "style is to let them [the commissioners] run their own departments, let them do their own thing, and hope that he's made the best choices possible." The skeptical reporter provided a word of caution, however, noting that Daley "is acutely sensitive to the critics' charges that he is destined to be the 'Son of Boss,' another Mayor Daley who will govern arbitrarily and rely on a tight-knit political circle" (*Chicago Tribune*, April 23, 1989).

As it turned out, the skepticism was warranted. Within a short time, a small inner circle had formed, consisting of four long-term Daley aides, none of whom held reform credentials, which shaped much of the administration's policy (ibid., April 12, 1989). Indications quickly surfaced that Daley's commissioners held little influence and had limited discretion. Harriet McCullough, the head of the city's board of ethics (a Washington initiative) resigned in frustration, complaining that she and her board had had no input on the mayor's new ethics bill (ibid., June 20, 1989). A week later, a long-time deputy commissioner of housing, highly regarded by affordable-housing advocates, was fired. According to insiders, the firing was carried out over the objections of Daley's blue-ribbon housing commissioner, Michael Schubert, raising questions, the reporter noted, "about who is in charge of the department" (ibid., June 26, 1989).

A short time later, the commissioner of cultural affairs, Joan Harris, was "forced out," after she had publicly criticized one of the mayor's policy decisions (ibid., November 1, 1989). Harris' termination undoubtedly had an especially chilling effect on other commissioners, because her husband was one of the mayor's prominent financial backers. Commissioners with less standing would have to keep their heads down and their opinions to themselves.

Daley also stripped the so-called ethnic advisory commissions of much of their independence and influence. The commissions— women, veterans, Hispanics, gays and lesbians, Asians, and so forth—had been created by Washington to provide him with information and policy recommendations. Daley consolidated them and put them under the human relations commission. The context for the decision provides another indication that the mayor would brook no opposing views by those within his administration.

The consolidation decision came on the heels of a heated encounter the mayor had had with a group of gays and lesbians who angrily opposed the city health department's inaction on AIDS. Daley arrived at their public meeting to cheers, but after an angry exchange ensued, the mayor stormed out of the meeting to boos and catcalls. Claiming he had been set up, Daley pointed to individuals on the podium with him: "There are people with political positions, and they obviously want to make them here. Adios" (*Chicago Tribune*, November 21, 1989).

Two months later a bill was passed in city council committee that consolidated the commissions and stripped them of much of their authority. All of the commissions strenuously opposed the bill, of course; however, public testimony was not permitted. On the day the bill was approved, the mayor addressed the Commission on Human Relations at its annual luncheon. The commissions, he said, "are spinning off in all directions. The Asians, Latinos, women, veterans, and gays and lesbians have set up their own enclaves. A system has been created that can divide us" (ibid., January 19, 1990).

Daley also extended the reach of his authority beyond city hall.

His old ally, Thomas Lyons, the only Northwest Side committeeman willing to openly side with Daley during the difficult Byrne days, was elected to take George Dunne's place as party chairman. Another close ally, Richard Devine, who had been Daley's top aide at the state's attorney's office, was placed on the independent and patronage-rich park district board and then elected president.

Daley did not take public positions on either of these developments. In the same way, he did not make an endorsement in the election for county board president in 1990, thereby avoiding any exposure on the dreaded "bossism" issue. However, several of his top aides and advisors worked on behalf of one of the candidates, Richard Phelan. Moreover, Phelan's campaign was amply aided by the party's decision to slate a Polish candidate, "Ted" Lechowitz, which badly damaged the prospects of another Polish candidate in the race, the front-running Stanley Kusper. With the Polish vote split, the contest became a two-man race between Phelan and black jurist Eugene Pincham, the Harold Washington party's candidate. The slating of Lechowitz also enabled Phelan to run as an independent "outsider" against the machine. Finally, the relatively unknown Phelan benefited from a huge outpouring of financial support that enabled him to run a strong media campaign against the financially strapped Pincham. With all that good "wind at his back," Phelan emerged the winner.

Judged, then, by the standards he espoused of open, accessible, and decentralized government, Daley's actions fall well short of the mark. A small inner circle of old allies is making many of the administration's critical decisions. Despite claims to the contrary, agency commissioners have been given little discretionary authority. Interest groups that had held considerable access and influence under Washington have been reined in. Notwithstanding Daley's apolitical public posture, the reach of the mayor's office extends well beyond City Hall, into the party and independent branches of local government. Thus, the rhetoric of reform masks a number of moves that have recentralized and closed government in the machine tradition.

Fair Government

Structure plays a critical role in determining who has access to and representation in a government. In turn, representatives and others with access can play an instrumental role in shaping a government's outputs, determining who is empowered by the government. As we saw, for example, when Daley consolidated the independent advisory commissions by placing them under the jurisdiction of another commission, he effectively disempowered groups that had been empowered by Washington. Yet when it comes to fair government in racially polarized Chicago, the central question is, of course, how well have blacks fared under Daley's rule?

Virtually the first words heard from Daley following his election expressed his commitment to maintaining Washington's affirmative action programs. A long history of racial discrimination is the city's great albatross and the heavy burden shouldered by young Daley in particular: The seeds of open racial discord were planted by his father, the bitter fruit grew more bountiful under machine mayors Bilandic and Byrne, and young Daley received virtually no black support in his mayoral election.

The mayor's record on the fairness issue has been decidedly mixed. Daley retained black commissioners in several agencies critical to black interests: the public schools, police, and public housing. He also brought in blacks from outside Chicago to head up the park district and economic development commission. However, as we saw, Daley's commissioners are given little discretionary authority, and the black commissioners are not exempted from the rule. Thus, after arriving in the city with much fanfare, little has been heard from either the parks or the economic development commissioner, and insiders report that neither man has much say in agency matters. Thus, plans for the city's third major airport, one of the administration's central policy developments, were devised with virtually no input from the commissioner of economic development.

Viewed in broader terms, Daley's administration has fallen far short of its stated goal of fairness in retaining black policy makers. When the mayor entered office, perfect parity existed between white and black top executives. Each held 45 percent of the policy-making positions, with Hispanics and Asians holding the remaining top posts. However, when the first headcount was taken under Daley, in November 1989, the white share had increased by 21 percent while the black share had fallen by 25 percent. Although Daley substantially increased the number of policy-making posts by 20 percent—from 753 to 903—the maldistribution remained basically unchanged. Figure 7 provides the particulars.

The troublesome issue was dealt with in a variety of ways. Initially, Daley's personnel director, Glenn Carr, one of the mayor's black commissioners, attempted to cover it up. Testifying before a city council committee, Carr submitted outdated hiring figures that made the distribution appear more equitable than it actually was.

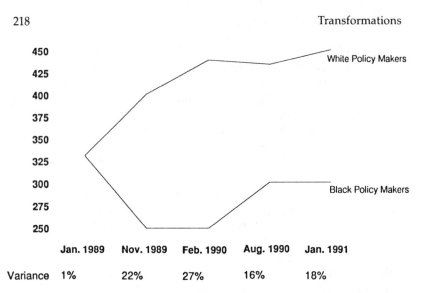

FIGURE 7.   Black and white policy makers in the Sawyer and Daley administrations. Source: *Chicago Sun-Times,* August 9, 1990; January 31, 1991.

Challenged later by reporters, the mayor's press secretary acknowledged the inaccuracy of Carr's data (*Chicago Tribune,* November 1,
1989). During another reporting period, Carr contended that several
blacks had turned down positions with the administration because
the mayor's critics had exerted "intense political pressure" on them
(*Chicago Sun-Times,* April 12, 1990).

Carr ultimately wound up arguing that the inequity was inevitable, the result of a natural racial preference: "Everybody would
accept that you would have a higher percentage of minorities in pol-
icymaking positions when the administration is headed by a black
mayor" (ibid., August 9, 1990). The peculiar explanation overlooked
the fact, of course, that racial parity had existed when Daley entered
office.

Finally, when black hiring took its first and only upward swing
in August 1990, Daley came to the fore and made the most of it. "You
gave me a lot of criticism in the last few weeks and months and
everybody keeps crying the same thing," he told reporters, "but I
am very committed to a fair and open administration. . . . We have
to move together. We cannot move isolated or separated from any
community" (ibid.).

Blacks experienced another critical setback when Daley revised
the city's set-aside program for minority and female contractors. The
plan was presented as "landmark legislation," which elevated Wash-

ington's executive order into law. However, the new legislation contained a new exemption. Personal services contracts would not be covered. This meant that about half of the contracts to be let—46 percent of $674,000,000 were the figures for 1989—would not be covered by the set-aside provision of 25 percent for minorities and 5 percent for women.

Daley defended the decision by claiming that Washington also had exempted personal service contracts (*Chicago Tribune*, July 27, 1990). However, Washington's corporation counsel, Judson Miner, denied that this had been the case (Miner interview, 1991). The bill's principal drafter defended the exemption on the dubious grounds that it was required in order to protect the city's interest. Granting personal service contracts on a low-bid basis meant, she said, that "you surely wouldn't get the best lawyers, who charge more for their services. In many situations, a government can't take that kind of risk" (*Chicago Tribune*, July 27, 1990). Yet, of course, the broad exemption also blanketed a wide range of low-risk contractors: public relations firms, banks, bond counselors, and lawyers performing routine tasks. Daley was simply making certain, under the guise of symbolic reform, that his "pin-stripe patronage" would go where it was going to do him the most good, that is, to friends, and not to enemies and strangers.

All in all, then, despite his public pledges to practice fair and open government in the Washington tradition, Daley is actually pursuing a mixed course, best understood as machine politics, reform style. Government has become more centralized under Daley, and the involvement of interest groups—ranging from neighborhood organizations to women and minorities—has been reduced. The distribution of top administrative and contractual benefits also has largely reverted to the machine style of rewarding friends and punishing enemies.[4]

That Daley rolled so easily to reelection in 1991 testifies to the skill he has displayed in steering his way along the contrary course he is pursuing. Blacks once again were the odd ones out in Daley's electoral coalition. Daley's media adviser, David Axelrod, crowed to reporters after the 1991 election that the rising level of black support (it increased from 9 percent in 1989 to 28 percent in 1991 in the 19 predominantly black wards) indicated the success of Daley's efforts to "reach out to all communities." Axelrod failed to note, however, that turnout in the black wards had fallen from 64 percent to 33 percent. Black voters were not turning toward Daley, then, so much as they were turning away from politics. No less divided in 1991 and even more demoralized than they had been in the wake of Washington's death, blacks once again were back in the peculiar political position that had been their lot for so many years. Politics had little to offer but bitter fruit.

In Perspective

Looking back over the full course of the black-machine electoral relationship, its rich texture and extraordinary variety contradict the conventional wisdom rooted in the economic perspective's assumptions and expectations. We saw that the Democratic machine was constructed during the 1930s with scant assistance from black voters, despite their dire socioeconomic circumstances. Deeply attached to the Republican "party of Lincoln, the emancipator" and repelled by the racist excesses of the Democratic party, blacks alone chose to remain outside the new "house for all peoples."

Moreover, when blacks finally did shift to the ascendant Democratic party, the realignment had far less to do with a new favors-for-voters nexus than is commonly supposed. Some black voters were connected in that way; a good many others were not. As the sociological and political perspectives would lead us to expect, black voters were driven not only by social and material needs but by political values as well, seeking representation in the party and empowerment from it.

Accordingly, divergent black Democratic paths emerged in the 1940s. Blacks moved into the national Democratic party in two great waves. In 1936 they were incorporated into the "party of the little man" on a social class basis, and when FDR finally addressed the issue of racial discrimination in 1944, blacks were incorporated on a racial basis. Yet while the national realignment was being sealed, large numbers of black voters were turning away from the local Democratic machine. The divergence was driven by the distinction many black voters began drawing between the national party's "New Deal" and the local machine's "raw deal" on the race issue.

It took twenty-five years for the Chicago machine to secure a commanding hold over the black vote, despite its long years of hegemony and the black community's terrible need for help. Yet again, as we saw, the local Democratic realignment was not produced by an influx of party agents bearing bigger and better favors. The sociopolitical perspectives point to the realignment's actual basis: The flight of the countervailing middle class left poor black voters behind and without any political choice other than what the machine was willing to provide, and when beleaguered Mayor Kennelly launched his racist campaign against Daley and the machine in 1955, the local black Democratic realignment was fixed.

Given the shaky foundation, then, on which the black-machine relationship rested, it is not surprising that the relationship came asunder when the civil rights movement swept into the city in the 1960s. A series of local racial upheavals added impetus to the move away from the machine: massive school boycotts; a devastating West Side riot accompanied by Daley's infamous "shoot to kill" order; a "police riot" at the Democratic convention; Black Panther leaders murdered by the police; and Daley's long and bitter feud with Congressman Metcalfe, who was transformed from a hack into a folk hero by the confrontation. Thus, the Democratic divergence that had marked the black wards during the 1940s reemerged in the late 1960s. By Daley's end in 1976, the legacy he left his successors included a party in marked decline and a black electorate suppressed and devoid of representation to the point where it was ready to explode.

The no less racially tumultuous Bilandic and Byrne mayoralties completed the bridge that enabled Washington to enter the mayor's office against virtually all odds. Building a novel coalition with a promise of representation and empowerment to a host of "have nots," Washington launched a reform government centering around redistribution of benefits, broader representation, and greater access to significant decision-making centers.

Thus, the black belt wards, once the Daley machine's electoral stronghold, became the "movement" wards under Washington. The West Side plantation wards finally were fully liberated from white control. Ironically, however, the great engine wards of the Washington revolution—the black middle-class wards—remained largely represented by machine loyalists, who paid public deference to the mayor's reforms, but privately yearned for the reform revolution's demise. The first Hispanic-controlled wards emerged under Washington, and the lakefront liberal wards received their first opportunity to put their reform aspirations into practice.

Yet no sooner had the reform revolution been firmly established, through the formation of a council majority and reelection, than it collapsed. Without Washington the center could not hold. The black loyalists he had left in place joined with their white counterparts and put one of their own into the mayor's office. The black nationalists

Washington had tolerated took over Evans' opposing campaign, transformed it into a black empowerment movement, and destroyed the reform coalition Washington had constructed.

The new black divide opened the way for Richard M. Daley's entry into the mayor's office. Behind a public facade of largely symbolic reforms, Daley is discreetly reconstituting what remains of the machine and putting it under his control. His machine politics, reform style form of governance is rolling back gains made by blacks under Washington, for they now have no representation to speak of in either government or the party, while the affirmative action and set-aside programs have been substantially cut back. Until blacks regroup and reconstruct a coalition with their Hispanic and white liberal allies, they are going to remain out in the cold.

Along the organizational dimension, the black-machine relationship has been no less complex, contradictory, and variable. We saw during the machine's faction-ridden formative stages that, contrary to the economic perspective's understanding, the black elite were not so much members of the machine, working on its behalf, but rather they were associates of rival factions within the machine, which served to often pit them against each, damaging the machine's interests in the process.

The sociopolitical perspective's concern for coalition-building and elite empowerment pointed to the critical role played by factional sponsors in the careers of the black elite. Skill and productivity usually counted for something, but abiding personal loyalty was everything. Thus, for all his skill, cunning, and boundless ambition, "Boss" Dawson's career was constructed by one mayor and destroyed by another, as it served the particular interests of each. The economic well-being of the black ward organizations was allowed to prosper and allowed to collapse in the same way.

When Daley entered the mayor's office, the black ward organizations emerged as the machine's electoral stronghold, displacing the poor white immigrant wards that had carried the machine since its inception. Yet for all the increased productivity, the black elite wound up receiving no more benefits under Daley than they had when they were only marginally productive under Kelly.

To insure against the possibility that the black elite would press the claim for more benefits warranted by their increased productivity, Daley instituted a novel form of elite recruitment. He brought in black ward leaders who possessed little political experience and had only marginal ties to the ward organizations they were to head. The high social standing the new elites also possessed provided Daley with a claim on the loyalties of the disaffected middle class; if modest favors had failed to win them over, then perhaps nominal representation would secure their support.

Daley's brilliant elite-recruitment strategy backfired, however, when the civil rights movement swept into the city, in whose wake came a long series of explosive racial upheavals. Some of Daley's civic-notable elites, with their high community standing, buckled under the pressure exerted by the movement and the upheavals. Accordingly, Daley abandoned the civic-notable strategy in favor of an elite recruitment strategy that would confine the black revolt to the electoral arena. The containment strategy involved recruiting from the lower and middle levels of the patronage ranks elites who possessed firm, multiple ties to the machine and its Irish Catholic leadership and who held little stature in the black community. The elevation of the new loyalist elite left the black community with even less representation in the government and the party.

It fell to Daley's successors to pay the price for the containment strategy, and in their respective fashions, by incompetence and through calculation, Bilandic and Byrne provided their own contributions to the black community's estrangement from the machine. The seeds of racial discord planted by Daley during the latter half of his mayoralty reached full bloom under Byrne. Blacks became pawns as Byrne tried to checkmate young Daley in her struggle to entice support away from her nemesis.

Through it all, the black machine elite remained loyal to whomever ruled, shifting their support from Daley to Bilandic and then to Byrne, regardless of the contrary preferences black voters expressed. Thus, we saw that during the post-Daley years Eugene Sawyer, for example, repeatedly failed to carry his ward for the machine's mayoral candidate; yet his loyalty never wavered. Even in 1983, under the compelling pressure exerted by Washington's candidacy, the black machine elite did little more than duck for cover, endorsing the black reform candidate if constituency pressure compelled them to, but doing little to actually help him.

The black machine elite wound up profiting no more under Washington's reform rule than they had under the Kelly-Nash machine's factional rule or Daley's dictatorial rule. Several even suffered, swept out of office by opponents more closely identified with Washington's reform agenda. Others complained, though usually privately, that more should be given than "a pat on the back," as one disappointed alderman put it, to those who had backed the mayor's candidacy. Others bided their time, waiting for the storm of revolution to pass or spend itself. As it turned out, they did not have long to wait.

With young Daley in the mayor's office, the shoe is on the other foot. The few black ward leaders with a genuine commitment to reform are now doing the suffering, ducking for cover, issuing private complaints, and waiting more or less patiently for happier days to arrive. With the reinstatement of the friends-and-enemies style of machine politics, hardly anyone is willing to speak out for fear of winding up on the dreaded enemies list. As for the machine loyalists, they simply transferred their loyalties yet another time. Accordingly, the black community once again remains essentially without representation, forced to deal with a mayor who gained office with scant black support. As the memory of Washington's reform mayoralty fades, the agenda he advanced—fair and open government—appears to be fading along with it, dimming the prospects for its revival. Thus, we end as we began, with blacks again reaping the bitter fruit of machine politics.

Notes

Chapter 1

1. There is an immense literature on machine politics and a fair amount on the black urban political experience, some of which looks at the relationship between blacks and the machine. Among the works I found most useful are: Bryce 1893; Ostrogorski 1902; Gosnell 1935, 1937; Drake and Cayton 1945; Merton 1949; Wilson 1960; Banfield and Wilson 1963; Allswang 1971, 1986; Katznelson 1976; Rakove 1975, 1979; Shefter 1976; Guterbock 1980; Gove and Masotti 1982; Bridges 1984; Browning, Marshall, and Tabb 1984, 1990; Erie 1988.

2. The seminal work in political science on the relationship between perspective and explanation is Graham T. Allison's *Essence of Decision: Explaining the Cuban Missile Crisis* (1971). Allison and I both use forms of economic, sociological, and political perspectives to develop distinct explanations. The content of our sociological and political perspectives differs, however, and I use the three perspectives to develop electoral as well as organizational explanations. I am indebted to my IIT colleague David Beam for recalling my attention to Allison's work.

3. In the analysis that follows, I identify three types of black machine-ward leaders; each type was recruited to serve particular and changing organizational and elite needs. Mayor Kelly (1933–47) and party chairman Jacob Arvey (1946–51) recruited black elites who possessed considerable political experience and demonstrated skill, the "politicians," as I call them. Mayor Daley recruited a markedly different type of elite, "civic notables," individuals with high standing in the community, but with little political experience. This provided the middle class with a nominal measure of representation, and it provided Daley with substantial control over the elites. The pressure generated by the civil rights movement, to which the civic notables were especially vulnerable, compelled Daley to begin recruiting a new type of elite, the "loyalists." The loyalists were drawn from the low and middle levels of the patronage ranks, they held limited standing in the community, and most of them were Catholic, which helped bind them to the machine's Irish Catholic leadership while it made them less vulnerable to the Protestant-based civil rights movement.

4. The irony is that Chicago's first and only full-blown machine was founded in large part upon a classic reform measure. Daley's predecessor, Kennelly, had assembled a Committee on City Expenditures, which called

for the establishment of an executive budget under the mayor's control. However, Kennelly lacked the political influence to even attempt implementing the proposal; it was Daley who brought the proposal to fruition (Gable 1953, 172).

Chapter 2

1. The ethnic rivalry thesis, classically stated by Gosnell (1937) and more recently advanced by Erie (1988), pits the Irish against later arriving ethnic groups (notably Poles, Italians, and Jews) seeking to move up the succession ladder. Yet virtually all of the leading rivals to Kelly and Nash were also Irish. The principal rivals were Tom Nash and his alderman John Duffy, who led the Southwest Side Irish bloc. Other powerful factions were headed by County Assessor John Clark and county board commissioner Dan Ryan (O'Connor 1975, 49–51, 57; Biles, 1984, 46).

2. Two inner-city Italian wards, the Twentieth and Twenty-eighth, also carried for Thompson, one barely and the other heavily. However, this had more to do with their ward leaders' close ties to Thompson than with the sentiments of the electorate. A year later, Roosevelt won nearly two-thirds of the city's Italian vote (Allswang 1971, 42).

3. Readers familiar with William Julius Wilson's work will recognize the parallel to his argument regarding the formation of the "ghetto underclass." As Wilson (1987, 49) says: "The movement of middle-class black professionals from the inner city, followed by increasing numbers of working-class blacks, has left behind a much higher concentration of the most disadvantaged segments of the black urban population." Thus, the departure of the middle class left poor blacks economically, as well as politically, disadvantaged.

Chapter 3

1. See chap. 2, note 2.

2. Just as Roosevelt was pushed to the liberal left by the prospects of Huey Long's candidacy, Henry Wallace pushed Truman in the same direction. Truman's advisers, Clark Clifford and James Rowe, argued that the course was a reasonable one to pursue: "The Negro voter has become a cynical, hard-boiled trader," while "as always, the South can be considered safely Democratic. And in formulating national policy, it can be safely ignored" (Memo cited in Sundquist 1983, 273–74).

3. The 1935 mayoral election sometimes has been misinterpreted as a critical turning point. Mayor Kelly's biographer, historian Roger Biles (1984, 94), who generally overestimates Kelly's popularity among black voters, maintained that "the 1935 mayoral election . . . substantiated Kelly's tremendous popularity among black voters." Dianne Pinderhughes' interesting study, *Race and Ethnicity in Chicago Politics* (1987, 79) goes even further, arguing that "the consolidation of patronage, political office, and electoral support in the new machine left them [black voters] with no alternative but to move into the Democratic party, which they did by the 1935 elections."

4. The political independence of the black church subsequently was undermined by Mayor Daley. He used federal poverty program funds to place several black ministers on the city payroll. According to former city officials, by the 1970s some sixty ministers were employed in a city program entitled Churches United (*Chicago Reporter*, December 1987, 7). The political course of the churches was undoubtedly influenced as well by contributions, assistance with mortgages, and the like, and by the negative sanctions available to a variety of city inspectors. As one minister said to me, "Just as soon as you apply for some help, any kind of help, it doesn't matter, they got you, brother, where they can hurt you. Guess that's why they used to call this place 'the city that works.' It sure worked for them, didn't it."

5. The other black ward, the Third Ward, also elected its first black Democratic alderman, Benjamin Grant, in 1939. Grant shared Dickinson's high social standing, and their election was "hailed as a more advanced and capable political leadership in the Negro community" (Henderson 1939, 24). Grant was a minister's son, and he and Dickerson were graduates of the University of Chicago. Thus, with the election of faculty member Paul Douglas as alderman of the Fifth Ward, 1939 constituted a political breakthrough year for the University of Chicago as well as for the black Democrats.

Chapter 4

1. The status of any given ward organization needs to be empirically determined. Rakove (1975, 106) characterized them as "fiefdoms, set within . . . a feudal structure." However, the ward organization in which Rakove worked, Vito Marzullo's Twenty-fifth Ward organization, was atypical. Its close ties to the crime syndicate provided it with far more discretion than most ward organizations are able to secure. Thomas Guterbock (1980, p. 67) described the ward organization in which he worked as an "administrative outpost." Its Jewish leadership had weak ties to the machine's ruling Irish Catholic elite, and all critical decisions were made from above. The black ward organizations I studied far more resembled administrative outposts than semi-independent fiefdoms.

2. See chapter 2, note 1.

3. In a campaign brochure Sneed issued in 1936, he reported that forty-five of his sixty-nine precinct captains held government jobs (Henderson, 1939, 78). Newspaper accounts indicated that Sneed and the other black ward leaders also relied on the black policy cartel to provide their ward organizations with jobs (*Chicago Daily News*, February 15, 23, 1939).

4. One of Dawson's protégés confirmed Dickerson's assessment of Dawson: "Some people want money, some want power. Bill Dawson eats power" (Weisman and Whitehead 1974, 44).

5. Dawson finally carried the Second Ward in 1944 with 59 percent of the vote. Before that, the best that a Democratic congressional candidate had done was 46 percent, in 1940 and 1942. Dawson's breakthrough was part of the black national Democratic realignment following Roosevelt's de-

cision in 1944 to address the issue of racial discrimination (see fig. 1 above). FDR received 64 percent of the black vote in 1944, up from 51 percent in 1940.

6. Reflecting the close ties between the black politicians and the black policy racketeers, Illy Kelly was the brother-in-law of the former Republican alderman of the Second Ward for many years, Louis Anderson, who served as Mayor Thompson's floor leader in the city council. Democratic committeeman "Mike" Sneed's brother also was involved in the policy racket. As for "Billy" Skidmore, he was characterized as "the foremost political fixer and underworld bagman during the Kelly-Nash regime" (Demaris, 1969, 124). He was convicted in 1940 for failing to report income of $1,103,545 for the years 1933–38 (Biles 1984, 110).

7. When Dawson made this statement to reporters, however, the white crime syndicate already had taken over the policy racket. The head of the Chicago Crime Commission, Virgil Peterson (1953), called Dawson's statement an effort to "perpetuate a myth that policy operations are controlled by Negroes and should not be disturbed." A white machine committeeman with close ties to the black ward leaders described Dawson's motivation much the same way: "No, Bill didn't get pushed aside by the white guys. Let me put it this way, Bill simply acquired new partners, that's all" (Korshak interview, 1982).

Chapter 5

1. In keeping with Robert Merton's (1949) classic thesis that businessmen often are prime beneficiaries, and therefore are supportive, of machines, Mike Royko (1971, 100–101) attributed the demise of the local Republican party to Daley's infusion of funds into downtown development and public works, which swung the development interests over to the machine's side. This, along with attendent support from the generally booster media, undoubtedly helped legitimize the machine in what often had been hostile quarters.

2. The population of the Douglas, Grand Boulevard, and Washington Park community areas actually increased by 43,549 between 1940 and 1950, reflecting the magnitude of the continuing migration to Chicago from the South. Overall, the black population rose by 77 percent, or 214,534, during this period (Hauser and Kitagawa, 1953). The black belt's population did not decline until 1960, and land clearance for public housing developments that would span the black belt had much to do with the population reduction.

3. Thus, for example, in the Woodlawn community area, which straddled the 63rd Street class divide, median rental was among the highest on the South Side, and its black population increased by 159 percent between 1940 to 1950. The residents of the Woodlawn community area had higher median years of schooling, median family income, and percentage employed in professional and technical occupations than residents in the three black belt communities (Hauser and Kitagawa 1953).

4. Steven Erie (1988, p. 165–68) makes the argument that Daley's ma-

chine used "Great Society programs to stabilize and build political support in the black community." The argument flows from his general thesis that the machine's well-being is shaped by intergovernmental relations; they thrive when the spigot of intergovernmental aid is turned on, and suffer when it is turned down. Erie is wrong on both counts as far as the Daley machine is concerned, for Daley's machine acquired solid black support well before the Great Society programs were launched. Indeed, black support of the machine was falling off by the time Congress approved President Johnson's War on Poverty in 1964. As for the machine's greater well-being, we shall see in the following chapter that this had far more to do with local race relations than federal-city intergovernmental relations.

5. Richard Keiser (1988) advances a radically different interpretation of black success at acquiring resources during the Kelly-Nash era. According to Keiser, the level of party competition determines the extent to which blacks can effectively bargain and thereby become "incorporated" (i.e., acquire substantial benefits and influence) into the local political system. The cutoff point for "competitive" is defined as a mayor winning by less than 70 percent. (In an unpublished subsequent paper, the cutoff point has been lowered to 60 percent.) Inasmuch as Kelly won by *merely* margins of from 55 to 59 percent, it follows that blacks acquired significant leverage in their bargaining with him. However, as I show, Keiser is on shaky ground empirically as well as theoretically. Blacks actually fared no better under Kelly, when the electoral system supposedly was competitive, than they did under Daley, when the system turned monopolistic.

6. A study (Baron 1968, 28, 33) directed by the Chicago Urban League's former research director found that in 1965 blacks held only 2 of the 156 "policy-making positions" in Chicago government. This was not out of line with how blacks fared in the study's sampling of private and non-profit organizations in the city. The study concluded with the observation that "realistically, the power structure of Chicago is hardly less white than that of Mississippi."

7. The *Chicago Defender* (February 17, 1955), typically firmly supportive of the Democratic party, used Metcalfe's inexperience as the stated basis for endorsing his Republican opponent, Archibald Carey, Jr., in 1955. It was noted that Metcalfe had only "entered politics three years ago as Democratic committeeman of the third ward."

Chapter 6

1. Daley won by 138,792 votes in 1963, and the seven wards headed by black aldermen supplied 68 percent of the mayor's margin. The "black" share of Daley's margin increases to 88 percent when the Twenty-seventh and Twenty-ninth wards are included, these being two West Side wards with large black populations but represented by white aldermen. The remaining 17,092 votes of Daley's margin very likely were provided by "pockets" of black voters in several predominantly white wards, notably the Fifth, Nineteenth, Twenty-first, and Forty-second.

2. The term "plantation wards" was coined by Don Rose (interview, 1984) and Timuel Black in Black's 1963 aldermanic campaign in the Fourth Ward against the machine, and it was used to characterize all of the black wards under the machine's control. The flamboyant Charlie Chew picked up the expression and denounced the Seventeenth Ward's white machine leadership with the term during his successful 1963 aldermanic campaign. Over the years, the term came to designate only the four black West Side wards under white control.

3. Several studies have explained the Daley machine's acquisition of a white ethnic electoral base in the 1960s on the basis of improved services to the wards. Thus, in *Rainbow's End* (1988, 161–63) Steven Erie maintains that "in Chicago, the Daley machine in the mid-1960s began shifting its policies and electoral base, replacing costly patronage and welfare services delivered to poor inner-city wards with efficient low-cost homeowner services delivered to outlying middle-class wards." Erie cites Petrocik (1981) and Fuchs and Shapiro (1983) in support of his argument.

However, there is no evidence of any late service improvement shift. To the contrary, as soon as he became mayor, Daley took control of ward services away from the ward bosses and improved them. Milton Rakove (1982, 221) explained the political basis for Daley's move: "If good city services and jobs for workers were the basic ingredients for electoral success, no ward committeeman could justify his failure to carry his ward in an election on any basis other than his own incompetency or his failure to avail himself of what the city government was providing to ensure success on election day." Moreover, as I have shown (1982, 72–73), the white ethnic shift to Daley was not uniform. Seven of the top ten wards in Daley's new white ethnic machine were Southwest Side wards, the most racially troubled area in the city.

Chapter 7

1. Bilandic joined Daley's Eleventh Ward organization in 1948. However, it was not until 1969 that Daley, after repeated appeals over the years, finally was able to persuade a reluctant Bilandic to run for alderman. Dunne was similarly self-effacing. Daley had to overcome Dunne's reluctance to run for committeeman and then for the county board. As Dunne put it, "Ambition is a laudable characteristic, but when that ambition consumes someone and you can't control it, then I say that you might be very well devoured in its flames" (Rakove 1979, 76–88, 396–99). Of course, it is not uncommon for politicians to "protest too much"; however, the accounts square with the view of insiders that both men were essentially good soldiers rather than ambitious leaders.

2. Byrne had some basis for turning on Carter, who had given the machine much less deference than it was accustomed to receiving. I participated with a group of anti-machine activists who persuaded the Carter campaign in 1976 to fund an independent campaign organization in the South Side black wards on the grounds that the black machine committeemen no longer could get out a big vote. As we realized, and as Carter's operatives

subsequently learned, Mayor Daley was infuriated by the intrusion of "outsiders" into what had been his exclusive campaign domain. As president, Carter antagonized party chairman George Dunne and other machine leaders with another unprecedented move: He appointed several individuals to federal posts without clearing the appointments with the machine leadership; whereas under Daley, all federal patronage dispensed by Democratic presidents had to be approved by the mayor.

Chapter 8

1. Daley's Southwest Side base and Washington's black middle-class base each consisted of eight wards. Since the late 1960s, the Southwest Side wards had been the machine's electoral stronghold. Thus, Bilandic carried 61 percent of the stronghold vote in 1979 against Byrne, who defeated him everywhere else except in the poor "river wards." Washington carried the black middle-class wards against Bilandic in 1977, but just barely. However, as the account below explains, Washington had a much larger electorate and far more momentum on his side in 1983.

2. Paul Kleppner (1985, 148, 279) estimated that there was a net gain of 127,000 new black voters registered between 1979 and November 1982, bringing the total number of black voters to 647,000. In the seventeen predominantly black wards, the gain was 120,922 amounting to a total of 552,993. By Kleppner's estimate, the black share of the city electorate stood at 42 percent; the seventeen black wards' share was 36 percent.

3. An interesting discussion of the black nationalist's complex role in Washington's campaign is provided in an "insider" account by Alkalimat and Gills, (1989, 59, 65). On the one hand, they contend that "the general assessment of many observers is that the movement for Harold Washington led to his victory, and was followed by organization." They go on to observe, however, that the principal nationalist organization, The Task Force for Black Empowerment, "was reduced to serving as an extension of the Washington campaign," and that it "provided little enduring leadership for the campaign." From my own observation, the Task Force's campaign office at 47th Street and Martin Luther King Drive was nearly empty on primary election day; but by then the "street heat" and heavy participation on black talk shows may already have done the job.

4. Shortly after Mayor Washington's death, one of his top political aides and a black reform alderman ran down the list of the aldermen for me, and they concluded that four black aldermen and an equivalent number of white and Hispanic aldermen were genuinely committed to Washington's reform agenda. A few more were identified as "borderline cases," but the bulk of the mayor's supporters were "only along for the ride," as the former aide put it.

Chapter 9

1. Acting Mayor Sawyer's press secretary, Monroe Anderson (1991, p. 112–13), provided a bittersweet account of Sawyer's administration and

campaign. He marks the reorganization of the city council, led by the white machine bloc, as the critical turning point in Sawyer's mayoralty. The leaders of the white machine bloc saw it the same way. Anderson quotes Alderman Burke saying to Alderman Mell in a city hall washroom right after the reorganization, "The niggers will never get together after this."

2. According to Monroe Anderson's "insider" account (1991, 109–10), Sawyer's campaign was ineptly managed. The principal fund raisers dictated many decisions by dispensing funds as they saw fit. Sawyer's campaign manager divided his time between Chicago and New Orleans (although from Anderson's estimation of the manager's skills, the frequent absences may have helped Sawyer more than they harmed him).

3. An "insider" account by Evans' media advisors, Don Rose and James Andrews (1991, 117, 129), describes the dominant influence acquired by the white radical and black nationalist factions in Evans' campaign. They attribute the decision to form a third party and run in the general election to the radical-nationalist factions.

4. John Mollenkopf's (1990, 80) insightful analysis of Mayor Edward Koch's administration provides a telling rejoinder to Browning, Marshall, and Tabb (1984, 1990). He points out that conservative administrations such as Koch's, in an effort to "keep a potential opposition disunited may produce some aspects of policy responsiveness that Browning, Marshall, and Tabb attribute to a biracial coalition. New York shows that a conservative dominant coalition can seek to contain the potential for an electoral challenge and manage the tensions arising out of underlying social inequality with the tools of political incorporation invented by the earlier liberal experimenters." I would simply add that the conservative strategy employed by Koch, Daley, and others is more likely to involve symbolic, rather than substantive, benefits, thus creating mainly the illusion of political incorporation.

References

Alkalimat, Abdul, and Doug Gills. 1989. *Harold Washington and the Crisis of Black Power in Chicago.* Chicago: Twenty-First Century Books.

Allison, Graham T. 1971. *Essence of Decision: Explaining the Cuban Missile Crisis.* Glencoe, IL: Scott, Foresman.

Allswang, John M. 1971. *A House for All Peoples.* Lexington: University Press of Kentucky.

———. 1986. *Bosses, Machines, and Urban Voters.* Rev. ed. Baltimore: The Johns Hopkins University Press.

Andersen, Kristi. 1979. *The Creation of a Democratic Majority, 1928–1936.* Chicago: University of Chicago Press.

Anderson, Alan B., and George W. Pickering. 1986. *Confronting the Color Line.* Athens: University of Georgia Press.

Anderson, Monroe. 1991. "The Sawyer Saga." In *Restoration 1989,* edited by Paul M. Green and Melvin G. Holli. Chicago: Lyceum Books.

Banfield, Edward C., and James Q. Wilson. 1963. *City Politics.* New York: Vintage Books.

Baron, Harold M. "Black Powerlessness in Chicago." *Transaction* 6, no. 1 (November): 27–33.

Biles, Roger. 1984. *Big City Boss in Depression and War: Mayor Edward J. Kelly of Chicago.* DeKalb: Northern Illinois Press.

Bridges, Amy. 1984. *A City in the Republic.* Cambridge: Cambridge University Press.

Browning, Rufus P., Dale Rogers Marshall, and David H. Tabb. 1984. *Protest is Not Enough.* Berkeley: University of California Press.

———, eds. 1990. *Racial Politics in American Cities.* New York: Longman.

Bryce, James. 1893. *The American Commonwealth.* New York: Macmillan.

Castells, Manuel. 1977. *The Urban Question.* Cambridge: MIT Press.

Chicago Crime Commission. 1953, 1954. *Annual Report.*

City of Chicago, Dept. of Planning. 1984. *1980 Ward Profiles.*

Clark, Terry Nichols. 1975. "The Irish Ethic and Spirit of Patronage." *Ethnicity* 2:205–59.

Clark, William G. 1979. Interview, by Milton L. Rakove. In *We Don't Want Nobody Nobody Sent,* ed. Milton L. Rakove. Bloomington: Indiana University Press.

Clayton, Edward T. 1964. *The Negro Politician.* Chicago: Johnson Publishing Co.

Day, Richard, Jeff Andreasen, and Kurt Becker. 1984. "Polling in the 1983 Chicago Mayoral Election." *In The Making of the Mayor, Chicago 1983.* Melvin G. Holli and Paul M. Green, eds. Grand Rapids, Mich.: Wm. B. Eerdmans.

Demaris, Ovid. 1969. *Captive City.* New York: Lyle Stuart.

Drake, St. Clair, and Horace Cayton. 1945, 1962, 1970. *Black Metropolis.* New York: Harper and Row.

Elkins, Stephen L. 1987. *City and Regime in the American Republic.* Chicago: University of Chicago Press.

Erie, Stephen P. *Rainbow's End.* 1988. Berkeley: University of California Press.

Etzioni, Amitai. 1960. "Two Approaches to Organizational Analysis: A Critique and a Suggestion." *Administrative Science Quarterly* 5 (September): 257–58.

———. 1961. *Comparative Analysis of Complex Organizations.* New York: Free Press.

Ferman, Barbara, and William Grimshaw. 1991. "Old Politics, New Politics: Divergence and Convergence Strategies." American Political Science Association Annual Meeting.

Fishbein, Annette. 1962. "The Expansion of Negro Residential Areas in Chicago, 1950–1960." Master's thesis, University of Chicago.

Fitzgerald, Kathleen Whalen. 1981. *Brass: Jane Byrne and the Pursuit of Power.* Chicago: Contemporary Books.

Frazier, E. Franklin. 1964. *The Negro Church in America.* New York: Schocken Books.

Fuchs, Ester R., and Robert V. Shapiro. 1983. "Government Performance as a Basis for Machine Support." *Urban Affairs Quarterly* 18, no. 4 (June): 537–50.

Gable, William Russell. 1953. "The Chicago City Council: A Study of Urban Politics and Legislation." Ph.D. diss., University of Chicago.

Geisler, R. Gene. 1958. "Chicago Democratic Voting, 1947–1957." Ph.D. diss., University of Chicago.

Gleason, Bill. 1970. *Daley of Chicago.* New York: Simon and Schuster.

Gosnell, Harold F. 1935, 1967. *Negro Politicians: The Rise of Negro Politics in Chicago.* Chicago: University of Chicago Press. (Reissued 1967, with Introduction by James Q. Wilson.)

———. 1937. *Machine Politics: Chicago Model.* Chicago: University of Chicago Press.

Gouldner, Alvin W. 1959. "Organizational Analysis." In *Sociology Today,* edited by Robert Merton, Leonard Broom, and Leonard S. Cottrell, Jr. New York: Basic Books.

Gove, Samuel K., and Louis H. Masotti, eds. 1982. *After Daley.* Urbana: University of Illinois Press.

Granger, Bill, and Lori Granger. 1980. *Fighting Jane: Mayor Jane Byrne and the Chicago Machine.* New York: Dial Press.

Green, Paul M., and Melvin G. Holli, eds. 1991. *Restoration 1989*. Chicago: Lyceum Books.

Greenstone, J. David, and Paul E. Peterson. 1976. *Race and Authority in Urban Politics*. Chicago: University of Chicago Press.

Grimshaw, William J. 1979. *Union Rule in the Schools*. Lexington, Mass.: Lexington Books.

————. 1982. "The Daley Legacy." In *After Daley*, edited by Samuel K. Gove and Louis H. Masotti. Urbana: University of Illinois Press.

————. 1984. "Is Chicago Ready for Reform?" In *The Making of the Mayor, Chicago 1983* edited by Melvin G. Holli and Paul M. Green. Grand Rapids: Wm. B. Eerdmans.

————. 1987. "Unraveling the Enigma: Mayor Harold Washington and the Black Political Tradition." *Urban Affairs Quarterly* 23, No. 2 (December): 187–206.

Guterbock, Thomas M. 1980. *Machine Politics in Transition*. Chicago: University of Chicago Press.

Harmel, Robert. 1989. "The Iron Law of Oligarchy Revisited." In *Leadership and Politics*, edited by Bryan D. Jones. Lawrence: University Press of Kansas.

Hauser, Philip M., and Evelyn M. Kitagawa, eds. 1953. *Local Community Fact Book*. Chicago: University of Chicago Press.

Henderson, Elmer William. 1939. "A Study of the Basic Factors in the Change in the Party Alignment of Negroes in Chicago, 1932–1938." Master's thesis, University of Chicago.

Hirsch, Arnold R. 1983. *Making the Second Ghetto*. Cambridge: Cambridge University Press.

Hogarth, Robin M., and Melvin W. Reder, eds. 1987. *Rational Choice*. Chicago: University of Chicago Press.

Holli, Melvin G., and Paul M. Green, eds. 1984. *The Making of the Mayor, Chicago 1983*. Grand Rapids, Mich.: Wm. B. Eerdmans.

————. 1989. *Bashing Chicago Traditions*. Grand Rapids, Mich.: Wm. B. Eerdmans.

Janowitz, Morris. 1952. *The Community Press in an Urban Setting*. Chicago: University of Chicago Press.

Johnston, Michael. 1979. "Patrons and Clients, Jobs and Machines: A Case Study of the Use of Patronage." *American Political Science Review* 73, no. 2 (June): 385–98.

Karnig, Albert, and Susan Welch. 1980. *Black Representation and Urban Policy*. Chicago: University of Chicago Press.

Katznelson, Ira. 1976. *Black Men, White Cities*. Chicago: University of Chicago Press.

Keiser, Richard. 1988. "Incorporation or Exclusion?" American Political Science Association Annual Meeting.

Kemp, Kathleen, A., and Robert L. Lineberry. 1982. "The Last of the Great Urban Machines and the Last of the Great Urban Mayors?" In *After Da-*

ley, edited by Samuel K. Gove and Louis H. Masotti. Urbana: University of Illinois Press.

Kennedy, Eugene. 1978. *Himself! The Life and Times of Mayor Richard J. Daley.* New York: Viking Press.

Kleppner, Paul. 1985. *Chicago Divided: The Making of a Black Mayor.* DeKalb: Northern Illinois University Press.

Kornblum, William. 1974. *Blue Collar Community.* Chicago: University of Chicago Press.

Lipset, Seymour Martin. 1966. "Introduction." In *Political Parties*, by Robert Michels. New York: Free Press.

Lipset, Seymour Martin, Martin Trow, and James Coleman. 1962. *Union Democracy.* Glencoe: Free Press.

Lodato, Raymond M. "From King to Washington: Political Realignment as a Consequence of Social Movement Activity." Unpublished manuscript, Political Science Department, University of Chicago, 1989.

Logsdon, Joseph A. "The Rev. Archibald J. Carey and the Negro in Chicago Politics." Master's thesis, University of Chicago, 1961.

Madigan, Michael. 1986. "Interview, by Bruce DuMont." *Chicago* 35, no. 8 (August): 112–33.

Matthewson, Joe. 1974. *Up Against Daley.* LaSalle, Ill.: Open Court.

McClory, Robert. 1984. "Up from Obscurity: Harold Washington." In *The Making of the Mayor, Chicago 1983*, edited by Melvin G. Holli and Paul M. Green. Grand Rapids, Mich.: Wm. B. Eerdmans.

Merriam, Charles E. 1929. *Chicago: A More Intimate View of Urban Politics.* New York: Macmillan.

Merriam, Charles E., and Harold F. Gosnell. 1924. *The American Party System.* New York: Macmillan.

Merton, Robert K. 1949. *Social Theory and Social Structure.* New York: Free Press.

Meyerson, Martin, and Edward C. Banfield. 1955. *Politics, Planning, and the Public Interest.* New York: Free Press.

Michels, Robert. 1962 [1911]. *Political Parties.* New York: Collier Press.

Mikva, Zorita. 1951. "The Neighborhood Improvement Association: A Counter-Force to the Expansion of Chicago's Negro Population." Master's thesis, University of Chicago.

Mollenkopf, John H. 1990. "New York: The Great Anomaly." In *Racial Politics in American Cities*, edited by Rufus P. Browning, Dale Rogers Marshall, and David H. Tabb. New York: Longman.

Morris, Harry Wesley. 1950. "The Chicago Negro and the Major Political Parties, 1940–1948." Master's thesis, University of Chicago.

Nie, Norman, Sidney Verba, Henry Brady, Kay Lehman Schlozman, and Jane Junn. 1988. "Participation in America: Continuity and Change." Midwest Political Science Association Annual Meeting.

O'Connor, Len. 1975. *Clout.* Chicago: Henry Regnery.

———. 1977. *Requiem.* Chicago: Contemporary Books.

Ogburn, William Fielding. 1935. Foreword. *Machine Politics: Chicago Model.* Harold F. Gosnell. Chicago: University of Chicago Press.

Osofsky, Gilbert. 1963. *Harlem: The Making of a Ghetto.* New York: Harper and Row.

Ostrogorski, M. 1902. *Democracy and the American Party System.* New York: Macmillan.

Peterson, Paul E. 1981. *City Limits.* Chicago: University of Chicago Press.

Peterson, Virgil W. 1953. *A Report on Chicago Crime and Criminals.* Chicago: Chicago Crime Commission.

Petrocik, John. 1981. "Voting in a Machine City: Chicago, 1975." *Ethnicity* 8:320–34.

Pinderhughes, Dianne M. 1987. *Race and Ethnicity in Chicago Politics.* Urbana: University of Illinois Press.

Preston, Michael B. 1982a. "Black Politics and Public Policy in Chicago: Self-Interest Versus Constituent Representation." In *The New Black Politics,* edited by Michael B. Preston, Lenneal J. Henderson, Jr., and Paul Puryear. New York: Longman.

———. 1982b. "Black Politics in the Post-Daley Era." In *After Daley,* edited by Samuel K. Gove and Louis H. Masotti. Urbana: University of Illinois Press.

Prewitt, Kenneth, and Alan Stone. 1973. *The Ruling Elites: Elite Theory, Power, and American Democracy.* New York: Harper and Row.

Rakove, Milton L. 1975. *Don't Make No Waves, Don't Back No Losers.* Bloomington: Indiana University Press.

———, ed. 1979. *We Don't Want Nobody Nobody Sent.* Bloomington: Indiana University Press.

———. 1982. "Jane Byrne and the New Chicago Politics." In *After Daley,* edited by Samuel K. Gove and Louis H. Masotti. Urbana: University of Illinois Press.

Reed, Adolph L. 1986. *The Jesse Jackson Phenomenon.* New Haven: Yale University Press.

Riordan, William L. 1963 [1905]. *Plunkitt of Tammany Hall.* New York: E. P. Dutton.

Rose, Don. 1984. "How the 1983 Election Was Won." In *The Making of the Mayor, Chicago 1983,* edited by Melvin G. Holli and Paul M. Green. Grand Rapids, Mich.: Wm. B. Eerdmans.

Rose, Don, and James Andrews. 1991. "How Evans Lost the Race." In *Restoration 1989,* edited by Paul M. Green and Melvin G. Holli. Chicago: Lyceum Books.

Royko, Mike. 1971. *Boss.* New York: Signet Books.

Shefter, Martin. 1976. "The Emergence of the Political Machine: An Alternative View." In *Theoretical Perspectives on Urban Politics,* edited by Willis D. Hawley and Michael Lipsky. Englewood Cliffs: Prentice-Hall.

Simpson, Dick, ed. 1988. *Chicago's Future.* Champaign, Ill.: Stipes.

Spear, Alan H. 1967. *Black Chicago: The Making of a Negro Ghetto, 1890–1920.* Chicago: University of Chicago Press.

Simpson, Dick, and others. 1991. "The Chicago City Council, 1971–1991." Political Science Department, University of Illinois at Chicago.

Skocpol, Theda, ed. 1984. *Vision and Method in Historical Sociology.* Cambridge: Cambridge University Press.

Smith, Michael Peter, ed. 1984. *Cities in Transformation.* Beverly Hills: Sage Publications.

Stone, Clarence N. 1989. *Regime Politics.* Lawrence: University Press of Kansas.

Stone, Clarence N., and Heywood T. Sanders, eds. 1987. *The Politics of Urban Development.* Lawrence: University Press of Kansas.

Sullivan, Frank. 1989. *Legend: The Only Inside Story of Mayor Richard J. Daley.* Chicago: Bonus Books.

Sundquist, James L. 1983. *Dynamics of the Party System.* Washington, D.C.: The Brookings Institution.

Suttles, Gerald D. 1968. *The Social Order of the Slum.* Chicago: University of Chicago Press.

Tillman, Dorothy. 1986. "Movement Activism from Martin Luther King to Harold Washington." In *Research in Urban Policy,* edited by Terry Nichols Clark. London: JAI Press.

Travis, Dempsey, J. 1987. *An Autobiography of Black Politics.* Chicago: Urban Research Press.

Walker, Daniel. 1968. *Rights in Conflict.* Chicago: National Commission on the Causes and Prevention of Violence.

Walton Jr., Hanes. 1972. *Black Politics.* Philadelphia: J. B. Lippincott.

Weisman, Joel, and Ralph Whitehead. 1974. "Untangling Black Politics." *Chicagoan* 1, no. 10 (July): 43–75.

Welch, Susan, and Timothy Bledsoe. 1988. *Urban Reform and Its Consequences.* Chicago: University of Chicago Press.

Whitehead, Ralph, and Joel Weisman. 1974. "Is LaSalle Street Grooming the Black Mayor?" *Chicagoan* 1, no. 11 (August).

Wilson, James Q. 1960, 1965. *Negro Politics.* New York: Free Press.

———. 1973. *Political Organizations.* New York: Basic Books.

Wilson, William Julius. 1987. *The Truly Disadvantaged.* Chicago: University of Chicago Press.

Wolfinger, Raymond E. 1972. "Why Machines Have Not Withered Away and Other Revisionist Thoughts." *Journal of Politics* 34, no. 2 (May): 365–98.

Zikmund, Joseph. 1982. "Mayoral Voting and Ethnic Politics in the Daley-Bilandic-Byrne Era." In *After Daley,* edited by Samuel K. Gove and Lois H. Masotti. Urbana: University of Illinois Press.

**Newspapers and
Periodicals**

Chicago (magazine).
Chicago Daily News.
Chicago Defender.
Chicago Reporter.
Chicago Sun-Times.
Chicago Tribune.
Reader.
Wall Street Journal.

**Interviews and
Personal Communications**

Caldwell, Lewis. 1982.
Davis, Corneal. 1979.
Despres, Leon. 1979.

Dickerson, Earl. 1979.
East, John. 1979.
Janney, Al. 1981.
Jones, Sidney. 1985.
Korshak, Marshall. 1982.
Love, Edison. 1979.
Martin, Peggy Smith. 1982.
Melas, Nicholas. 1985.
Parks, Sam. 1979.
Patch, Sam. 1982.
Raby, Al. 1983.
Rather, Ernest. 1979.
Robinson, Renault. 1984.
Rose, Don. 1984.
Washington, Harold. 1979, 1982, 1985.

Index